UNDERCOVER

ROB EVANS has been a reporter for the *Guardian* since 1999. He has won awards for his work both on corruption scandals and for promoting freedom of information, including the Paul Foot award for investigative journalism. He is also the author of *Gassed: British Chemical Warfare Experiments on Humans at Porton Down*. He previously worked for the *Sunday Telegraph* and the *Financial Times*.

PAUL LEWIS is Washington correspondent for the *Guardian*. His investigations into undercover policing in the UK took place when he was working as the newspaper's special projects editor, between 2010 and 2013. Paul has won 10 major journalism awards since joining the *Guardian* as a trainee in 2005. He is currently co-writing a second book about the English riots. He studied at Cambridge University and Harvard University.

UNDERCOVER
The True Story of
Britain's Secret Police

ROB EVANS
& PAUL LEWIS

First published in Great Britain in 2013

This paperback edition first published in 2014
by Guardian Books, 90 York Way, London N1 9GU
and Faber and Faber Ltd, Bloomsbury House,
74–77 Great Russell Street, London WC1B 3DA

10

A CIP record for this book is available from the British Library

ISBN: 9781783350346

Typeset by seagulls.net

Printed in England by CPI Group (UK) Ltd, Croydon, CR0 4YY

FSC
www.fsc.org
MIX
Paper from
responsible sources
FSC® C013604

CONTENTS

To Caroline. I love you.
Every day I am glad that you are with me. Rob

To Barry and Ramona,
who would have been very proud. Paul

CHAPTER 1

The Secret Unravels

They were in their safe house, sitting on worn-out sofas in the lounge.

A team of undercover police officers had spent the evening drinking and chatting in the London apartment. It was late one night in 1994.

They turned on the television to catch a news report from Germany. Tens of thousands of Germans were trawling through secret files compiled on them before the Berlin Wall came down. There was a wave of revulsion at the scale of surveillance perpetrated by the Stasi, the East German secret police. They had as many as 100,000 informants; teachers were reporting on their students, neighbours snooping on friends, doctors on patients. Even husbands and wives were found to have been informing on each other. The files also revealed the identities of thousands of professionally trained spies. Men and women had been given new identities before being scattered across East Germany to quietly seek out opponents of the communist regime. The TV report showed the distraught face of a woman in Berlin who had discovered the man she had loved for years was a spy.

There was silence in the lounge. Then one of the undercover police officers said what the others must have been thinking.

'You do realise, this is going to happen to us one day,' he said. 'We're going to open a book and read all about what we've been up to.'

1

It was a chilling thought. The men lounging on the red sofas were members of the Special Demonstration Squad, a top-secret unit within London's Metropolitan police. Their undercover work was so secretive that most senior police officers in the land had no idea they even existed. Their job was to monitor British subversives. And to pull it off, they needed to transform themselves into the people they were spying on and live among them for years. Each police officer had forfeited his warrant card in return for a whole new identity, complete with fake passport, driving licence and bank account. Most of them grew beards and long hair, giving rise to the unit's unofficial nickname, the Hairies.

Twice a week, they met in safe houses to laugh, drink and share anecdotes about their undercover lives. These were bonding sessions. One classified document drawn up at the time defined the purpose of the meetings as the creation of a 'developed sense of team spirit'. On this particular night, they were in a flat in Chiswick. It was on the second floor of an apartment block called Beaumont Court, which they codenamed West London OP. It was standard practice during these gatherings for the police officers to remain in their undercover roles throughout. It led to some bizarre encounters. A bearded anarchist engaged in angry debate with a fascist skinhead. Animal rights activists tried to persuade their colleagues to give up meat. Campaigners from rival left-wing groups would argue over the finer points of Marxism. But unlike in the real world, when the spies would be expected to clash with each other, the safe house meetings were intended to foster camaraderie.

'The first time you go to one of the meetings is an experience you never forget,' says one spy in the Chiswick safe house that night. 'Nothing can prepare you for it. Whatever your perception of the police is, you lose it when you see them. They simply do not look like police officers at all. One of them even brought his dog with him. It's the equivalent of turning up at a conference for people selling the *Big Issue*. Some of them have cans of Carling in their hands because they cannot get out of role.'

He recalls how the television report about the activities of the Stasi in Germany triggered an awkward discussion. Of course, the SDS operation was on nothing like the scale of surveillance perpetrated in East Germany. But some of their methods were perhaps not that different.

'It was an uneasy conversation,' the spy recalls. 'I think we realised that none of us would like to ever see a book about this come out. We were part of a black operation that absolutely no one knew about. Only the police had actually agreed that all this was all OK. We felt one day there would be a reckoning. Would the British public be happy if they knew this was happening?'

It was another 17 years before the reckoning. Even then, the process of realisation was a gradual one. There was no sudden deluge of revelations, no decision from on high to come clean about the dark truth of covert policing. None of those who were spied upon were granted permission to visit a police warehouse, open their file and discover which friends and lovers had betrayed them. All of that is perhaps still to come.

Instead, one of the most tightly guarded secrets the British police had ever kept from the people unravelled slowly, like an old jumper finally worn thin. The first frayed thread appeared in October 2010, when a curious blog post appeared on a website. It was an update on Indymedia, a site used by political campaigners to disseminate news.

The page contained two pictures of a strange-looking man. In the first, he was smiling from beneath a fluffy Russian hat. He had a damaged left eye looking sideways. The second photograph showed the same man beside a river, an idyllic country scene behind him. He had shoulder-length hair and the sun was twinkling off his bright gold earrings.

The caption said it all. 'Mark "Stone" has been an undercover police officer. We are unsure whether he is still a serving police officer or not. His real name is Mark Kennedy. Investigations into his identity revealed evidence that he has been a police officer and a face-to-face confession has confirmed this.'

Although no one knew it at the time, Kennedy was just the latest in a very long line of undercover police who had been living in protest groups. The history of the infiltration of political campaigns stretched way back, long before even the team of officers who were sitting in that lounge in 1994.

But Kennedy was unique. He was the first spy ever to be identified as a police officer and unmasked in public. He would, within a few months, become Britain's most infamous undercover police officer, setting in train a cascade of revelations that would shock the establishment to its core.

Kennedy was 41 years old, brought up in the commuter belt of London, and married with two children. His alias, Mark Stone, was a tattoo-covered man of the same age but cut from a very different cloth. Stone was a cocky, gregarious eco-activist with a taste for adventure. Based in Nottingham, he travelled across Europe, infiltrating almost every major anti-capitalist and environmental protest.

Kennedy seemed to have licence to do whatever was necessary to manipulate activists into trusting him. He had an endless supply of cash, earning him his nickname, Flash. He had two long-term activist girlfriends and countless other sexual liaisons. One of the women remained his partner for six years.

Not long after the blog post appeared on the internet, senior police began to realise the severity of the situation. They quickly established that Kennedy had crumbled in front of his activist friends and admitted his real identity. If that was not bad enough, Kennedy had also compromised another police spy, revealing that a woman eco-activist who pretended to work in care homes in Leeds was actually another undercover officer. Kennedy had gone rogue.

A team of senior officers was dispatched to the United States, where Kennedy had gone to ground somewhere in Ohio.

They arrived too late. Weeks earlier, he had picked up the phone and called an activist friend in England. The man on the other end of the line was a lecturer who used a dictaphone to record Kennedy admitting the entire operation had been 'like a hammer to crack a nut'.

'I am just so sorry, for everything,' Kennedy said. 'It really hurts. I am really sorry … The way I feel, I really want to make amends. I fucking hate myself so much. I betrayed so many people.'

Before he hung up, Kennedy asked the lecturer to tell their mutual friends that he was sorry for what he had done. His voice was trembling.

'I haven't just run away, you know?' he added. 'I want to face up to what has happened and I want it addressed.'

'Yep,' the lecturer said.

'You are the first person I have really spoken to. I'm glad it's you because you are a sensible guy. I don't know. It's just the loss. It's been huge. It was my life for so many years. It's just empty now.'

'All right, Mark.'

'I am not going to start blubbing down the phone.'

'It's weird, because there is just so much to say.'

'There is,' Kennedy said finally. 'And it has to be said.'

When details of Kennedy's life undercover began seeping into the newspapers, there was the kind of public uproar that police chiefs have nightmares about. The controversy quickly stretched way beyond British shores. Kennedy had used his fake passport for more than 40 foreign missions, from Poland to New York, and the story of the libidinous British spy was making headlines in France, Germany, Ireland and Iceland.

Eventually, Kennedy sold his story to the press. 'Both sides have been waiting for my statement – the police and the activists,' he told a tabloid newspaper. 'This interview is my statement.' What followed was a mixture of truth, embellishment and fiction, but all of it helped fan the flames of publicity. 'People like to think of things in terms of black and white,' Kennedy said. 'But the world of undercover policing is grey and murky. There is some bad stuff going on. Really bad stuff.'

Kennedy said he was one of a dozen undercover operatives infiltrating protesters for a squad called the National Public Order Intelligence Unit. Each spy was costing the taxpayer £250,000. Kennedy claimed to have been hung out to dry by his supervising officers. He said he was on the brink of suicide. The picture Kennedy painted was of a rogue police unit abusing its power, hiring luxury apartments and driving around in expensive blacked-out vehicles. 'If we all had a meeting it looked like the CIA had turned up or something – seven identical flash cars in the car park of a pub,' he said. Police had spent £7,000 modifying a Casio G-Shock watch so he could use it to record conversations with protesters he was spying on.

Police chiefs were holding daily crisis meetings to deal with the fallout. Each time a new detail about covert operations emerged into the public domain they had to manage the consequences. The throwaway remark about his Casio watch, for example, resulted in an immediate order to undercover operatives across the country who were wearing the same device. Their watches were now compromised. They were instructed to immediately remove them from their wrists.

For police, ordering a new brand of covert listening devices was the least of their worries. Politicians were demanding to know what on earth had been going on. That was a difficult question to answer. Police chiefs had been running their own fleet of spies for a very long time without ever consulting parliament. It was a secret, designed to enable them to keep an eye on the politically troublesome individuals in society. Now the whole operation was starting to come apart at the seams.

Still more threads kept appearing. Each detail made the story seem even more surreal. The female undercover officer who served with Kennedy had infiltrated a community centre in Leeds, before suddenly disappearing to Lithuania. An overweight truck driver who had recently been sleeping with women in Cardiff turned out to be another undercover cop from the same unit. There were disclosures about undercover police with punk haircuts, smoking weed, posing as animal rights fanatics and organising illegal raves. All of them had vanished without a trace. Many had women they left behind. Some had even fathered children.

Controversies involving the British establishment tend to follow a familiar arc. It has been honed over centuries. The first response from those in power is to ignore public disquiet, and wait to see if the storm runs out of energy.

If the pressure builds to a point where the authorities can no longer remain silent, there is a public declaration of wrongdoing and a promise to learn lessons. Individuals are blamed, never institutions. If there is still a demand for answers, the state deploys a potent weapon. It is a technique that has stood the test of time, allowing those in power to duck responsibility and silence critics with one fell swoop and kick a controversy into a field of long grass, where they hope it will be forgotten.

Inquiries are strange phenomena. They lend the appearance of probity, but rarely achieve much, except the avoidance of awkward questions. There are exceptions, of course: full-blown public inquiries like the Leveson inquiry into the press or the Macpherson inquiry into racism in the police. Mostly, though, inquiries take place behind closed doors, allowing those in power to determine what the public should be told, and what must remain secret.

The more a controversy persists, the greater the number of inquiries that are launched. It is a game that can last for years. The overall number of inquiries that are announced can be a barometer of how hard the authorities are trying to quell a scandal.

The first inquiry into undercover policing of protest groups was launched in January 2011, just after the details of Kennedy's deployment were made public. By the spring of 2013, a further 14 inquiries had been announced. None had come close to answering the most basic questions.

How did Mark Kennedy manage to spend seven years living a double life? How was he found out? Who were the other undercover police officers and what happened to the friends and lovers they left behind? How long has all of this been going on? And why?

CHAPTER 2

Starter for 10

He was one of life's larger personalities. 'A big guy with a booming personality' was one description. Born in 1927 to an army family, educated at a Wiltshire public school and Oxford University, he joined the Royal Marines at the end of the second world war and after a brief stint at a football pools company was recruited to the Metropolitan police. A fortnight later, Conrad Hepworth Dixon was called to an austere police section house in Beak Street in London's Soho, stripped naked and ushered into a small room. 'A man in white coat came in and stared at his lower half, examined his feet, and went wordlessly away. Shortly afterwards, Dixon was transferred to Special Branch,' records his obituary. The branch only selected those it considered to be the finest specimens. In its view, it was the Met's elite, revered and feared in equal measure, and Dixon was one of its most experimental leaders. It was Dixon, a chief inspector, who first had the ingenious idea of turning police constables into pretend political activists. The story starts with him.

It was 1968, a rather iconic year for protest. It is perhaps difficult nowadays to understand just how turbulent the late 1960s really were. Across the globe, governments were convulsing. Workers and students were taking to the streets in Paris, Prague, Berlin, Madrid, Mexico City and Chicago in spontaneous bursts of civil unrest. They had similarities and differences; they did not all have the same philosophy or aim, but they were loosely progressive or left-wing. They were united by their opposition to America's war in Vietnam. And they shared what one historian called 'the common spirit of youthful rebellion'.

In Britain, the establishment trembled as government ministers and police chiefs grew worried that protesters had the power to tear down Britain's political and economic system. A revolutionary mood was in the air; many young people hoped there was more than a whiff of actual revolution too. They were enjoying the benefits of a good education and the prospect of a good job and they wanted to do things differently to their parents' generation. They were more idealistic, free-spirited; they felt the world was theirs to shape. They rebelled against a society they saw as intransigent, drab and paternalistic. They distrusted authority – politicians, college administrations and police. It was a time of radical change in the arts, music, film and fashion. It felt like the old certainties were giving way to a new world. For the young, protest was the exciting engine of this change. For the authorities, it was a dangerous and very real risk to the established order.

A mood of panic gripped Whitehall as the protests over the Vietnam War intensified in 1967 and 1968. There were frequent marches in London, but one in particular shook the government: the Grosvenor Square demonstration of March 1968. Following a large rally in Trafalgar Square, thousands marched on the US embassy, which was surrounded by police. There was a standoff as the protesters refused to back down and mounted police rode into the crowd. Demonstrators broke through police ranks and streamed onto the lawn of the embassy, tearing up barriers and uprooting sections of the fence. More than 200 were arrested during a prolonged battle as stones, firecrackers and smoke bombs were hurled at the building.

Public disorder as ferocious as this had not been seen on the streets of London for many years. For some of the younger generation, it was a totally alien sight – and intoxicating. Black and white television pictures showing the police struggling to control the demonstrators, and punching and kicking them, shocked the country. One MP later complained about the 'violent use of police horses who charged into the crowd even after they had cleared the street in front of the embassy'. In Scotland Yard, there was alarm – a sense that senior officers had been caught on the back foot.

That day was a watershed moment. When the protesters started to organise a second large demonstration scheduled for October that year, politicians and police were determined to clamp down. Two months before the scheduled march, Special Branch was sending weekly reports to the Home Office, chronicling how the protesters were preparing for the event. The dispatches reveal deep anxiety in police about what some feared was an impending insurrection. In one update, Dixon wrote that 'a group of about 50 anarchists from Liverpool' intended to attack an army recruiting office when the march snaked through Whitehall. Around 160 demonstrators from Glasgow, he reported, were 'being advised to wear crash helmets and urged to carry ball-bearings, fireworks, hat pins and banner poles for use as weapons'.

One informant claimed that protesters would tie fishing line between parking meters to trip up police, while anarchists were reported to be devising a plan to loot shops, restaurants and travel agencies along Oxford Street. The list of buildings police believed were under threat was continually expanding and included the Bank of England, the Ministry of Defence, Home Office, the Hilton Hotel and even the Playboy Club. Bomb disposal experts were mobilised in case explosives were found. Ministers were so worried that they considered deploying soldiers – a suggestion rejected by senior officers at the Met who insisted they could control the streets.

Meanwhile the press inflamed the febrile atmosphere with lurid but dubious articles about protesters manufacturing and storing Molotov cocktails and attempting to buy small firearms. Privately, Dixon informed a senior officer the press reports were 'a carefully constructed pastiche of information, gathered from a number of sources and spiced with inspired guesswork'. Brian Cashinella, one of the journalists who reported the claims, says the information had actually come from Special Branch. If the purpose was to discourage people from joining the protest, the strategy appeared to work, as more and more activists distanced themselves from the scheduled march.

Still the hysteria spread. Mary Whitehouse, the self-appointed guardian of British morals, breathlessly told police about a hot new piece of intelligence she had acquired. 'I have received information from an American friend of mine that an organisation called "The Doors" who are a political extremist organisation are now in England. I do not think that their arrival here in the United Kingdom is a coincidence.' A police constable dutifully recorded the tip-off, which, like much of the melodrama, was amusingly wide of the mark about the intentions of Jim Morrison and his fellow band-members.

When the big day of the second Grosvenor Square demonstration finally arrived, it was a huge anti-climax. Thousands of protesters came and marched, listened to speeches in Hyde Park and then quietly went home. One section of the demonstration again attempted to break the police cordon around the embassy, but without success. As for the arsenal of Molotov cocktails, one of the demonstrators found three milk bottles containing petrol and a piece of rag and handed them in to police.

However, hearsay can be as relevant as truth when it comes to influencing a national mood and the atmosphere remained volatile. Many still believed the country was on the cusp of social unrest. One damp squib of a march was not going to discourage Dixon, who was already determined to invent a new tactic to help quell the upheaval.

On September 10 1968, the Special Branch chief inspector had crafted a six-page memo. Stamped 'Secret', it was sent to a select group of the most senior officers in Scotland Yard. 'The climate of opinion among extreme left-wing elements in this country in relation to public political protest has undergone a radical change over the last few years,' Dixon warned. He spelled out how this change had escalated. 'The emphasis has shifted, first from orderly, peaceful, co-operative meetings and processions, to passive resistance and "sit-downs" and now to active confrontation with the authorities to attempt to force social changes and alterations of government policy.'

He continued: 'Indeed, the more vociferous spokesmen of the left are calling for the complete overthrow of parliamentary democracy and the substitution of various brands of "socialism" and "workers' control". They claim that this can only be achieved by "action on the streets", and although few of them will admit publicly, or in the press, that they desire a state of anarchy, it is nevertheless tacitly accepted that such a condition is a necessary preamble to engineering a breakdown of our present system of government and achieving a revolutionary change in the society in which we live.'

Revolutionary times called for revolutionary solutions. When Dixon was finally asked by his superiors what could be done about the protests, he unveiled his grand plan. In Special Branch folklore, the ebullient commander is said to have replied: 'Give me £1 million and 10 men, and I can deal with the problem for you.'

He got what he asked for. The framework for covert surveillance that Dixon constructed that year remained intact throughout his lifetime and beyond.

His radical plan was nothing less than a new concept in policing. The police had dabbled in undercover work before. By the late 1960s, the police had been deploying undercover officers to infiltrate and catch street criminal gangs, but had only done so sporadically. Officers impersonated drug dealers, robbers, contract killers, gamblers or antique fraudsters. But they only did so for short periods – usually just a few days or weeks. In between these covert assignments, officers would return to their station and resume their normal duties.

What Dixon had in mind was infiltration of a different order. He wanted Special Branch officers to transform themselves into protesters and live their fake identities for several years. For the whole time they were undercover they would never wear a uniform or set foot in a police station, unless, of course, they were dragged in, kicking, screaming and handcuffed, in character as a protester. They would be equipped with false ID documents, grow their hair long, and melt into the milieu of radical politics, emerging to feed back intelligence on any gathering conspiracy. These men, who would only penetrate political groups, would have a close-up, front-row view of what was really going on.

It is unclear how Dixon alighted on such a radical idea, but it was approved precisely because the authorities were so alarmed by the threat of the burgeoning protest movement. Labour prime minister Harold Wilson's government was so supportive of the initiative to gather more reliable intelligence that it agreed to fund Dixon's plan directly from the Treasury.

For his new recruits, Dixon had in mind a distinctive type of police officer. They needed to be skilled manipulators who were resilient, resourceful and sharp. They would find flats or bedsits, preferring those at the back of houses in case fellow activists went past at night and noticed the lights were off and no one was in. They would take up jobs with flexible working hours and travel, such as labourers or delivery van drivers, so they could disappear for, say, a day with their family, without arousing suspicion.

The elaborate pretence would count for nothing unless the physical appearance of the police officers was dramatically changed. The usual tidy short-back-and-sides haircut would have been an easy giveaway. These officers were required to grow their hair long, often down to their shoulders or even longer. Their hairstyles and resplendent beards fitted in with the alternative fashions of the day. One squad member recalls that he grew his hair out and put on John Lennon-style round glasses, but struggled to produce anything more than wispy facial hair. Another spy's hair was so fine that he had to go to the hairdressers and have a perm. 'I ended up looking like Marc Bolan – big hair!' Years later, members of the unit had their hair shorn as they were sent to infiltrate Nazi skinheads.

The ragged appearance adopted by many of the police operatives gave rise to nicknames for their specialist unit within Special Branch. They were occasionally called the Scruffy Squad, but were more commonly known as the Hairies. More formally, the official name for Dixon's new unit was the Special Demonstration Squad, usually shortened to SDS. Its official role was to provide 'sufficient and accurate intelligence to enable the police to maintain public order'.

SDS officers evolved their own ritual over the years before crossing the threshold into their undercover lives. There were three parts to the ceremony. The first was to have a big leaving party to say goodbye to their Special Branch colleagues. For the restricted number within the branch who knew of the existence of the SDS, it was the unit into which police officers vanished.

'It was a shadowy section where people disappeared into a black hole for several years,' recalls one officer who infiltrated the revolutionary Socialist Workers Party in the 1980s.

Second, the would-be spies were taken into a room and interrogated by two senior members of the squad to test their cover stories. Another undercover officer remembers his test well: 'What's the name of your employer? What's his phone number? Right, I am going to ring him now, and so on. They ask the kind of questions you might get tripped up by and make sure your cover is as solid as it can be.' The last symbolic gesture was for SDS officers to hand in their warrant cards; it was too risky for them to be kept, even at home.

It was the final act in their transformation and it meant that police spies would never be able to arrest suspects, a factor that was key to the plan devised by Dixon. Normal undercover police who infiltrated criminal gangs gathered evidence in far shorter operations that could be presented in court as part of a prosecution. Like other branches of the constabulary, their job was to nail criminals. But the SDS was different: they were solely required to gain inside intelligence from political groups and slip it back to their handlers over a period of many years.

They would never be tasked with collecting evidence for use in a trial or called to be a witness in court. The reason was obvious: if any SDS officer disclosed their true identity to testify against activists from a witness box, the whole edifice of the spy operation would come tumbling down. For Dixon's plan to work, it was essential for political activists to believe that the state would never go so far as to plant spies to live among them for years on end.

As with any closed group, the SDS quickly developed its own culture and language. The more accomplished members of the squad – those capable of totally submerging themselves into their undercover roles – became known as 'deep swimmers'. Less committed spies were 'shallow paddlers' and derided for not managing to access the heart of their selected political movement. The SDS, which was 10-strong for many years, also had a nickname for the targets they were spying on. Political activists were called 'wearies', in recognition of what police saw as their 'wearisome' dedication to a political cause.

The SDS cherished their reputation as the Hairies, but insiders had another nickname for the unit. 'The 27 Club' was a name that recognised the date of the unit's official foundation on October 27 1968, the day of the second large demonstration against the Vietnam War. The club even had its own unofficial motto that encapsulated the squad's approach to undercover policing: 'By Any Means Necessary'.

There is no doubt that many squad members relished the adventure of espionage, the thrill of constantly living on the edge at risk of being found out. Managing to make friends with activists and gaining their confidence was only half the battle. Protest groups were often on the lookout for infiltrators and the slightest slip-up by the police officer could stir suspicions. One spy says he was nervous every time he changed clothes and converted himself into his activist persona.

Life is full of weird, unpredictable coincidences, and the spies always ran the risk of unexpectedly bumping into someone they knew in their real life while undercover. SDS officers knew that at any moment they could be walking along the street with activists and randomly bump into someone who knew them as a police officer.

According to SDS folklore, that is precisely what happened to one officer who went undercover in the Socialist Workers Party in the 1970s. He was on a demonstration when a uniformed colleague recognised him through his dishevelled disguise. The

SDS man's reaction was instinctive and decisive: he attacked the police officer, grabbing his balls until he backed off. The spy then quickly slunk away.

These stories about what had gone wrong with past deployments were relayed to new recruits as a warning. Another cautionary tale handed down through the years concerned an undercover officer who was embedded in a tiny Trotskyist group, the International Marxist Group. A telephone tap had revealed to the SDS that his targets were growing suspicious about him. He was later invited to a pub by his activist friends, plied with alcohol and asked detailed questions about his past.

'I remember drinking something in the region of nine or 10 pints of beer,' he says. 'I was very concerned that I was getting to the point where my guard would slip, that I would reveal something which would give something away or expose a colleague and I remember my mind seeming to stay ice cold. The rest of me felt like jelly but they had drunk along with me so they were showing considerable signs of wear as well, and I don't know if I satisfied them or not but I was allowed to go and then I was met shortly afterwards by a colleague, then I just collapsed. I was absolutely drunk as a skunk, but I'd held it together until then.'

The episode told the SDS spy and his managers that it was time to quit. He had not enjoyed the undercover life and, in any case, it was affecting his family life. Every SDS officer knew that if the suspicions grew and they were compromised it would mean the end of their mission. They only ever had one chance; it was plainly too risky for a spy who had been rumbled to disappear and then reappear in a new group.

After the anti-Vietnam protests, one of the next movements to attract the attention of the SDS was the campaign against apartheid in South Africa. In the late 1960s, opposition to the regime was growing. A coalition of students, liberals and Christians sprang up to confront and disrupt white South African sportsmen competing in Britain. In late 1969 and early 1970, the activists laid siege to the South African rugby team with imaginative forms of civil disobedience.

Buying tickets like ordinary spectators, campaigners would gain access to grounds and jump over the barriers, past police and onto the pitch to interrupt the game. The battle of wits between the protesters and the police lasted months. Authorities deployed more police to form a barrier to guard the pitch and keep watch for activists leaping out of the crowd. At one game, barbed wire was laid down to deter incursions.

Campaigners adapted their own tactics. One slipped into the South African team's hotel and glued the door-locks to their rooms. Another disrupted the tour by dressing in a smart suit and telling the driver of the team coach that he was needed inside the hotel. When the driver was gone, the activist sat in the driver's seat and chained himself to the steering wheel.

Among those who were placed under surveillance by the nascent SDS was Peter Hain, an activist who would later become a Labour cabinet minister. One of the SDS spies who joined Hain's campaign was called Mike Ferguson. The SDS operative's handler, a fellow Special Branch officer named Wilf Knight, says the mole used cunning to climb the ladder of the anti-apartheid campaign. Knight recalls how, at one meeting, Hain told the group he believed they had been infiltrated by a spy. 'There was one poor devil that Mike Ferguson looked down the room at and said, "I think it's him,"' says Knight. 'He got thrown out, and Ferguson survived – bless him.'

Finger-pointing at bona fide activists, and wrongly accusing them of being infiltrators, become a well-used technique among the SDS officers who wanted to deflect attention. Ferguson survived any suspicion anti-apartheid campaigners may have had and completed his undercover tour. He later progressed to become the head of the SDS.

Another early target of the SDS was the International Marxist Group, a collection of left-wing revolutionaries at the vanguard of the campaign against the Vietnam War. 'A small group numerically, but significant as an idea-producing faction,' was how Dixon summed them up in one of his reports. Prominent in the group was a well-known radical of the time, Tariq Ali, who had, in Dixon's view, 'natural gifts as a mob orator'. Ali would later become a leading left-wing figure for many years.

The SDS spy who targeted Ali and his friends was sufficiently trusted to be allowed to guard the office of the anti-Vietnam war campaign. 'I was aware that some of the keys that I was holding when I was babysitting those offices gave access to offices that we, or the Security Service, might be interested in,' he recalls. When activists were out of sight, the SDS officer pressed keys into some Plasticine to make a mould from which copies could later be made. The filing cabinets of the campaign group were later apparently rifled through by MI5.

Breaking into the premises of campaign groups would become another common tactic for the SDS. The legality of such a tactic was dubious, but this was the SDS, the unit which believed 'any means' were justifiable and took its cue from the security services. This kind of stuff was routine for MI5, and they had long been assisted by reliable men from Special Branch. The former MI5 operative Peter Wright famously wrote in his bestseller *Spycatcher*: 'For five years we bugged and burgled our way across London at the state's behest, while pompous bowler-hatted civil servants in Whitehall pretended to look the other way.'

Dixon was given a free hand to develop the tradecraft of the undercover unit. The squad was buried so deep within Special Branch that it was immune to many of the grudging reforms undergone by the rest of the force. The branch operated on the traditional principle of 'need-to-know' – only those officers involved in an operation would be briefed on its details. Intelligence provided by SDS spies would be shared with other departments in the Met without anyone disclosing how it was obtained.

The SDS turned out to be a surprisingly easy secret to keep. Its spies were out of the office and out of sight, meeting only in safe houses across the capital. It is perhaps a cliché to call the SDS an elite squad, but to an extent it was. It prided itself on recruiting only the very best officers within Special Branch, which considered itself a cut above the rest of the Met. The covert squad did not operate like the rest of the police. There were very few rules and the spies did not feel bound by their rank when they discussed operations. The operatives were expected to approach problems in a creative way, eschewing the obedient, plodding mindset of a bobby.

The spying game was initially considered a man's world. It appears that SDS operatives were all men until the early 1980s, when women police officers were needed to infiltrate the women-only peace camp set up outside the American nuclear weapon base at Greenham Common in Berkshire. Two female police officers were selected and duly dispatched to join the women protesters. Even after that, women were rarely recruited to the SDS. Insiders describe the unit as macho and competitive, a team in which it was frowned upon to discuss emotional issues despite the very obvious psychological strain being placed on operatives.

The unit was not just the brainchild of Dixon, but very much a product of Special Branch, which already had a controversial reputation for conducting a covert war against enemies of the state. The branch was founded in 1883 to capture Irish republicans who were planting bombs in London. Since then, its primary job had been to gather intelligence to protect the nation's security. Some of its work was relatively uncontroversial. It included protecting public figures considered to be at risk, monitoring ports and airports for unwanted visitors, carrying out surveillance on embassies and helping to vet foreigners applying to become British citizens. But Special Branch, with its close links to MI5, was considered by many to be Britain's political police. Its officers were characterised as foot soldiers for the security services, acting as their 'eyes and ears' on the ground.

Over the years, Special Branch had spied on suffragettes, pacifists, unemployed workers, striking trade unionists, anti-nuclear activists, anti-war campaigners, fascists, anarchists and communists. The job of Special Branch, as the then home secretary Merlyn Rees put it – perhaps too honestly – in 1978, was to 'collect information on those who I think cause problems for the state'. In more formal terms, Special Branch spied on those deemed to be 'subversives'. But the definition of subversion was a contentious one and there was always the concern police would target people they should not.

In 1963, five years before Dixon founded the SDS, subversives were officially defined as people who 'would contemplate the overthrow of government by unlawful means'. By the late 1970s, the net had been cast wider and the definition amended to include all those who 'threaten the safety or well-being of the state, and are intended to undermine or overthrow parliamentary democracy by political, industrial or violent means'. By 1985, concerned MPs on the home affairs select committee noted that the branch was acquiring 'a sinister reputation of a force which persecutes harmless citizens for political reasons, acts in nefarious ways to assist the security services, is accountable to no one, and represents a threat to civil liberties'.

When Dixon was putting together his squad, Special Branch was expanding to cope with the perceived growth in the subversive threat. Indeed it seemed that the branch was constantly grow-ing. The 225 officers attached to the Special Branch in the early 1960s had expanded to 300 by the end of the decade. By 1978, there were 1,600 Special Branch officers. Originally based only in London, branch officers spread out across the country into provin-cial forces. Much of the increase was a consequence of the urgent need to deal with the Irish terrorist threat following the outbreak of the Troubles in the late 1960s.

But the expansion was also attributed to the growing surveil-lance of political campaigners, thousands of whom ended up in confidential Special Branch files. Much of the intelligence in these files was generated from publicly available information. For exam-ple, desk officers scoured press clippings, noting down names of activists quoted in articles or recording the names of people who had signed petitions.

When the homes of activists were raided, branch officers would comb through the contents of address books, letters and cheque-stubs to work out whom they were in contact with. Moving up the scale, phones were tapped and mail was opened. This was the routine, systematic work of the branch.

SDS officers had the more glamorous role. They left office duties behind them to inveigle themselves into key positions in protest groups. Becoming the treasurer was an established method of quickly gaining access to financial records. So too was becoming secretary, or minute-taker. The spies were told to avoid rising so far up the hierarchy of a group that they became its leader. 'As a rule of thumb, you could allow yourself to run with the organisation, but you had to stop short of organising or directing it,' recalls an SDS spy who infiltrated the Socialist Workers Party at the time of the Falklands War. The best position was that of a trusted confidant, a deputy who lingered in the background.

Although Dixon brought the SDS into existence, he did not hang around for long. In 1973, just five years after constructing the apparatus for long-term infiltration of protest movements, the chief inspector quit policing altogether. He did not want to be desk-bound, grinding his way up the police hierarchy for the rest of his career. The former police officer went to Exeter University to study economic history and then completed a doctorate in the working conditions of merchant seamen. Bizarrely, in 1975 Dixon was a contestant on the popular television quiz show *University Challenge*. A black-and-white photograph shows the Exeter team seated in the familiar line-up of the show, waiting to answer questions, or as the programme's famous catch-phrase would have it, their 'starter for 10'.

Dixon's young team-mates reflect the look of the era: long hair, moustaches, polo necks and big collars. The 48-year-old student stands out with his thinning black hair and bushy beard. His small eyes stare directly at the camera with the imposing air of someone who was not to be messed with. Dixon later lectured at maritime history conferences about the practices of foreign seamen and wrote a slew of books about yachting, one of which explained the intricacies of an electronic navigation system for boats. Each year, he spent a few months out on the open sea, sailing his boat off the coasts of Europe. He died in 1999, leaving behind a wife and four children. He was rewarded with a discreet obituary in *The Times*, the newspaper of record favoured by the establishment.

Prior to his death, Dixon did not disappear altogether from the SDS. He had chosen a new life but kept in touch with his old colleagues. Every five years, the spies, past and present, gathered to remember old times. In 1993, Dixon attended an SDS reunion to mark the 25th anniversary of the squad. Around 50 ex-spies and their managers came together at London's Victory Club, near Marble Arch, and heard a speech from their founder. One attendee recalls Dixon looked like 'a shanty old seaman'.

Over dinner, feeling secure that they were within a trusted circle, the spies traded tales of derring-do from their covert days. Revered among their number was of course Dixon, the founder of the squad. But there was another man who had gained the special respect of his colleagues – Bob Lambert. Suave and manipulative, Lambert's own tour of duty as a spy a few years earlier was considered one of the most impressive deployments in the history of the SDS.

CHAPTER 3

The Slippery Fox

The seasons were on the turn; Londoners were reaching for their jumpers beneath a cobalt blue sky. A little before lunchtime on September 19 2011, a debonair academic was preparing to give a scholarly talk on the fifth floor of a prestigious think-tank overlooking the River Thames. Around 50 people had come to hear the presentation at the International Institute for Strategic Studies, which styles itself as the world's leading authority on political–military conflict. Nigel Inkster, a director of the institute, praised the academic's 'encouragingly youthful demeanour' and paid tribute to his 'long and distinguished career' in the Special Branch.

Up to the podium stepped Dr Robert Lambert, a tall, composed man in his late 50s, wearing a well-tailored dark suit and tie. Lambert delivered his hour-long lecture, about progressive alternatives to combating the threat from al-Qaida terrorists, with the confidence of a practised public speaker. He spliced his thoughtful presentation with a few jokes, sending ripples of appreciative laughter through the audience, and waved his hand in the air as he expounded the arguments in his newly published book. This was a carefully written manuscript that charted selected parts of his 26-year career in Special Branch 'countering threats of terrorism and political violence in Britain', but made no mention of the darker periods of his past. There was nothing to puncture his image as a progressive academic, the recipient of an MBE for 'services to policing'. When Lambert stepped off the podium, he contentedly absorbed the applause from the audience, just one of many that had been convened from Singapore to Aberystwyth as part of his book tour.

He might have felt he was reaching the pinnacle of his career. In fact, the opposite was true. Over the next few months Lambert's reputation would be left in tatters.

Lambert began his career in the police in 1977, aged 25. He joined the Metropolitan police, following in the footsteps of his grandfather, Inspector Ernest Lambert, who spent a quarter of a century in the force. Within three years, Lambert was in the Special Branch and soon after recruited into the SDS, joining the ranks of Conrad Dixon's secret unit. Time and again Lambert would prove himself a master in the art of deception, a risk-taker with flair.

His undercover persona was Mark 'Bob' Robinson, a disarming, intelligent radical with a taste for danger. In 1983 – the first year of his deployment – Lambert met Charlotte, a vulnerable 22-year-old woman at an animal rights demonstration outside Hackney town hall in east London. Around 100 campaigners were outside the 1930s Art Deco building to put pressure on the council to sign up to a charter pledging an end to animal cruelty.

Lambert wandered over and asked Charlotte why she was wearing a stewardess-style colourful uniform, scarf and hat. She replied that she had come straight from work. The second time they met was more memorable: a demonstration against foxhunting in the Essex countryside. Charlotte started to fall for the older man. Lambert began picking her up before protests and dropping her back at her flat in east London, where she lived alone. 'He told me that he worked as a gardener in north London,' she says. 'He got involved in animal rights and made himself a useful member of the group by ferrying us around in his van.'

Looking back, Charlotte feels she was targeted by the man she knew as Bob Robinson. 'He was always around,' she says. 'Wherever I turned he was there trying to make himself useful, trying to get my attention. I think he was about 12 years older than me. It now seems that he worked to build a relationship with me, which developed into an intimate friendship and which became sexual. I believed at the time that he shared my beliefs and principles.' Lambert was Charlotte's first serious boyfriend and before long she was besotted.

Lambert always gave the impression of being a committed political activist. He chided his girlfriend for not doing more to stop the abuse of animals and encouraged her to take a more radical stance. He said that lobbying MPs and town councils would never bring radical change, arguing that only revolution would end the oppression of animals and humans in a capitalist society. 'He would tease me for not being committed enough,' she said. 'I was a vegetarian but he encouraged me to become a vegan and he got me to become more involved in "direct action".'

The police spy liked to flirt with the radical end of protest – and gave the impression he would break the law to further his cause. At weekends he visited London markets to stop traders selling and slaughtering chickens on the street, or stood outside butchers harassing customers. A friend of Charlotte says Lambert's persona was seductive: 'It was really an aphrodisiac that you had someone who wanted to do everything with you, who kind of took the risks that he took, and so it was a real rollercoaster in her life.' After a few months, Lambert and Charlotte appeared inseparable at demonstrations; friends commented they had an air of Bonnie and Clyde. Lambert was often protective of his younger partner too. He once rushed to help her when some foxhunters threw her into a lake.

Within a few months, the pair were an established couple among radical protesters in London. Rather than sitting in the back of the van, Charlotte was now in the front seat, beside the charismatic driver. 'Although Bob had a bedsit, he would stay with me. We set up home together. He would sometimes go off for a short while saying he had to visit his dad with dementia in Cumbria and sometimes he went off saying that he had a gardening job. Most the time while we were together he lived with me.' It was of course a double life. Lambert's father did not have dementia and did not live in Cumbria. His periods away from Charlotte were instead spent living a more conventional life with his wife and children in suburban Herefordshire. For at least five days a week, however, Lambert was with Charlotte.

Many SDS officers struggled to maintain their double lives. Not Lambert. He appeared to relish his duplicity, switching effortlessly between two worlds that were poles apart. Lambert was an ambitious man. He knew that a successful deployment – one in which he accessed the furtive underground networks of animal rights campaigners – could propel him up the ladder at Special Branch, and Charlotte was a key part of his equation. One of the hardest challenges for covert officers is turning up out of the blue without friends or family to vouch for them. They arrive in their late 20s or early 30s with sometimes feeble excuses for their sudden interest in politics.

Acquiring a girlfriend was an easy way to fill the gap, making an undercover police officer seem like a real person. Having Charlotte by his side helped Lambert to douse any questions about who he really was. Although she was not the most radical campaigner, she was a recognisable face, and had been interested in animal rights issues for around two years. Lambert exploited the credibility his girlfriend had already earned. 'One day, Bob wasn't there,' recalls a friend of the couple. 'And then Bob was there. He was everywhere.' There seemed no protest Lambert was not interested in. Unlike some of his more highly strung comrades, he had a relaxed charm about him.

'Bob was not extreme in his language,' says Martyn Lowe, a radical librarian. 'He was calm, reasonable, smiling. In politics you get nutters who sort of rant and rave – he was the complete opposite to that.' Paul Gravett, another activist, recalls Lambert as 'an affable, nice, fun guy who knew a lot about things. He was not a cardboard activist, he had real depth to him.' He remembers Lambert as 'very convincing as a sort of alternative person' who rejected the greedy individualism associated with Thatcherism, claiming instead to embrace a non-materialist lifestyle. He claimed to be into music – attending Glastonbury Festival and sharing Van Morrison albums with friends – and showed a keen interest in the left-wing literature stocked at Housmans, the radical bookshop near King's Cross station.

Lambert was well versed in political theory, and, according to one of his friends from the time, was 'pretty well organised intellectually', able to debate the finer points of anarchist philosophy. The spy quickly developed the right patter. Adopting the doctrines of the animal rights movement, he condemned speciesism – the idea that humans have more moral rights than animals – and claimed he did not believe in keeping pets because he rejected the idea he should control an animal. In a letter he sent to a campaigner in 1986, Lambert wrote about a campaign to stop trains carrying nuclear waste through London. He called them 'nukiller trains' – the favoured term of derision among anti-nuclear campaigners. One another occasion, when scuffles broke out between protesters and police at a demonstration, Lambert immediately took out his camera to record what he called 'police repression'.

Soon Lambert was throwing himself into several different strands of political activity, becoming involved in squatting, free festivals and anti-nuclear weapon camps. The mid-1980s were a tumultuous time in British politics as Margaret Thatcher sought to impose her will on the British people. Lambert and Charlotte were among those who resisted. 'They were like warriors trying to fight against it all,' recalls a friend of the couple. 'It was a really unjust time, a really divisive time. You either made loads of money or you were living in real poverty.' One of the big clashes took place in Wapping, east London, where the newspaper magnate Rupert Murdoch took on the print unions by sacking 6,000 workers. There were regular confrontations between police and supporters of the strike – more than 1,200 people were arrested. Lambert and Char-lotte were often at the heart of the protests. The group Lambert seemed most interested in was a small, environmental group called London Greenpeace, which bore no relation to the larger campaign with the same name. London Greenpeace was a radical anti-capitalist group and Lambert quickly found his niche, speak-ing eloquently at meetings and writing the group's propaganda.

Although he made a convincing activist, Lambert was never dour. His friends considered him a great drinking companion who liked to socialise at pubs like the Rising Sun in Euston Road. In the summer of 1986 he hosted a party at his flat on Talbot Road in Highgate when he moved out. He claimed to be earning a cash-in-hand income as a gardener in well-heeled properties in nearby Hampstead and elsewhere. A photograph from the era shows a lean, topless Lambert in white jeans and dirty trainers mowing a lawn. One day, to bolster his cover story, he hired two fellow activists to help him clear a garden in Surrey. He also told friends he had a side job driving mini-cabs, touting illegally for customers. True to his non-conformist lifestyle, he claimed he didn't have a bank account and preferred working in the black economy to stay off the government's radar and avoid paying tax.

*

Tracing the development of Lambert's undercover deployment shows a master at work. He began on the fringes of radical protest, made friends, persuaded activists that he was useful, and then began the gradual process of working his way into the heart of the action. In the early part of his time in the field, Lambert just turned up at the kinds of publicly advertised demonstrations that rarely attracted more than a handful of uniformed police. One – a protest against food manufacturers Unigate – took place outside central London's Dorchester Hotel in September 1984. Photographs show Lambert among a smattering of campaigners passing out handwritten leaflets and berating company share-holders en route to an annual meeting. He had even penned the leaflet that called on activists to make a stand against Unigate's directors. 'Let them know that there is no place for callous meat production in a caring society,' the leaflet said. 'Animals would prefer not to end up as Bowyers Pork Sausages.' Lambert ended the leaflet with the popular animal rights slogan: 'Meat is murder.'

However, from the outset Lambert was adept at cultivating the impression that his moderate exterior belied a more radical edge. 'Bob gave off the impression he was doing a lot of direct action but one could never put one's finger on it,' says Lowe. 'One always had the suspicion he was into something heavier. He never talked about it directly.' Gravett remembers that soon after he met him, Lambert 'let it be known' that he dabbled in illegal protest. He said that Lambert even told him he had once dressed up as a jogger and poured paint-stripper over the car of a director of an animal-testing laboratory. Truth or fiction, the story helped Lambert portray himself as a secret firebrand. It was the persona he needed to fulfil what had become the main objective of his mission – penetrating the intensely furtive, hard-core wing of the animal rights movement: the Animal Liberation Front.

Since 1976, the ALF has carried out thousands of unlawful protests to stop what it perceived to be the abuse of animals. It has a reputation for extreme acts of sabotage that have caused millions of pounds of damage. Police view the group as an underground terrorist network. ALF activists have targeted laboratories, abattoirs, butchers' shops, fast-food restaurants and factory farms. Their more radical tactics have included arson, break-ins, destruction of equipment, harassment of scientists, death threats and hoaxes. Campaigners in the ALF have been best known for the photographs in which they were disguised in black balaclavas and camouflage jackets triumphantly posing with rabbits or dogs they claimed to have 'liberated' from laboratories. For many years, the group was personified by its figurehead: the diminutive Ronnie Lee, a man widely recognised by his round glasses, beard and flat cap.

In the 1980s, the ALF was growing and its attacks were becoming more destructive. The ALF claimed it only attacked property and made sure that people were not harmed, but conceded its approach was combative. Keith Mann, an ALF activist jailed in 1994 for 14 years for sabotage, told the BBC: 'One man's terrorist is another man's freedom fighter. Call us violent, call us terrorists, call us anarchists, they're all used regularly. All we're asking for is change. We want people to stop using violence against animals.' The ALF was an obvious target for the SDS – one of the most important political groups the unit had to monitor. But the group presented a headache for senior officers.

ALF campaigners operated through a diffuse subterranean network of small activist cells. The ALF had no membership and no leaders. It encouraged the idea of autonomy; any activists could organise their own direct action and claim responsibility for it under the banner of the ALF. With no obvious structure, its followers worked in a fluid, loose way, coming together to execute a direct action and then quickly dispersing. Often attacks were carried out by solitary individuals. Each disparate cell waxed and waned according to the enthusiasm of its members and the ability of police to detect what they were up to. By 1985, police felt they were losing the battle.

A special squad was set up to catch ALF campaigners, who were subjected to telephone taps and extensive surveillance. Special Branch recruited an ever-expanding team of informants from across the animal rights movement in a desperate bid to find out what was going on. By the 1990s, police were running around 100 informants in animal rights groups, according to Ken Day, a former Special Branch man. He says some were being paid as much as £10,000 a year for intelligence on the ALF and its associates.

A confidential Special Branch document reveals that the SDS first deployed one of their operatives to the animal rights movement in April 1983. 'At this time, the major related policing problem was public disorder at large-scale demonstrations. Hence it was a relatively easy matter for him to infiltrate ... and obtain useful intelligence concerning public order events,' the document notes. It says of their spy: 'Essentially, he was working amongst well-meaning, idealistic campaigners ... Within their ranks was a small but growing number of militant activists prepared to take the law into their own hands.' Not long after that first deployment, the SDS deemed it necessary to send in a second operative and chose Lambert, one of their brightest young recruits. The document contains Lambert's own assessment of the task ahead, in which 'hard-won credibility and trust are prerequisites to high-grade intelligence'.

After first establishing himself among more moderate activists, Lambert set about befriending campaigners suspected of being in the ALF. One was called Geoff Sheppard. 'In my eyes he was a totally credible activist,' Sheppard says. 'I felt no doubt what-soever, you might say, that he was one of us.' Sheppard recalls how Lambert drove protesters around the country to support fellow ALF activists who were being prosecuted. They travelled up to Sheffield when Ronnie Lee and others were put on trial for conspiracy to commit arson. Lee, a former trainee solicitor, was jailed for 10 years in January 1987. Sheppard, Lambert and others complained that the sentence was harsh, telling each other that the treatment of their comrade should spur them on to carry out further attacks.

Just as he had done with Charlotte, Lambert made Sheppard feel the pair had a special connection; they were locked together in the struggle. A photograph captures the two men together in Lambert's van. The long-haired police spy is at the wheel of his battered vehicle, looking out the back toward his friend. 'I believed in him, and I liked him, and I thought he was a friend of mine,' says Sheppard. 'I trusted in him 100 per cent.' Both men were frequently seen at demonstrations and were involved in what Sheppard calls 'the legal stuff'. But few knew that they were also committed ALF activists. According to Sheppard and Gravett, Lambert even produced a well-known ALF leaflet from the era which summed up the group's philosophy under the stencilled headline: 'You are the Animal Liberation Front.' 'You wouldn't leave it to others if your friend was being beaten up in the street,' it said. 'In the same way you can't stand by as thousands of animals are slaughtered every day.'

It was this uncompromising approach that led the ALF to wage a sustained campaign aimed at economically damaging companies that sold animal products and provided Lambert with an opportunity to make his name. The ALF was turning its attention to chains of department stores like House of Fraser, Debenhams and Allders, all of which sold fur. Over three years from 1984, activists had planted more than 40 incendiary devices to set fire to shops up and down the country. In one particular spree, there was a series of co-ordinated attacks on House of Fraser stores across northern England, from Altrincham in Cheshire through to Blackpool, Harrogate and Manchester.

The media called the arson attacks 'firebombs', but in reality the homemade contraptions, designed to cause tiny ignitions, were rather basic. Devices the size of cigarettes boxes were placed under flammable objects such as an armchair or settee in the stores. The ALF insists that the devices were designed to go off at night so that people were not harmed – typically, they would be laid in the afternoon and timed to ignite just after midnight. The aim was to cause enough of a fire to set off the sprinkler system, avoiding a full-scale blaze but flooding the store extensively and ruining the stock. The top floor was favoured as all the floors underneath would be drenched.

The ALF hoped the campaign would inspire copycat actions around the country. A step-by-step guide on how to make the devices was quietly circulated around cells of activists. Under the misleading rubric 'Interviews with Animal Liberation Front activists', the closely typed booklet contained intricate diagrams involving nails, batteries, nail varnish, tweezers, watches and washing-up liquid. The instructions could be mastered by a clever activist with enough time on their hands, while all the household ingredients were available in regular high-street shops.

Sheppard recalls the moment in 1987 that a trio of ALF activists concocted a plan to set fire to three branches of Debenhams in an attempt to force the department store to abandon its fur products. 'Myself, and Bob, and one other person got together and formulated a plan,' he said. According to another confidential source who knew about the plot, the components for the attacks on branches of Debenhams in and around London were assembled in an empty squatted property. After a period of experimentation, the trio believed they had improved the rudimentary design stipulated in the booklet.

Lambert was in a prime position for a covert agent. He confided to one friend he was 'deeply involved' in the ALF and spent hours defending the ethics of its hard-line tactics. Another friend recalls Lambert telling her that he was going to set fire to the department store. She says she 'spent ages trying to persuade him not to, that it was a bad idea'. Lambert was unmoved: he portrayed himself as being willing to undergo a heroic sacrifice, risking his own freedom to prevent the sale of fur. The question was: how far would the undercover police officer go?

According to Sheppard, his friend Lambert was intimately involved in the conspiracy. Sheppard's testimony about the attack on the Debenhams store – and the part he alleges Lambert played – was highlighted in a parliamentary speech by Caroline Lucas MP in June 2012. Lucas told the House that Sheppard had claimed that he, Lambert and a third activist were part of the plan to target three branches of Debenhams. The trio each collected two devices during the day on Saturday, July 11 and then headed off to their designated branch. One was in Luton, another in Romford. The third, which Sheppard said the police spy was going to target, was the Harrow branch in north-west London.

That night, Lucas reported, Sheppard says he returned from setting fire to his allotted store and turned on the radio to listen to the BBC World Service. The newsreader announced that three Debenhams stores had been subject to arson attacks – including the branch in Harrow. According to Lucas, Sheppard said in his testimony: 'So obviously I straight away knew that Bob had carried out his part of the plan. There's absolutely no doubt in my mind whatsoever that Bob Lambert placed the incendiary device at the Debenhams store in Harrow. I specifically remember him giving

an explanation to me about how he had been able to place one of
the devices in that store, but how he had not been able to place
the second device.'

Lambert has consistently denied planting the incendiary device
in the Harrow store. Whatever the truth, the simultaneous strike
that night had by far the biggest impact of the ALF's campaign for
all the wrong reasons. Although police would have had advance
notice of the plan, through Lambert, the sprinkler system at
the Debenhams store in Luton's Arndale shopping centre had
been turned off to be repaired. There was nothing to douse the
small fire ignited by one of the incendiary devices in the mens-
wear department. Firefighters discovered the fire at 1.50am on
Sunday. It took 80 of them, pumping water from 10 engines, until
6.39am to bring the blaze under control. Four floors of the store
were gutted, and the store was shut for weeks. A black-and-white
photograph from the morning after shows a fireman hosing down
a mass of smouldering debris that looked like the scrunched aftermath of an earthquake. Insurers later calculated that the damage,
including loss of trading, amounted to £6.7m at the Luton store
alone – far more than any of the other arson attacks in the ALF's
campaign against the sale of fur by high street stores.

The store at Harrow was also badly hit, costing Debenhams
£340,000. The fire alarm went off just before 1am, alerting the
police and the fire brigade. Police constable Simon Reynolds from
Wealdstone police station arrived within minutes and found 'a
thick blanket of smoke'. With the help of a torch, PC Reynolds
and a colleague discovered the sprinklers working in 'an area badly
damaged by fire and water' in the section of the store selling luggage
on the first floor. The carpets, clothing and goods were sodden.

John Horne, of Scotland Yard's anti-terrorist branch,
confirmed that 'an improvised incendiary device had functioned
against the wall in a display area'. He told the court: 'Amongst

the debris I was able to identify the heavily charred remains of a small cardboard box, an alarm clock and what appeared to be the remains of a vehicle light bulb, and a dry cell battery.'

Police testified only one device was planted at the Harrow store. Two devices in the other Debenhams stores had failed to ignite and so police found them intact. Care had been taken to ensure no fingerprints were left on the small homemade devices, which had labels stuck to the side: 'Warning – Do not touch, ring police, Animal Liberation Front.' In Sheppard's version of events, Lambert had again earned his spurs as an ALF activist during the attack on Debenhams. 'I was already confident in him anyway but after that, I would have had absolutely no doubts whatsoever that he was a genuine ALF activist, because it simply would not have entered my mind that a police officer would carry out such an action.'

The attacks bore all of the characteristics of an ALF mission executed without a trace. If it were not for Lambert, detectives might never have worked out who planted the devices. Police made their arrests a couple of months later, bursting into the ground-floor bedsit of a corner house in Hillside Road in Tottenham in north London at 4.50pm on Wednesday September 9.

Sheppard and Andrew Clarke, the other ALF activist who would ultimately be convicted over the attacks on Debenhams, could not have been caught at a worse moment. They were in the middle of assembling a fresh round of incendiary devices for another wave of attacks. They were wearing rubber gloves, to keep their fingerprints off the devices, and sitting around a table in the tiny, spartan room. Spread out in front of them on pages of the *Guardian* newspaper was the paraphernalia for making four more devices – dismantled alarm clocks, copper wire, bulbs, batteries and nail varnish. The soldering iron being used by the pair to make the devices was still hot.

As Sheppard puts it: 'There was a kick on the door at which point the door came swinging open very violently. At least four or five large suited men came through that door and we were caught red-handed.' Lambert, however, was not with them. He seemed to have been the lucky member of the trio who had got away.

Months later, Sheppard and Clarke were sat side by side again, this time in the dock at the Old Bailey, listening as the prosecution laid out their case against them. 'They were in the process of what was clearly a well-practised method of constructing incendiary devices similar in every significant respect to those used at Harrow, Luton and Romford,' Victor Temple, for the prosecution, told the court. He explained how, after arresting Sheppard and Clarke, detectives seized a black woollen mask, 'incriminating' ALF literature, press cuttings of the previous attacks on Debenhams, and 'lists of butchers, fur shops etc'.

Looking back, Sheppard says that the tip-off for the raid was so accurately timed that it 'obviously came from Bob Lambert'. The police spy was one of the few people who knew that his friends Sheppard and Clarke would at that very moment be constructing more devices in the flat. But at the time, Sheppard never suspected Lambert. Indeed, for another quarter of a century, despite years languishing in jail trying to work out who the grass had been, Sheppard never once considered that his friend Bob Robinson had betrayed him.

In part, that can be explained by Lambert's deceptive skill when his friend was put behind bars: feigning empathy for his comrade and supporting him at every step. In a letter to another activist in March 1988, Lambert explained how he was desperate to ensure that enough supporters were visiting Sheppard, who was on remand. 'I just had a feeling that no one would be visiting him on the Sunday and I was getting very frustrated,' he wrote.

Behind bars in Wandsworth jail, Sheppard felt grateful when Lambert visited him and gave him a gift – a book about philosophy. 'I remember thinking, "Bob's still there for me." Actually he was the guy who put me there,' says Sheppard. However, at the time, Sheppard and others had no reason to wonder why and how the third man in their cabal had got away. 'For 24 years I have believed that my friend, what I thought was my friend Bob Robinson was on the run and had most likely gone to a different country and probably made a new life for himself,' says Sheppard. 'And I just thought – good for him, he was the lucky one that managed to get away.'

In June 1988, Sheppard and Clarke were convicted of the arson attacks on all three Debenhams stores, which caused £9m damage. Sheppard was jailed for four years and four months, and Clarke for three and a half years. Judge Neil Denison told the pair: 'I am not going to spend time pointing out to you what in my view are the errors of your ways for the very good reason you wouldn't pay attention to what I'd say.' Sheppard and Clarke already had a record of breaking the law in protest against animal cruelty. At the time of their arrests over the Debenhams attacks, Clarke had a conviction for damaging property during an anti-fur trade demonstration, while Sheppard had breached a suspended sentence for smashing a butcher's window. In the 1990s, Sheppard spent another four years in jail after he was caught with components to make incendiary devices and a shotgun. Both men say they no longer take part in illegal protests.

Sheppard and Clarke made an odd pair. Sheppard was an unemployed 30-year-old who professed an unwavering dedication to his cause, even if that meant breaking the law. Taciturn and straightforward, he says it as he sees it. Clarke, a gardener for a London council, was younger at 25, and, as he now admits, a touch naïve. He is often given to long, involved explanations of events. The pair would not naturally be friends, but any movement needs all sorts of people.

One interpretation of Lambert's infiltration of the ALF is that it was a superb triumph for the police. The undercover operative had been buried deep enough in the group to secure intelligence that jailed two committed campaigners in the midst of an arson spree involving a well-known department store. And Lambert did it with aplomb, displaying a cunning that cemented his reputation as one of the finest spies ever to serve in the SDS. His escapades would be recounted for years to come, burnishing his credentials as one of the most committed 'hairies' ever deployed in the field. There is even grudging respect from Sheppard. 'There is part of me that does feel betrayed by Bob because I genuinely felt that we were mates,' he says. 'But on the other hand, now I know that he was an undercover officer doing a job of work, I suppose you have got to, in that sense, hand it to him in a way. He was very clever at what he did.'

But would an officer in Lambert's position who did carry out a criminal act cross a line? Broadly speaking, police chiefs can authorise an undercover officer to participate in criminal acts if they can show that it would help detect or prevent a more serious crime. They are not usually permitted to be involved in the planning, instigation or execution of crime. Nowadays covert policing is regulated by the Regulation of Investigatory Powers Act 2000, which requires advance authorisation from senior officers. But in Lambert's time, the rules were more vague. The SDS considered the arrest of its spies, and their occasional participation in crime, a hazard of the job that could always be ironed out with a quiet word with someone senior at Special Branch.

A practice had emerged in which SDS officers who committed crimes quickly reported what they had done to a supervising officer. They were then provided with retrospective authorisations, recorded over the years in top-secret green files, known through their filing code: 588. It was not *carte blanche* approval to commit any crime, but it gave SDS spies licence to blur the lines when out in the field. Most of the time, the crimes they were committing involved trespass, breaches of the Public Order Act or minor acts of criminal damage.

The accusation levelled against Lambert is of a different order: that he encouraged and even participated in an arson campaign that caused millions of pounds of damage. Lambert has firmly denied that he planted the incendiary device at the Harrow store of Debenhams but takes credit for jailing Sheppard and Clarke. In a carefully worded statement, he says: 'I was deployed as a Met Special Branch undercover officer in the 1980s to identify and prosecute members of the Animal Liberation Front who were then engaged in widespread incendiary and explosive device campaigns against vivisectors, the meat and fur trades. I succeeded in my task and that success included the arrest and imprisonment of Geoff Sheppard and Andrew Clarke.' Denying the accusation over the arson attacks, he adds: 'It was necessary to create the false impression that I was a committed animal rights extremist to gain intelligence so as to disrupt serious criminal conspiracies. However, I did not commit serious crime such as "planting an incendiary device at the Harrow store".'

On one reading of the contrasting accounts, Lambert should be believed over Sheppard. It is the word of a long-serving, decorated police officer against that of a convicted animal rights campaigner with an obvious axe to grind.

Even if that is the case, there remain a host of difficult questions for Lambert and the SDS. If Lambert was involved in the arson campaign because it was deemed necessary to avert a more serious crime, who authorised his mission? Two former SDS officers say the unit would never have countenanced one of its spies taking part in sabotage of that severity as it would have been too risky and foolhardy.

And there were of course other options. Given they had advance warning of the plot against the three Debenhams stores, why did the SDS allow the arson attacks to go ahead? Why did they not intervene sooner, arresting Sheppard and Clarke as they were about to carry out their first wave of attacks?

Finally, there is the mystery of the fire in the Harrow branch of Debenhams. The luggage section of the department store was undoubtedly scorched by flames. If Lambert did not start the fire, then who did?

CHAPTER 4

Fatherhood

In the autumn of 1985, Bob Lambert was standing in a hospital holding his newborn son. Surrounded by nurses and medical equipment, he looked the archetypal proud father. His eyes were fixed adoringly on the infant he had just watched being born. But this was not one of the children he had with his wife. Lambert was in the cosy red jumper and jeans of his alter ego, Bob Robinson. In a nearby bed, recovering from the painful labour, was Charlotte, the activist he had been sent to spy on and now the mother of his child.

The birth of a first child is an unforgettable moment for any couple, and Lambert and Charlotte seemed no different. Lambert came and visited his tired girlfriend in hospital. He held her hand at her bedside as she floated off to sleep. 'Bob was there by my side through the 14 hours of labour in the autumn of 1985 when our son was born,' Charlotte says. 'He seemed to be besotted with the baby. He was a great dad and I had no reason to believe that our son was not his first. I didn't realise then that he was already married with two other children.'

Lambert was not the first SDS officer to father a child in the field. At least one other child had already been born to a member of the squad in the early 1980s. Rather than receive any reprimand for his actions, that SDS officer was later promoted to a senior post in the squad. But on the whole, fathering children was not what police spies were supposed to do. It made life exceptionally complicated.

A few days before the birth was due, Lambert announced that he needed to urgently visit his father, whom he pretended lived on the other side of the country, in Cumbria. Charlotte was devastated – she wanted the father of her child to be by her side. The birth was already a few days overdue and doctors had warned her that there was a growing risk of problems with the pregnancy. Lambert initially insisted he needed to go. Part of the SDS officer's cover story was that his mother had died of cancer, while his father, who had dementia, was alone. It was a convenient excuse for Lambert to disappear from time to time.

Charlotte's parents chastised Lambert, pleading with him to remain in London. But he refused to hang around. Instead, shortly before he claimed to be leaving for Cumbria, Lambert picked up Charlotte's mother and drove her to her daughter's flat in Hackney, so she could look after the heavily pregnant woman while he was away.

On the Sunday afternoon, Charlotte felt sufficiently well to tell her mother it was OK for her to leave her in the flat alone. Lambert was due to return that evening. After half an hour on her own, Charlotte began to suffer contractions and the pain was far worse than she had expected. She started to panic.

Lambert arrived home just in time to rush his girlfriend to hospital in his beaten-up old van. Charlotte started giving birth that night, oblivious that her boyfriend had not, as he claimed, been in Cumbria while he should have been looking after her.

Instead, Lambert had spent the weekend in Herefordshire, wearing the regular clothes of an off-duty cop and enjoying the company of his wife and kids. In the evening, Lambert had said goodbye to his family and told them he was going to work. None of them suspected anything untoward. They would never have imagined that when he said he was going to work, Lambert meant he was actually en route to a maternity ward to watch his secret child being born.

The challenge of juggling two separate family lives was just one of the dilemmas faced by Lambert, now he was the father of an activist's child. There were some difficulties, like the tricky question of the child's birth certificate, that were virtually impossible to overcome.

Because he and Charlotte were unmarried, they were required to sign the birth register together. The spy initially gave the impression that he wanted his son to take his surname – that of 'Robinson' – rather than Charlotte's. He then evaded several attempts by Charlotte to get him to sign the form.

At the hospital, Lambert disappeared when the registrar came around. He let Charlotte down on the handful of occasions when they made appointments to visit the registrar's office. On the last afternoon before the six-week deadline for registering the child, Charlotte stood waiting outside the office for Lambert to turn up. He never did. Charlotte registered her son under her own name but without any reference to Lambert. The section of the birth certificate used to list the name of the father was left blank.

In hindsight, Lambert's refusal to sign the document may seem odd. But at the time it appeared in keeping with the beliefs of a radical activist who eschewed any connection to the state and refused to wed Charlotte, arguing he did not want their relationship stamped with the institution of marriage. A friend of the couple recalls: 'Bob didn't believe that people should own each other and have some sort of legal hold over each other.'

Charlotte had fallen pregnant with the child toward the end of 1984. It was not an unwanted pregnancy. On the contrary, Charlotte wanted the baby and she got the impression that Lambert felt the same. 'Bob seemed excited by the news and he was caring and supportive throughout the pregnancy,' Charlotte says. The SDS man appears to have done nothing to persuade his girlfriend to terminate the pregnancy. He was caring and supportive, by her side during hospital appointments and antenatal classes. The couple went shopping together to buy clothes, a cot and pram for their child. Lambert insisted they undertake a practice drive from Charlotte's flat to the hospital, so they could be certain of the route.

What was Lambert thinking? He knew that his life with his son would be short-lived. At the time, he was near the start of his deployment, still trying to build his credibility as an activist. Lambert had another three years undercover ahead of him. But after that, he would be gone, likely never to set eyes on mother or child again. Charlotte, the woman he claimed to love, would be left in a life of poverty, raising their child as a single mother.

Perhaps Lambert was seduced by his undercover life and unable to think through the consequences. Maybe he thought there would be a way to straddle his two worlds long into the future, that he would find a way to retain some kind of presence in his second family's life. A less charitable view is that Lambert calculated that having a child with an activist would cement his cover story. No one would suspect he was an undercover police officer if the mother of his child was an animal rights campaigner. The child would be his own flesh and blood. Evidence – if ever it were needed – that Bob Robinson was a real person.

Cynical as it may seem, some people who know Lambert well believe he probably had his undercover operation in mind when he decided to have the child. To penetrate groups like the Animal Liberation Front, his fake persona had to be totally believable. The child, his son, was a convenient prop.

Initially, Lambert gave every impression of being a devoted father. For a few months he betrayed no hint that he would vanish from the family's life, doting on the boy and supporting Charlotte. He took the child with him on father and son outings and spent most of his spare time with his new young family. One photograph from the time shows Lambert and other activists building an animal sanctuary. They are in a muddy construction site, pushing wheelbarrows and carrying planks of wood. Lambert is leaning against a wall, holding his son in one arm and staring at the ground.

Lambert knew he would need to terminate his relationship with Charlotte and prepare the ground for his departure months or even years before he disappeared. In 1987, at the height of his infiltration of the Animal Liberation Front, Lambert became more distant from the mother of his child. One of the perceived strains on their relationship was lack of money. Charlotte came from an unstable background and was struggling to support herself and their newborn son. Lambert claimed never to earn much in wages from his cash-in-hand jobs doing bits gardening and cabbing. Besides, he told Charlotte that his efforts were better spent campaigning against animal cruelty.

Friends of Charlotte recall how she was initially happy to take the greater responsibility for earning money, allowing Lambert to dedicate his time to politics. After a period on benefits, she took on some part-time work, making arrangements for friends and family to look after the baby. But Charlotte could not escape the feeling that Lambert should have done more to provide for them. It was a constant source of friction. Another reason for the arguments was more intimate. Eighteen months after the birth of his son, Lambert was complaining that Charlotte was neglecting their sex life. 'The relationship was a slow death – arguments, scenes, all the things of a breakdown of a relationship,' says a friend of the couple.

Charlotte believes that Lambert deliberately provoked her and started wearing her down, causing arguments when there was no reason to quarrel. 'With the benefit of hindsight I can now see how he orchestrated the breakdown of our relationship,' Charlotte says. 'It was a very hard time for me.'

Desperate, she would shout at the father of her son and say she was disappointed in him, that she needed him to start working to put food on the table. Friends recall how Lambert remained calm, even Zen-like, and refused to talk to her unless she calmed down. 'That would make her even more wild, as you could never wind Bob up,' the friend adds.

Charlotte was one of four sexual relationships Lambert had when he was undercover. A second was little more than a one-night stand, and a third lasted some months. His fourth intimate relationship was curious because it was not with an overtly political campaigner, but a woman who Lambert believed could lend his undercover identity further credibility.

Karen met Lambert at a party in Tottenham in north London in May 1987, around the time his relationship with Charlotte was falling apart. Karen was a 24-year-old who had come to the capital to find work and was intrigued by Lambert's endearing smile. They fell easily into conversation and before long, she was smitten. Evidence of the love she felt for Lambert rolls easily off her tongue. He was, Karen says, 'polite, considerate, very romantic, attentive, charismatic'. She recalls he smiled a lot and was non-judgmental. And he was cute. 'I thought I had found my Mr Right. He was very charming and I thought I could take him to meet my parents,' she says. Throughout their 18-month relationship, she was struck by one particular trait in the man she knew as Bob Robinson. 'I thought he had a high moral code,' she says.

Very quickly they were spending most of their free time together, attending concerts and spending long, lazy weekends at home. Karen was aware that Lambert had a young son from a previous relationship and he occasionally brought him along when he saw her. But on the whole he came across as a free spirit with a politically rebellious streak. Lambert confided in Karen that he was deeply involved in campaigning for animal rights and even admitted he was part of the ALF. Karen in contrast had little interest in political activism. 'He was always asking me to go to meetings. He introduced me to lots of activists. I did not realise what the ALF was,' she says. At the time Karen was working as an administrative assistant at the state-owned Central Electricity Generating Board. She kept quiet about her job as she feared Lambert's activist friends would take against her because the CEGB was running nuclear power stations.

Karen had less idealistic hopes for the future. She wanted to develop her career and settle down to a family life, ideally with Lambert. The SDS man gave every impression that life together was a possibility.

After more than a year together, Karen felt their relationship was moving forward. She had made it clear that she wanted to start a family with Lambert and he appeared to feel the same way. He had been to see her parents three times. But when Karen eventually broached the question of conceiving children head on, Lambert surprised her by saying that he was not interested. She wrote in her diary that it had been a 'black day'. 'I remember crying a lot that day,' she says. 'I was just so shocked.'

The couple were spending most of their time together at her house in east London, which she shared with seven others. Lambert lived in what she remembers as a grotty flat above a barber's in Graham Road, Hackney. 'He had a single man's room with a shared kitchen,' she says. It was almost completely empty. 'He claimed to be not interested in possessions,' Karen says. It was the same line Lambert had used on Charlotte when she had visited his threadbare Highgate flat a few years earlier.

There was a time during the summer months of 1987 when Lambert was maintaining a complex web of deception involving women. He spent at least one day of the week with his wife and two children in the suburbs. The rest of the week was either spent with Karen or Charlotte, whom he was still sleeping with. Charlotte was desperate to rekindle her relationship with the father of her son. Lambert would often come around to her flat with a 'takeaway and a bottle of wine', a code they developed for a night of romance.

Lambert must have known he was toying with Charlotte's emotions, giving her false hope. There was no chance of a reconciliation. He knew that Bob Robinson was soon going to have to vanish for good. His duplicity was becoming more intricate. Lambert made sure that Karen and Charlotte never met each other and told both women different stories. He told Karen that his son was the result of a brief fling with a woman who had tricked him into having a baby by claiming she was taking the contraceptive pill when she was not. Whenever he picked up his son from Charlotte, he made sure that Karen stayed in the van, parked around the corner.

There was a reason for Lambert to maintain ties with both women: they would be useful when he was manufacturing the end of his deployment. Every SDS officer needed a plausible excuse to drop everything and disappear – and it was important that there were people close enough to them to vouch for their vanishing act.

Following the arrests of Geoff Sheppard and Andrew Clarke over the Debenhams attacks, Lambert began to arrange his departure. He told Karen, Charlotte and other friends that he could be next in line to be arrested and he believed that Special Branch were hot on his trail. He told Karen about a 'big crisis' in the ALF; there was talk of an infiltrator in their midst who was providing police with detailed information about the group's activities. Lambert said he feared he would be arrested and charged with some kind of conspiracy, meaning a jail term as long as 10 years.

Lambert was considered something of an expert when it came to smoking out informants. A few times before he had made accusations about other ALF campaigners, accusing them of facilitating police. He had even written a guide for animal rights activists to work out how to spot infiltrators. Now he was telling friends that he believed their clandestine group had been so successfully penetrated that the law was closing in around them.

In 1988, the SDS pulled off a clever ruse to convince Lambert's friends that his anxieties were justified. By then Karen had moved into a flat in a high-rise block on the Nightingale Estate in Hackney with two of Lambert's friends.

Early one morning, detectives raided the flat, letting slip that they were 'looking for Bob'. He was not there, and neither was Karen, but the news quickly filtered out that Special Branch were hunting for Lambert. The fake raid was, according to one former Special Branch officer, 'done for maximum effect' to add credibility to Lambert's cover story. It was a trick the Special Branch was to orchestrate on other occasions.

Over the last few months of 1988, Lambert and Karen discussed what to do. It appeared obvious that Lambert had to make himself scarce for a few years. Karen said she wanted to join him on the run, but he insisted he would have to go alone. He said that she should not waste her life as a fugitive, constantly looking over her shoulder. He said she deserved better: the rewarding career and family that she wanted so badly. Karen remembers her boyfriend saying: 'I am not good enough for you.'

Lambert abandoned his flat and stayed for a couple of weeks in what he called a 'safe house' with one of Karen's friends. She remembers meeting him once. 'There was still a lot of electricity between us,' she says.

In December 1988, Lambert and Karen spent a week alone together in another friend's house in Dorset to say goodbye. 'I was heartbroken,' she says. 'Even when he left, I could not imagine that it had finished because we loved each other so much. I wanted to go on the run with him. I was prepared to do that for him.' Lambert's apparent sacrifice in not taking Karen with him made her admire him even more. He said he was going to Spain. In early 1989, Karen received a long letter from Lambert post-marked Valencia, saying he was not coming back but raising the possibility that she could join him out there. It was the cruellest of false hopes, but Lambert knew it would make his disappearance seem more genuine.

Earlier he had been having similar discussions with Charlotte. On one visit to her flat, he entered his son's bedroom, leaned over his cot and told him that he loved him, whispering goodbye. 'He said he had to "go on the run" to Spain, owing to him being involved in the firebombing at the Debenhams store in Harrow,' Charlotte recalls. 'He promised he would never abandon his son and said that as soon as it was safe I could bring our baby to Spain to see him.'

Lambert knew that was never going to happen. Charlotte too received a letter from Lambert from Spain. It was the last she, or her son or Karen ever heard from Bob Robinson. He was gone.

Life for Charlotte as a single mum was never easy. With Lambert suddenly out of contact, she felt emotionally bruised and vulnerable. Later, she began a relationship with another man and married him. Her new husband treated his stepson as his biological son and to some degree was like a substitute father in Lambert's absence. For a few years they had a happy family life. But just five years into the marriage, Charlotte's husband tragically died. She was grief-stricken, but particularly worried for her son, who was then aged just eight. The boy had now effectively lost two fathers.

Distraught, Charlotte became desperate to find Lambert, believing that he could help their son get through the mourning process. Lambert had always promised he would return to look after his son; now they were in dire need of his assistance. One of Charlotte's friends recalls how the young woman was sure that Lambert would return, reuniting the family. 'She needed him so much in her life, she was so devastated,' the friend says. 'She was so damaged that she just wanted Bob to help her with her son.'

Charlotte enlisted the help of social services and the Child Support Agency, the government department responsible for tracking down absent fathers and making them pay their share of child maintenance costs. Time and again, official state records drew a blank. It was as if Bob Robinson didn't exist. Charlotte's only remaining hope was that Lambert would keep his promise and get in touch. Although she had moved house, her parents lived in the same property, and she knew it would be easy for Lambert to quietly return from Spain to track the family down.

When she realised Lambert was not coming back, Charlotte felt she was at fault. 'I felt guilty,' she says. 'At that time I blamed myself a lot for the break-up and for the fact that my son had lost his father.'

By then of course Lambert was not in Spain, but just a few miles away, behind a desk at Scotland Yard. Following his SDS deployment, Lambert was transferred to a Special Branch department known as E Squad, which investigated terrorist threats from around the world. By the time Charlotte had lost her husband, and begun searching in vain for Lambert, he was back at the SDS in a senior position. Lambert's infiltration of the ALF and London Greenpeace was considered a stellar performance and he was recalled to work as an SDS manager around 1994. The titular head of the SDS was by then a detective chief inspector, Keith Edmondson. But it was Lambert – controller of operations – who had the respect and the day-to-day control of the squad.

Lambert was now a spymaster, using wisdom gleaned from his years undercover to guide the next generation of SDS spies. He was adamant that other spies should follow his example in disappearing abroad at the end of their deployment. One classified SDS report written by Lambert once he was in the post stressed the importance of managing 'carefully crafted withdrawal plans' to convince 'increasingly security-conscious target groups of the authenticity of a manufactured departure'. He added: 'Inevitably this entails travel to a foreign country. Given our collective experience of problems which can arise when less careful attention is given to withdrawal strategy this policy appears manifestly justified.'

To many of the new SDS officers, Lambert was a patriarchal figure, whose reputation was an inspiration for those who served under him. He took to the role with ease, giving his men practical and philosophical advice about espionage. He informed his squad that 'with experience and expertise comes legitimacy and credibility'. Lambert was the gaffer, deciding when, where and how SDS operatives should be deployed. He was pulling the strings like a puppet-master.

One undercover officer who looked up to Lambert was a young, headstrong recruit with a ponytail who used the alias Pete Black. At the time he was full of praise for the man he describes as the 'operational governor' of the SDS. 'I chatted to Bob about everything, everything,' he says. 'You used to go in with any sort of problem, and if he could not work out how to get you out of the shit, then you were fucked.'

Lambert stepped down from the SDS in the late 1990s, after managing dozens of undercover officers. His career, like that of the Special Branch, took a dramatic twist in the wake of the 9/11 terrorist attacks on the United States. Law enforcement on both sides of the Atlantic believed they had been caught off guard by the attacks and there was a major shake-up of counter-terrorism policing.

Lambert claimed to believe that the 'war on terror' developed by US president George Bush, and supported by Tony Blair, was a misguided approach. He publicly advocated that police should develop an outreach approach, engaging with Muslim groups to isolate the more fundamentalist elements that advocated terrorism.

He and two other former SDS spies were given the resources to set up the Muslim Contact Unit, which was ostensibly designed to build relations with Islamic groups in London. Lambert ran the unit between 2002 and 2007, publicly arguing that policing of Muslim communities should be based on trust, transparency and voluntary civic duty. He claimed to want to empower Muslims and reduce the influence of al-Qaida propagandists in mosques.

It was a decidedly liberal position for Lambert to take, and a far cry from the culture of intrusive surveillance he had perfected during his many years in the SDS. Indeed, some have asked whether the Muslim Contact Unit was in fact a front for a more sinister intelligence-gathering exercise – an accusation Lambert denies.

After his retirement from Special Branch, Lambert made an extraordinary decision that would sow the seeds of his downfall. For many years he impressed on his men that discretion was absolutely key to intelligence work. Under Lambert, SDS officers were reminded of the importance of keeping a low profile, even years after their deployment had ended. Lambert made clear this was an obligation for all of his men. He wrote in one Special Branch document that the continuation of cover, even after a deployment is completed, was 'the golden rule' of SDS tradecraft.

The message, in Lambert's words, was clear: SDS officers had to 'maintain cover in all situations and at all costs, and later, when returned to normal duties, do nothing to compromise the integrity of the operation'.

It was with some astonishment then that fellow SDS officers noticed Lambert take on such a public profile after leaving the Met police. It was as though he could not help shuffling himself into the limelight. Building on his professed theories about the policing of Muslim communities, Lambert became an academic. He took on postings at St Andrews and Exeter universities. He became a regular fixture on the speakers' circuit, giving passionate talks at conferences. He even appeared on television.

Lambert grew into his latest incarnation as a progressive academic. He now had a grey beard and liked to wear jackets with a shirt and no tie. He spoke at public rallies, joining campaigns against racism and Islamophobia. It was like a small part of him was becoming Bob Robinson again.

Of course Lambert never concealed the fact he was a former detective inspector from Special Branch. His policing career provided him a certain cachet. Lambert wrote a book, *Countering Al-Qaeda in London*, which airbrushed his SDS years from his long career as a police officer. He began touring the country to promote his book. He was becoming a public face.

Lambert's golden rule about never compromising the integrity of the SDS, repeated to spies over the years like a mantra, was going out the window as he basked in the attention of his newfound career as an academic.

Every time he made a public appearance, the veteran spy was playing with fire. Many SDS officers had murky secrets they hoped would never see the light of day. But few had as many skeletons in the cupboard as Lambert.

*

Almost a quarter of a century after Bob Robinson disappeared, pretending he was going on the run to Spain, Charlotte had moved on in life. Her son was now a strapping 25-year-old man. She was proud of what he had achieved, despite his difficult childhood. After those postcards, Lambert had ceased contact altogether. There were not even any child maintenance payments to support Charlotte. 'He abandoned me to support our son alone and to explain to him the disappearance of his father,' she says. 'I tried to track Bob down countless times over the years but those efforts were doomed to failure as I did not even know his real name.' Both Charlotte and her son had been searching for Bob Robinson, a man who no longer existed. They presumed he had started a new life somewhere in Spain, still fearing arrest by Special Branch. They realised that Lambert might be anywhere, if, that was, he was still alive.

Thursday, June 14 2012 had been an ordinary day for Charlotte. 'I came home from work at about 4pm. As I don't work Fridays, Thursdays are the start of my weekend. I made a pot of coffee and because the weather was good, I took the *Daily Mail* and the coffee out to the garden. As I flicked through the paper I saw the picture of Bob Robinson in the 80s – it was "my" Bob, my son's dad. I had not had news of him for approximately 24 years and there was his face staring back at me from the paper. I went into shock, I felt like I couldn't breathe and I started shaking. I did not even read the story which appeared with the picture.'

In the end, it was veteran activists from the now-defunct London Greenpeace who had joined the dots and realised Bob Robinson was not a fugitive still hiding in Spain, but an academic touring lecture theatres in Britain. It was not hard for them to find Lambert's photograph on the internet toward the end of 2011. The world had changed immeasurably since the days when Lambert and his comrades used old printing machines to produce political leaflets. Now they were staring in amazement at YouTube videos. The man they knew as Bob Robinson was thinner than the middle-aged academic on the screen. His hair was shorter and greyer, and he now had a beard. But it was his mannerisms that gave Lambert away. His disarming smile, his smooth voice, the inimitable way he held the attention of an audience.

Some of the veteran campaigners were out of practice. They had not taken part in direct action protests for years. One afternoon in October 2011, they had a good reason to come out of retirement.

Lambert was giving a speech in London alongside an impressive line-up of MPs, writers and musicians at a conference organised by two anti-racist groups, Unite Against Fascism and One Society Many Cultures. It was the kind of event Lambert was getting used to – a rally to 'celebrate diversity, defend multiculturalism, oppose Islamophobia and racism'.

That morning, five former London Greenpeace members met in a café near the rally to plan their confrontation. At lunchtime, two of them, Helen Steel and Martyn Lowe, came out of the sandwich shop, and walked directly into Lambert. For a moment, they thought he might look at them in horror, realising they were the activists he infiltrated years ago. But there was not even a flicker of recognition in his face as he strode confidently past.

Shortly after, Lambert took his familiar position behind the podium and looked out at the 400-strong crowd at the Trades Union Congress building. Lowe, Steel and three other campaigners took seats dotted around the audience. Lambert gave a short, pugnacious speech castigating David Cameron, Tony Blair and other politicians for alienating Muslims. He walked a few metres back to the top table of speakers. Before the applause could die down, a man in the audience rose to his feet.

'I have one question from the floor. Dave Morris, London

Greenpeace. Is he going to apologise for organising disgusting undercover police infiltration of campaign groups including
anti-fascists and my own group, London Greenpeace, for five
years as Bob Robinson?' There was confused whispering in the
audience.

The chairwoman tried unsuccessfully to quieten Morris down.
But he was not going to stop – he had been chosen by the group
to speak out because he had the strongest voice.

'We are publicly outing you today because you were involved
in this activity and we want to ensure that you are not informing
on groups that are here today,' he says. 'OK, will you apologise for
infiltrating London Greenpeace for five years and, as an inspector,
overseeing other police officers infiltrating environmental groups
and other campaign groups?'

Lambert sat impassively, giving nothing away. He sipped from
a glass of water. His old comrades looked older now, but he must
have known these were the former associates he had infiltrated in
another life.

The chairwoman interjected: 'Apologies for the disruption to
the conference. Our next speaker is…' Lambert left the building.

A few days later, aware that the *Guardian* was about to run a
story on his past, Lambert released a statement, admitting he had
once been an SDS officer. 'As part of my cover story, so as to gain
the necessary credibility to become involved in serious crime, I
first built a reputation as a committed member of London Greenpeace, a peaceful campaigning group. I apologise unreservedly
for the deception I therefore practised on law-abiding members
of London Greenpeace.' He added: 'I also apologise unreservedly for forming false friendships with law-abiding citizens and in
particular forming a long-term relationship with Karen, who had
every reason to think I was a committed animal rights activist and
a genuine London Greenpeace campaigner.'

Lambert made no mention of Charlotte, their son or the murkier aspects of his deployment as an animal rights activist. Neither was there any mention of the many other SDS officers who, as their commanding officer, Lambert knew had behaved in much the same way as he had. Presumably, these were secrets that Lambert was hoping would remain intact.

'I should point out here that the vast majority of Met Special Branch undercover officers never made the mistakes I made, have no need to apologise for anything, and I deeply regret having tarnished their illustrious, professional reputation.' He later added: 'I always knew that if details of my earlier role as an undercover police officer became public my own credibility and integrity would come under close scrutiny. I fully appreciate that many dedicated anti-racism campaigners who know me will find revelations about my prior undercover police work anathema and disturbing. I can only hope to regain the credibility and trust I have lost in the fullness of time and on the basis of what I do as well as what I say.'

If anything, however, Lambert's reputation has gone from bad to worse. Three months later, in January 2012, the *Guardian* revealed he had fathered a child while undercover, although the newspaper had been unable to locate Charlotte or her son. Amid speculation about the real purpose of Lambert's Muslim Contact Unit, he was forced to deny it was a front for surveillance. 'I did not recruit one Muslim Londoner as an informant nor did I spy on them,' he said.

Six months later, the Green MP Caroline Lucas stood up in parliament to make a speech about Lambert's infiltration of the ALF. She raised some awkward questions about those 1987 arson attacks against Debenhams. '[Geoff] Sheppard and [Andrew] Clarke were tried and found guilty – but the culprit who planted the incendiary device in the Harrow store was never caught,' she said. 'Bob Lambert's exposure as an undercover police officer has prompted Geoff Sheppard to speak out about that Harrow attack. Sheppard alleges that Lambert was the one who planted the third device and was involved in the ALF's co-ordinated campaign.'

The MP added: 'There is no doubt in my mind that anyone planting an incendiary device in a department store is guilty of a very serious crime and should have charges brought against them. That means absolutely anyone – including, if the evidence is there, Bob Lambert or indeed the people who were supervising him.'

It was an explosive revelation. Lambert denied the accusation, but the story was carried by dozens of newspapers, including the *Daily Mail*, which ran the headline: 'Undercover Officer "Set off Firebomb in Debenhams"'.

It was this story that Charlotte came across when reading the newspaper in her garden that Thursday in June. 'I describe 14 June as the day of the earthquake and a big hole opened up,' she says. 'All my security, everything I took for granted fell down the hole.' Stunned by the picture of Bob Robinson in the newspaper, Charlotte could barely move. She managed to stand up and walk inside her house to phone her parents.

'My dad got the paper from their nearest shop and my mum got out the photos of Bob and our son, at the birth and when he was a toddler. They confirmed to me that by comparing photos, it was definitely Bob. I didn't sleep all that night. My head was full of memories and questions. I was examining every memory again looking for clues that I should have seen that would have revealed his identity. I needed to know if I was just a part of Bob's cover story, and if our son, who he'd abandoned, was also just a part of his cover story.'

The next morning, Charlotte spent the day frantically trying to track down Lambert. She knew he was now an academic at St Andrews. 'I called the university and asked for Bob Lambert. I was put through to a woman in his office. She was understandably cagey but I burst into tears and told her that I was the mother of his son. She could hear that I was in a state and said to me she would call Bob, tell him I'd phoned and she would call me back if there was any message.'

Ten minutes later, the phone rang. 'It was Bob,' she says. 'This was the first time I had heard his voice for 24 years but I recognised it. It was very emotional. I remember asking him: "Why me?"' Charlotte recalls asking Lambert several other questions during that call. Was she chosen as his target by the SDS? Did he choose to abandon their son? Was their whole relationship the product of orders from a commander at Special Branch? She says Lambert sounded emotional but failed to help fill the gaps. 'He could not answer my questions,' she says. 'I could no longer believe a word he said.'

That day would leave a deep emotional scar for Charlotte. The trauma of discovering Lambert was a police spy led to months of psychiatric treatment at the Priory Hospital in London. Friends say Charlotte has not been the same since. She is fragile and constantly on edge and has had suicidal thoughts.

Charlotte has not been helped by the behaviour of Lambert, who has met her a few times since their first telephone conversation. Friends say that during their first encounter, Lambert arrived with flowers. He told her that she was a special woman, a great mother to their son, and that during his undercover deployment he had tried his best to protect them.

'I feel so confused and hurt by what has happened,' Charlotte says. 'I don't understand what I am supposed to have done that I was chosen by the state to be treated like this. I was no threat to national security. And what was my child – collateral damage?'

CHAPTER 5

McSpies

The epic legal battle 'McLibel' is a remarkable tale about how a group of powerless protesters challenged and embarrassed a mighty corporation. It is an incredible story, worthy of a movie script. Indeed, the story was made into a film and has already been the subject of a book and thousands of column inches in newspapers. The plot involved a tiny environmental group that produced a roughly typed leaflet castigating the world's biggest hamburger chain, McDonald's. The activists had so little money that they could only afford to distribute a few hundred photo-copied versions.

Instead of ignoring what was little more than a pinprick in the reputation of a restaurant chain whose commercial empire spanned most of the world, McDonald's executives decided to crush the criticism by exploiting England's notorious defamation laws and suing the activists for libel. They presumed the impecunious campaigners would bow to their demands, withdraw the leaflet and say sorry. Fifty media outlets, ranging from national newspapers to student magazines, had already decided it was too expensive to fight a full-blown libel case through the courts and had apologised for criticisms they had made about the fast-food chain.

Against all expectations, two of the campaigners stood their ground and took on the corporate power in what turned out to be England's longest-ever civil court case. The two – an unemployed postman and a part-time bartender – could not afford solicitors or barristers, so they had to defend themselves. By contrast, the multinational corporation, flushed with profits from selling Big Macs and fries to 35 million customers a day around the world, spent up to £10 million on the most expensive lawyers money could buy, including a £2,000-a-day barrister. The gruelling court battle, spread over 313 days between 1994 and 1996, was a David and Goliath contest.

In legal terms, McDonald's largely won the case, but in the court of public opinion, they lost badly. For years, they had spent billions to make their Golden Arches one of the most recognisable brands in the world. Yet the court case exposed the company to searing scrutiny, revealing embarrassing stories about the quality of its food and business practices. Millions of copies of the infamous leaflet were reprinted around the world, and McDonald's heavy-handed use of the law was seen by many as a disaster for its image. It prompted one expert to call it 'one of the most extended own-goals in the recent history of public relations'.

McLibel is now celebrated as a triumph for the activists who inflicted great damage on a corporate behemoth. But there is an untold story at the heart of the McLibel tale, and it involves the SDS. The group behind the McLibel leaflet was London Greenpeace. It rarely numbered more than around 20 anti-capitalists. Yet it was one of the most spied-upon political groups in modern history.

London Greenpeace was unconnected to the better-known (and much larger) campaign sharing a similar name. It comprised a mixture of environmentalists, anarchists and libertarians, who believed in a do-it-yourself philosophy.

For those who heeded the call, becoming part of London Greenpeace was simply a matter of turning up to informal, open meetings that were held each week near Euston station. Founded in 1971, the group concentrated mainly on campaigning against nuclear power, the arms trade and capitalism. By the mid-1980s it was turning its attentions to McDonald's.

The first protest was held in January 1985 when activists handed out a leaflet excoriating the multinational outside one of their restaurants in the Strand. Among the first campaigners pressing the leaflet into the hands of passing shoppers was Bob Lambert, who was then midway through his SDS deployment. Lambert was already making inroads in the network of animal rights groups at the time he infiltrated London Greenpeace.

On that cold winter's day, campaigners felt buoyed by the reaction to their message from passers-by. They decided to plough on and soon afterwards produced the now infamous six-page leaflet, railing against the burger chain and all it stood for. Headlined 'What's Wrong with McDonald's – Everything They Don't Want You to Know', it featured a cartoon American capitalist hiding behind a mask of the chain's mascot, Ronald McDonald. The corporation's golden arches were rebranded with insults such as 'McTorture', 'McGreedy' and 'McMurder'. The leaflet castigated McDonald's for promoting animal cruelty, paying low wages to its workers and exploiting children in advertising campaigns.

During the seemingly interminable libel case that followed, years later, in the mid-1990s, the judge, Mr Justice Rodger Bell, was not required to establish who exactly had written the leaflet. The proceedings revolved around who had distributed it. But if the judge had been interested in the question of who exactly penned the notorious leaflet he might have stumbled across an alarming discovery.

As with most London Greenpeace literature, the McLibel leaflet was a collective effort, pulled together by a few of the more enthusiastic writers. The tasks were shared, with activists creating different parts of the leaflet. Fittingly for a group where there were no leaders and decisions were taken by consensus, the work of pulling together the material for the leaflet was shared by about five people and took several months.

Remarkably, one of those responsible for writing the offending leaflet was the SDS spy, Bob Lambert. The police officer was not the sole author of the leaflet, but, according to several key members of the group at the time, Lambert co-wrote it. 'He was really proud of it,' recalls one of Lambert's friends. 'It was like his baby – he carried it around with him.' Paul Gravett, an activist in the group, says that while several people had input into the leaflet, Lambert was 'one of the most prominent people in the group at the time'. Lambert even confided in his then girlfriend – Karen – that he was behind the leaflet, although he appeared more reluctant to admit as much around others. 'He did not want people to know he had co-written it,' she said. 'He did not want to draw attention to himself.'

Put at its lightest, it means a police spy helped compose a leaflet that defamed a multinational corporation, costing it millions in legal expenses and causing severe damage to its reputation.

Lambert was not the only SDS spy to infiltrate London Greenpeace. As his deployment came to an end, senior officers at the SDS decided to send a second operative into the tiny group. The spy they chose was John Dines, a rugged sergeant, who went undercover with the alias John Barker.

In the early part of his mission, he lived in at least two squats in Hackney, north London for months on end. It was considered by the SDS to be evidence of his commitment to the job. It meant that day and night, he had to be constantly on guard among politically minded squatters. The slightest wrong comment or reaction and he could have fallen under suspicion. Even the most committed members of the SDS would normally retreat to their own flats. Dines plunged into an alien world of radicals, and in the parlance of the SDS, became another 'deep swimmer'.

Another sign of Dines's commitment was his physical transformation. He grew his hair long and had it cut in a harsh version of a mullet: the sides of his head were shaved completely, leaving a shaggy tail flowing down the back of his head. His dark eyes and thick jaw gave him an imposing, even sinister look.

Despite appearances, campaigners within London Greenpeace thought he was a likeable and rather chatty fellow. One activist recalls Dines as 'easy to get along with', although he did not exude the same 'air of confidence' as Lambert. Dines told his friends in the political group that he had moved to New Zealand as a teenager. He said that when he was there, he had campaigned against apartheid. He told them he had once been jailed for assaulting a policeman during a protest against a tour by the South African rugby team. Since his return to London, he claimed to have been living in a campervan near Waterloo station. He quickly became known among activists as 'New Zealand John'.

In the SDS, Dines had a different nickname: 'Sergeant Yob'. Dines tried to nurture an undercover reputation as a tough activist who would not shy away from a bit of rough and tumble on the streets. He was well built and extremely fit; his thigh muscles were so big that he was unable to cross his legs. In some ways he was the polar opposite of the suave and calculating Lambert, who was as thin as a rake. Handing out leaflets criticising a right-wing Christian preacher in Wembley Stadium, he once punched a random punter who was uttering racist insults. The victim crashed to the ground and Dines told his fellow activists that he 'hated fascists'.

It was useful for Dines to follow Lambert around 1987. The older officer could give the new spy a detailed briefing of all the personalities and dynamics within London Greenpeace. But Lambert did not introduce the newcomer to the group or make it appear that he already knew him. If one of the spies was rumbled, the SDS did not want suspicion being thrown onto the other spy.

The man activists knew as John Barker seemed to be made for the group's particular brand of politics: he was a friendly, practical, hands-on kind of a man, and he claimed to loathe capitalism. However, he was not the only new recruit to London Greenpeace at this time; in fact, by 1989 the ranks of the group were beginning to swell. There was a host of newcomers and they all seemed surprisingly willing to muck in and do the kind of boring jobs that some other campaigners showed little interest in. They helped run street stalls and crèches at gatherings, handed out leaflets on the high street and laboriously answered letters from school children asking for more information about their anti-Big Macs campaign. There was even a romantic liaison involving one of the new recruits. Old hands in the group sensed that there was something not quite right about the new arrivals. Some did not appear to have very strong political views. Others just seemed too keen.

Dines would probably have recognised these new recruits to London Greenpeace as rival infiltrators. However, these new spies were not working for the SDS, security services or any other state body. They were private eyes, working for McDonald's.

The corporation had a reason to spy on the small campaign group it was about to sue for defamation. It wanted to identify who the key players were within London Greenpeace and serve writs on them. McDonald's security department hired two private detective agencies to plant spies in the group. Executives at McDonald's stressed to both of the firms that the surveillance had to be conducted with absolute discretion. However, the multinational corporation did not tell these private detectives that it had hired two agencies.

As a result, London Greenpeace became saturated with spies, who ended up snooping on each other. It was a farcical situation, resembling something out of GK Chesterton's classic novel, *The Man who was Thursday*, in which all the members of an underground anarchist network turn out to be undercover police officers. Only in this case, just one of the spies was a cop – the rest were corporate infiltrators. The restaurant chain was forced to admit at the McLibel trial that the two detective agencies embedded at least seven spies in the group between October 1989 and spring 1991.

On at least two occasions, there were as many corporate spies at meetings of the small group as genuine activists. The number of real activists in the meetings had by then dwindled to between five and ten, and sometimes fewer. The spies had an incentive to put more effort into building their credibility in the group and so often attended more meetings than bona fide campaigners. Remarkably, agents working for McDonald's were effectively helping to hold its arch enemy London Greenpeace together.

In January 1990, activists were pondering whether to close down the group because attendance at meetings was so poor. The influx of what they thought were genuine activists encouraged them to keep going, believing that new life was being breathed into their radical campaign. One activist felt that London Greenpeace was 'on a roll again'.

Dines was one of the London Greenpeace activists who raised suspicions about these new activists and helped to work out if they were moles. Dines told another regular London Greenpeace member, Helen Steel, who would later become his girlfriend, that he had noticed he had been followed home after a meeting. The two of them decided to leave the next gathering together and keep their eyes peeled. As they travelled on an underground train, they realised they were indeed being tailed by a man. After leaving the Tube, Steel says: 'We walked to this estate and he was still following us. We ran up an external flight of stairs to the top and we hid up there, and we could hear him looking for us, opening doors and looking around. Then it went quiet and so we came down and he was standing there.'

Dines and Steel continued walking and were stunned when the man continued to pursue them. 'You would have thought he would have twigged that we obviously knew that he was following us,' she says. They then walked around a corner and hid behind a stairwell. As the corporate spy walked past, Steel and Dines jumped out and started taking photographs of the imposter. Unsure how to react, the man pretended to be inebriated, placing his hands over his face and saying, 'Leave me alone, I'm drunk.'

By the autumn of 1990, McDonald's had selected five London Greenpeace activists as the targets of their legal suit and served writs on them. The rest of the campaigners escaped and were left wondering why the corporation chose to sue some and not others. Dines for example was not part of the quintet subject to the legal action, even though he was as involved in the campaign as everyone else.

The chosen five activists found themselves facing the daunting prospect of taking on the legal might of McDonald's lawyers in the high court. Under England's notoriously restrictive libel laws, the onus was on the defendant to establish the truth, meaning London Greenpeace had to prove every allegation made in its leaflet. Their largest obstacle was money. They had hardly any, while McDonald's had lots. The activists had to defend themselves in their long and complicated legal battle without training or specialist expertise. They did so in the knowledge that if they lost, they could expect to pay the eye-popping costs incurred by McDonald's in hiring the best lawyers in the land.

It all seemed terribly unfair. McDonald's was using its financial muscle to browbeat political activists into apologising and retracting their criticisms of the multinational. The defendants were in desperate need of help, which arrived, mercifully, in the form of a square-jawed young barrister called Keir Starmer. Named after socialist icon Keir Hardie, the human rights lawyer was radical and idealistic and willing to offer his services. Years later he would become Director of Public Prosecutions, one of the most senior positions a lawyer can occupy in England and Wales. Starmer could not represent the London Greenpeace activists in court, but he was prepared to give them advice, free of charge, on how to conduct their defence.

As the pressure mounted, three activists decided it was hopeless trying to take on McDonald's and backed down, apologising to the restaurant chain. But two others, Helen Steel and Dave Morris, dug their heels in. For much of their legal battle, the duo would often go to Starmer's chambers and consult him privately about their strategy. They would then return to other London Greenpeace members and relay his advice.

One of those privy to the private guidance Starmer was giving the activists was Dines, the group's treasurer for some years. 'He was present at virtually all the meetings of the group at that time,' says one key activist. 'He was very much part of the group.' He took part in their discussions in their office, pub or each others' homes.

The SDS had once again secured itself a front-row view. One of its spies – Lambert – had helped write the notorious leaflet that so enraged executives of McDonald's in the first place.

Now another SDS spy, Dines, was secretly watching the repercussions unfold.

It is not known whether intelligence picked up by Dines, including the confidential legal strategy the activists were receiving from Starmer, was passed on to McDonald's. However, that seems highly probable. The McLibel trial revealed that Special Branch and McDonald's were at various points colluding and exchanging information about London Greenpeace. Morris and Steel eventually sued the police for unlawfully passing intelligence, including information about their home addresses, to McDonald's. The Met apologised and agreed to pay the pair £10,000 in an out-of-court settlement. It was the price police paid to keep secret uncomfortable details about its co-operation with McDonald's.

Certainly within the SDS, Dines' deployment, including his infiltration of London Greenpeace, anti-fascist campaigners, and anti-poll tax protests would have been considered a triumph, and there was particular praise for the mullet-haired spy. Lambert provided a glowing tribute to the operative, commending his apparently taxing stint in the squats. '[Dines] emerged from four years deployment (1987–1991) bruised, battered, and outstandingly successful,' Lambert wrote in a confidential SDS report. 'His professionalism and spirit [were] unquenched, despite enduring the most arduous working conditions in the history of the SDS.'

CHAPTER 6
Going Rogue

It was gone midnight when police found the abandoned Ford Sierra on the seafront of the West Sussex town of Worthing. The owner was nowhere to be seen. Officers feared the driver had crashed the car in Marine Parade and then run into the sea; an act of desperation by someone running out of options. They quickly alerted the coastguard and instigated an emergency search. All the available lifeboats were launched to search for the missing man. They were joined by a helicopter that hovered over the shore, its darting, searching beams lighting up the black sea.

Together, rescue teams on the boats and the helicopter frantically criss-crossed an area of sea four miles off Worthing Pier, as police with torches scuttled along the beach, barking dogs in tow. The commotion continued for two hours, disturbing what would ordinarily have been a peaceful Sunday night in a quiet town in the south of England. Eventually, the search for the owner of the abandoned car was called off. There was no sign of anyone alive and there seemed to be little point in continuing to look. Lifeboats and the helicopter returned to base, as forlorn police retired from the beach. Their feelings of dejection would have been amplified if they had known that the missing owner of the crashed Ford Sierra was an officer serving with Special Branch.

Mike Chitty was quite unlike the clean-cut, sensible men from the suburbs of London who normally swelled the ranks of Special

Branch. He was tall and slim with a thick head of curly hair and soft eyes. Among police colleagues, his hobby of driving racing cars was well-known. He once won the Caterham Seven car race at Brands Hatch. The victory was captured in a photograph in which he was congratulated by rock star Chris Rea. In the 1970s, he worked in Bermuda's Special Branch, where he was snapped posing with a gun after winning a shooting contest against the Royal Navy and the US Marines, during a visit by Princess Margaret. Chitty was an indepent thinker who apparently liked to carve his own path in life.

That was one interpretation. An alternative view, contained in the assessment of one disapproving manager, is that Chitty was the victim of his own 'predilection for cannabis, a carefree lifestyle, heavy rock music and laid-back women'. But somewhere in the echelons of Special Branch, managers saw potential in Chitty. In the early 80s, he was asked to make SDS history, becoming the first police officer ever tasked with spying on the Animal Liberation Front, paving the way for other spies, such as Bob Lambert. But it seems Chitty never quite lived up to expectations. Now, on a cold night in March 1994, the crashed car by Worthing Pier symbolised all that had gone wrong with this particular spy operation.

In the centre of down-at-heel Streatham, south London, lies a grand, pale building which has housed the neighbourhood's library since 1890. The two-storey building is a fine example of classical municipal architecture. It was in this prosaic setting that Chitty made his debut as an SDS operative posing as an animal rights protester.

He attended meetings at the library with a few dozen animal rights campaigners involved in what they called the South London Animal Movement (shortened to SLAM). It was an archetypal gathering of activists, mobilised by some of the prominent issues of the 1980s: combatting vivisection, the fur trade and, in a more local campaign, objecting to Battersea Park Zoo.

'It was like a group of friends really, like a close-knit bunch of friends. We would go leafleting in the week, and then to a demonstration on the Saturday,' says Sue Williams, a one-time SLAM member. 'There was quite a big social side to it: cooking food, meeting up at someone's house and drinking copious amounts of beer.'

Chitty, who grew a beard for his deployment, first turned up in the spring of 1983. He introduced himself as Mike Blake. 'I liked him,' says Williams. 'He was quite a nice bloke, quite laid-back, quite chilled.' In his 30s, Chitty looked a bit older than the other activists, most of whom were around 10 years younger. He once tried to chat up Williams with a 'cheesy line' at a fancy-dress party.

'I remember thinking, "Oh no, he's old enough to be my dad" or something,' she says. Chitty lived in a tiny bedsit in Balham, a short bus journey from Streatham Library and within easy distance of the homes of other SLAM activists. Over time he started taking part in demonstrations and handing out leaflets on the street. Like many SDS officers, he had a vehicle, and one weekend drove five campaigners to Blackpool in Lancashire to protest outside a circus.

During the long drive back to London, Williams recalls how the activists got 'some beers and went camping'. Another time, Chitty drove some of them to Devon to join a camp protesting against government plans to kill badgers. 'We had a nice camping holiday with Mike in the summer,' she recalls. 'We went skinny dipping in the river.'

A photograph shows Chitty and four other younger activists; he has his arm around the only woman in the group. The beard around his square chin has white tinges. He is wearing a sleeveless red T-shirt and blue beret. His appearance gives a hint of Wolfie Smith, the well-known revolutionary character from the 1970s sitcom, *Citizen Smith*.

Throughout the three years Williams knew Chitty, she always found him a curious character and difficult to fathom. 'He did not give much away,' she says. 'He had an air of mystery.' Her verdict chimes with other people who knew Chitty in his undercover role.

Robin Lane, another SLAM activist, says: 'We all thought he was a bit mysterious. He never seemed to have a proper job or particular line of work. He said he was a driver or mechanic, or some sort of odd-job man.' Lane found Chitty inscrutable, even though he socialised with him more or less weekly in the mid-1980s.

Chitty never talked much about politics and, unusually for this group of friends, did not look after animals. 'He was not an animal person,' says Lane. 'He did not have any pets. He was not particularly active, just did the odd demo, did the odd [bit of] leafleting. He was not a real hard-core campaigner like I was.' Williams, who personally steered clear of unlawful forms of protest, was also struck by how inactive Chitty was politically. 'He did not really do that much. He was just there.'

While he never seemed a particularly vigorous campaigner, Chitty appears to have enjoyed his covert life. He had friends – some of whom became girlfriends – and became fond of one woman in particular. One person with knowledge of his deployment says Chitty had 'a lack of interest in his home life' – an apparent reference to his wife.

When he had achieved a transfer from Bermuda to London, Chitty had spent his first year doing boring administrative work in Special Branch, vetting individuals who were applying to become British citizens and monitoring arrivals and departures at

Heathrow Airport. In 1982, when popular support for Margaret Thatcher's government was beginning to grow in the aftermath of the Falklands War, and the animal rights movement was gaining traction, Chitty was looking for another transfer. He arrived at a job interview, thinking he was applying to join the surveillance team that followed suspects on foot and in cars. Halfway through he realised that it might have something to do with undercover policing. Not long after that Chitty found himself introduced to the strange world of the SDS and was given a new identity to get inside the ALF.

It was a mission that, for one reason or another, Chitty never seemed to quite pull off. The main part of the problem was that Chitty only immersed himself in the moderate end of the animal rights movement, or in the words of one Special Branch source, 'in relatively tranquil waters'. They were not the dangerous cells of ALF saboteurs and vandals the police had really wanted him to keep tabs on.

The closest he seems to have got was his friendship with Robin Lane, who was one of the spokespeople for the ALF. Lane says police were often raiding him and he has no doubt he was a police target. In 1988, he was jailed for conspiring to incite others to commit criminal damages.

Lane said he and others never discussed ALF activities with Chitty, who was always considered to be on the periphery. There was little suggestion that Chitty himself wanted to be involved in illegal direct action. 'I don't think he was picking anything up really,' Lane says. All told, Chitty's undercover deployment appears to have been a relatively unremarkable tour of duty. In May 1987, he told his activist friends that he was leaving England for good to start a business in the United States.

Unlike most SDS officers, the real adventure for Chitty began once his deployment ended. When he returned to Special Branch, colleagues recall how he found it difficult to adjust to desk work and routine intelligence gathering. Within a few years, he was redeployed to a new role protecting VIPs.

It was a job that gave Chitty more freedom than other Special Branch officers and it enabled him to keep a remarkable secret from his superiors for several years. Unbeknown to the senior command at Special Branch, Chitty regularly slipped away from his bodyguard duties outside of London and drove many miles across country.

There, he would change out of his work clothes, swap into another car, and drive on. It was the strange ritual by which he shed his police officer identity to return, temporarily, to his previous life as the animal rights activist, Mike Blake. He lived the life of Mike Blake, on and off, for more than two years after his deployment was supposed to have come to an end. Chitty was like a mole who had burrowed deep into the earth before surfacing into an uncomfortable daylight. He stayed above ground, blinking in the sunlight for a few moments, before returning to his comfortable underground world.

Special Branch became aware that something was not quite right through the expenses he was claiming. An observant colleague noticed something odd about the number of miles Chitty was clocking up in his car. Compared to his partner in the bodyguard unit, Chitty was driving far greater distances. The details of his receipts raised further questions.

Chitty was found to have purchased fuel from a petrol station in Redhill in Surrey, near his home, at the precise time he was supposed to have been on duty in Wiltshire. In June 1992, Chitty was confronted by a manager over the alleged discrepancies in his petrol expenses. He provided no explanation or defence. Instead, Chitty is said to have shouted angrily at the senior officer, breaking down in tears before being escorted home. An internal inquiry was launched and Chitty was put on sick leave and had his gun taken from him.

Special Branch chiefs were faced with a puzzle. One of their officers, formerly a spy, had been caught claiming expenses miles from where he was supposed to have been deployed but was unable to account for the discrepancy. Chitty had then more or less fallen apart.

They needed to find out exactly what Chitty had been up to. It was essential they chose the right Special Branch detective to discreetly study the rogue officer and work out his secret. Their answer was Bob Lambert, the ambitious former SDS man who had the advantage of having once served alongside Chitty.

Lambert was by then one of the SDS's stars. His undercover tour had achieved legendary status among the ranks of the squad. The intriguing case of Mike Chitty was a chance for Lambert to prove that he had the managerial skills and cunning required for a future leading the unit. It worked. In 1994, Lambert returned to the SDS as the squad's head of operations.

However, it seems that the assignment to solve the Chitty enigma was not just a professional challenge for Lambert, it may have been personal too. Just a few years earlier, Lambert and Chitty had served together in the field, working alongside each other as animal rights campaigners. Both men were dispatched to infiltrate the ALF at about the same time, Lambert's deployment beginning just a few months after Chitty turned up at Streatham Library.

The similarity in their missions invited comparison and the SDS was notoriously competitive. Lambert believed that he had succeeded where Chitty failed. In Lambert's view, while Chitty was enjoying the social scene, living it up with a bunch of largely harmless animal rights campaigners in south London, he was making every sacrifice to inveigle his way into the murkier waters of the ALF.

It was Lambert, not Chitty, who ultimately succeeded in jailing two animal rights activists for setting fire to department stores. At the end of their deployments, the two men seemed on different career trajectories. Lambert was soon made a detective inspector and tapped up for senior roles; Chitty was still only a detective sergeant.

Of course, other thoughts may have been playing in Lambert's mind. Chitty was swimming in the same circles as Lambert at the same time. How much did Chitty know about the lengths Lambert went to in order to establish his cover identity? Was he aware of Lambert's secret child and the way in which he had infiltrated the arson attacks on Debenhams? From Lambert's perspective, Chitty may have been a spy who knew too much. He had an incentive to work out Chitty's motivations in order to preserve his own secrets.

Rarely, if ever, have details of these hushed, internal Special Branch inquiries been made public. Lambert's investigation into Chitty is laid bare in a highly confidential 45-page report stored under lock and key in a Scotland Yard archive. It is a top-secret report, headed with a stern warning that the document 'must be passed by hand under secure cover at all stages and retained in the SDS office'. It makes for compelling reading.

Written by Lambert in May 1994, the report contains the detail of his 18-month investigation into Chitty, leading up to an incredible discovery. It shows another side of Lambert; carefully, methodically and with some panache, he dissects Chitty's psychology, gradually unravelling the mystery of the former SDS officer's strange car journeys.

It is a document that should be interpreted with caution. Very possibly, Lambert's report is little more than the jaundiced opinion of a manipulative SDS spy with his own secrets to hide. It certainly reveals much about the cunning of Lambert, who spent several months gaining the trust of Chitty, under the guise of a caring friend.

Setting the context of his report, Lambert strikes a philosophical, even whimsical, note. He writes like an old sage. 'Like all families, the SDS has, over the years, rejoiced spontaneously in the successes of its members,' he said. The majority of the 'ex-hairies' had returned to Special Branch 'without fuss or favour; enlightened if not necessarily enriched by the undercover experience'.

A 'significant minority' had left the police for successful jobs elsewhere; one had recently become a lawyer and another a psychoanalyst. But the SDS had also 'no doubt, quite typically' struggled at times, Lambert said. It was important to face up and come to terms with those failures. 'If we accept, as Ray Davies put it in "Celluloid Heroes" (The Kinks, 1971, RCA Victor), that success walks hand in hand with failure, then perhaps we have a duty to tend to our casualties as well as fête our heroes.'

Clearly, Lambert was casting himself not as ruthless spycatcher, but a charitable and understanding colleague who had the interests of the SDS at heart. 'Accidents will occur in the best-regulated families … and if the family doesn't care for the victim, who else will?' he observed. 'And if the casualty is embittered; rejected by the family that once nurtured him, should anyone be surprised if he, with apparent malice, seeks to bring the old family home crashing to the ground?'

Lambert appreciated the danger presented by dissident, unhappy spies. They needed to be mollified. State secrets were theoretically protected, but the controversy over the publication, in the late 1980s, of *Spycatcher*, written by the ex-MI5 officer Peter Wright, highlighted the threat of rogue operatives. Nearly every spy had enough knowledge in their head to harm or even destroy the SDS if they chose to go public. That went for Chitty too. Like a true servant of the secret state, Lambert makes clear that 'the security of the SDS operation must take precedence over other less crucial considerations'.

At the time Lambert began his investigation, Chitty was on sick leave and in an unco-operative mood. Lambert knew he needed to get close to the ex-spy without inflaming the situation or isolating him further. Lambert wrote he was 'a strong believer' in a particular approach to dealing with runaway spies. It was an extension of the old adage about keeping your friends close but your enemies closer: sidling up to rogue operatives to offer them friendship and support.

'At best it helps inhibit further unprofessional behaviour and at the very least it provides access to their schemes and disruptive activity,' he said. Feigning empathy for Chitty was never going to be hard for Lambert. Duplicity was what Lambert was brilliant at. One Special Branch colleague who worked alongside Lambert around that time says he was 'able to lie as easily as he breathes'.

For more than a year and a half, Lambert befriended Chitty, pretending to be a sympathetic and loyal colleague. Lambert calculated that perhaps the 'old SDS bond still counted for something' in his dealings with the unrepentant officer. During his many encounters with Chitty, Lambert says he was met with 'a never-ending stream of ranting against persecution'. The visits to Chitty's home to check on his welfare he describes as 'a hazardous affair'.

On one occasion when Lambert and another ex-SDS spy went to visit Chitty, they ended up having to escort him from a 'saloon bar in a public house in Redhill when the licensee could no longer tolerate [his] loud profanities'. Chitty was expressing his fury for the senior officer who had confronted him over his expenses claims. Lambert believed the falling-out between Chitty and his senior officer had turned into something of a vendetta by the former SDS spy.

In his report, Lambert portrayed Chitty as aggressive and ready to snap. He said the Police Federation, which represents officers when they are in dispute with their employers, 'received short shrift' from Chitty. He was even angry toward colleagues in the VIP bodyguard unit, whom he accused of treachery, telling Lambert that they 'dared not go within a mile' of his home in Surrey. According to Lambert, Chitty had developed a 'remarkable fixation with a conspiracy theory' and said he was worried that Special Branch wanted to get him on a trumped-up charge of expenses fraud.

At first, Lambert did not realise that Chitty had secretly returned to his old friends, unable to relinquish his second life as Mike Blake. But over time Lambert began to piece together the jigsaw.

Chitty's appearance and behaviour seemed to be reverting to that of his alter ego. Once, during their long meetings, Lambert picked up a newsletter for a rock band left lying around at Chitty's home. Formed in south Wales in the late 1960s, Man played a mixture of progressive rock and psychedelia. Lambert knew that the band's small fanbase included a woman who Chitty had slept with while undercover. When Chitty said that he was going to go to a Man concert, Lambert warned him that he ran the risk of bumping into activists from the 1980s. Chitty replied truculently: 'So what?'

Later, Lambert would concede ruefully that the significance of this statement was lost on him at the time. 'Perhaps a better clue was to be found in his frequent references to his preparedness to go back to his former undercover associates,' Lambert wrote. 'This involved a simple but subtle shift from reality. He was keen to make the threat but at the same time to obscure the truth that he had already gone back.'

In search of clues, Lambert delved back into the past, revisiting Chitty's undercover deployment. Lambert's verdict on his rival's performance infiltrating animal rights activists was scathing. He described the intelligence Chitty obtained as 'reliable, if largely irrelevant'. Chitty's intelligence assessments about the 'ineffectual' meetings of the SLAM were 'filed briefly in Special Branch records'. Lambert pulled no punches. He noted how Chitty 'contributed wholeheartedly to the social and legitimate campaigning activities' of the animal rights movement 'without ever once providing intelligence that led to the arrest of any of their activists or the disruption of any of their activities'.

The intelligence procured by Chitty 'shed little light' on the ALF protesters, Lambert added, and 'certainly had no adverse impact on their criminal activities'. In Lambert's view, his fellow spy had been so ineffective that, had the activists he was spying on 'then or now' been told he was a police officer, they would be 'inclined to dismiss the claim as absurd'. In another cutting observation, Lambert said his rival's cover had been 'entirely sound', but only because no one would have suspected that someone so inactive was an infiltrator.

Lambert was not shy in pointing out that his colleague's apparently lacklustre performance undercover paled in comparison to his own penetration of the 'more security-conscious' ranks of the animal rights movement. He believed Chitty had spurned the opportunity to follow his lead. 'In fairness, Chitty was not unique amongst field officers at the time, in wishing to avoid the risks and hassle inherent in criminal participation.'

Lambert did have some positive things to say about his former colleague. He conceded for example that Chitty was regarded as being 'consistently shrewd in maintaining cover', at a time when paranoia about police surveillance was rife among activists. Lambert also described his colleague as an 'ideal officer to manage – reliable, punctual, co-operative, never rocking the boat like some of his more outspoken field colleagues'.

Yet, all told, Lambert's assessment of Chitty's deployment was harsh and condescending. From his own knowledge of the animal rights scene, Lambert believed that ALF activists 'would remember Chitty, vaguely, as one of the many middle-of-the-road campaigners who just didn't have the "bottle" or the inclination to get involved in direct action, and, thus, by their standards, was of no use whatsoever. Quite simply, he was never aware of their clandestine, criminal activities because they had no reason to tell him and he had no inclination to find out.'

However, it was when Lambert scrutinised Chitty's life after his deployment that he came to realise what had happened. Lambert showed no reservation about sifting through Chitty's personal letters, a search that yielded intimate correspondence with a woman from his days as an animal rights activist.

Lambert does not say in his report exactly how he came to inspect the 'pile of long-hidden, treasured love letters' between Chitty and the woman. He states only that they were secreted inside a padlocked toolbox in Chitty's garage. Either Lambert persuaded his colleague to let him read the cache of letters, or he broke into the box and read them without permission.

Either way, the correspondence contained incontrovertible evidence that Chitty was fraternising with the enemy. It turned out that Chitty was socialising with activists long after he was supposed to have resumed life as an ordinary Special Branch officer. One occasion was the 40th birthday party of a campaigner in 1991. Posing as Blake, the ex-spy partied with old friends. Lambert observed how the party was low risk for Chitty. 'No danger here of Chitty bumping into current SDS operatives who, he might rightly have guessed, were more gainfully employed infiltrating elusive cells [of ALF activists].'

Using the letters as a trail of evidence, Lambert documented the ebb and flow of Chitty's relationship with his girlfriend. She was 'best described as an old hippy whose life is built around trendy causes, cannabis, alcohol and sex'. Lambert added that the woman had a 'sharp intuition', not least about Chitty, who she thought was prone to 'mercurial behaviour and mental instability'.

Locked in the box beside the letters, Lambert found a collection of 30 photographs which contained further evidence of Chitty's double life. One recorded what Lambert describes as 'a dirty weekend' when the couple's relationship 'was very clearly on a high'. What exactly the photographs revealed is not stated, but Lambert said one image showed Chitty's girlfriend 'holding up a newspaper in which Margaret Thatcher's downfall as Prime Minister is headlined'. That was November 1990, three years after he was supposed to have ended his deployment.

Once Lambert had established that his former colleague had returned to his activist friends and gone native, the next question was why. When Chitty's deployment had ended in 1987, he was ordered to tell activist friends he was leaving for good. In keeping with SDS policy, it was imperative that he made a clean break with his undercover romances. Instead, Chitty appears to have given the impression that he might one day return.

'Perhaps she thought he was gone for good or perhaps, as now seems likely, he gave her cause to believe he might return to England if his "business plans" in the States did not work out,' Lambert said. When Chitty reappeared in August 1989, two years after disappearing, his girlfriend was 'surprised and bewildered'. She had moved on in her life and, according to Lambert, had got Mike Blake 'out of her system after a passionate affair'.

Upset, she confided her intimate feelings in a private letter to Chitty. Of course, she had no idea that he was a police officer – or that her emotional outpouring would later be scrutinised by a rising star in the Special Branch. Lambert analysed her words scrupulously. 'It is a letter that testifies to a serious romantic liaison,' he wrote. Chitty and the woman had evidently had a relationship of considerable meaning. Chitty had even asked the woman to marry him.

The implications of Chitty's proposal are hard to fathom. He could never have married using his fake ID. As it turned out, there was never any need to commit identity fraud in a marriage registry office. 'She pondered,' Lambert noted wryly, 'before declining.' Following that rejection, the pair had a 'slowly cooling' relationship, Lambert said, but an 'abiding friendship' until at least November 1991. Lambert's conclusion was that Chitty returned to his former life 'prompted by romantic and social considerations, rather than an ideological attachment to the cause of animal rights'.

But how exactly had Chitty pulled off such a stunning act of heresy without Special Branch finding out? In returning to his undercover role, Chitty had committed a serious breach of security. In Lambert's judgment, the SDS officer's behaviour was 'totally unacceptable' and showed a 'reckless disregard for the safe running of the SDS operation', but he concluded that the blame should not be placed entirely on his shoulders.

Lambert felt there had been mistakes in the handling of Chitty, from the moment he was removed from his undercover duties. For a start, he was placed behind a desk doing mundane intelligence analysis – 'such an enclosed, covert environment is none too healthy for an ex-SDS officer; certainly not for one who is hankering after his old lifestyle,' Lambert said.

When he was given a less pressured assignment at a section of the Special Branch in Putney, south-west London, Chitty suddenly had more room to manoeuvre. In Lambert's view, Chitty had the 'freedom he was searching for' and was able to prepare the 'documentation and logistical backup required to return convincingly to the field'. Lambert added: 'Suffice to say he appears to have had sufficient "down time" between operations to devote ample time to his "second" life'.

As Lambert discovered, there was considerable work and perhaps even some premeditation involved in reviving the identity of Mike Blake. When SDS officers completed their undercover tour, they relinquished all the fake documents in the name of their alias. Chitty handed back to managers the passport and birth certificate bearing the name of Mike Blake when his undercover tour ended in 1987.

However, he had never returned Mike Blake's driving licence, claiming he had lost it. Then, between 1989 and 1990, he somehow managed to get hold of a new passport and birth certificate in Mike Blake's name. Once his time undercover had drawn to a close, Chitty appears to have bought a car at an auction and then registered it in the same fake name. Chitty said that the car was not registered in his real name because it was used for official covert duties, an arrangement he said had been approved by his superiors.

But Lambert was sceptical. He concluded that Chitty had kept the driving licence 'for future use' and therefore apparently planned to return to his undercover life all along. He noted how Chitty later went on to acquire a home address in the name of Mike Blake. Lambert said that obtaining the use of a house in his fake name was 'no doubt the most difficult' part of Chitty's deception. Chitty seems to have elicited the help of a friend who allowed him to use a house in Hampshire. If he needed letters sent to Mike Blake, they would be posted there. Elliptically, Lambert wrote that Chitty 'appears to have been able to take advantage of one of the bedsit rooms for entertaining purposes'.

However, even equipped with ID documents, a car and an address, Chitty still needed a new cover story to explain to his activist friends how he could afford to live a 'comfortable and highly mobile lifestyle'. Lambert noted how his former colleague told activists that he was making a living as a racing driver. It is true that Chitty was an accomplished driver and a handy mechanic.

Chitty appeared to have pulled the wool over the eyes of his bosses in the SDS and was soon enjoying his double life. But he began to run into difficulty in 1990. Recalled from his assignment in Putney, which was relatively close to where his activist friends lived, Chitty was placed on more routine duties at Scotland Yard in central London.

Colleagues in Special Branch recall how much Chitty resisted being moved away from south London. 'One can see how, for example, a three-month stint as reserve room controller must have cramped Chitty's style!' Lambert wrote. 'He was notable for his poor work return and frequent absences from the office "on enquiries".' Not long after, Chitty secured his job protecting VIPs, a move that Lambert said must have made him feel 'a mixture of relief and anticipation'.

Lambert continued: 'Here again, was a posting that would allow him unlimited time away from home, and if he was clever, scope to give free rein to his alter ego's lifestyle. Another important factor which the officer would not have overlooked was that the posting was likely to boost his overtime earnings – an essential ingredient in his activities.'

It was a job which did indeed give Chitty more room for manoeuvre. Perhaps too much. It was the conspicuous 100-mile journeys from Wiltshire, where he was supposed to be protecting a VIP, to his home in Surrey that were Chitty's undoing in 1992. Chitty had become 'too clever and careless', according to Lambert.

By that time, Lambert calculated that the former spy 'had enjoyed leading a secret double life without being found out by his employers or his wife' for more than two years. Remarkably,

Chitty had been able to do his official police work without it being hindered by his second secret life. By February 1994, the Metropolitan Police's internal investigators had separately decided that Chitty should face a disciplinary hearing. They had interviewed hotel managers in Wiltshire and petrol station staff in Surrey. They had no idea precisely why the officer was claiming expenses in the wrong place at the wrong time. But it didn't smell right.

Chitty took the pressure badly. Soon afterwards, he vanished from his home for a week. For at least some of that period, Chitty was suspected to have travelled to Scotland to seek advice from another former SDS officer who had fallen out with the squad – a man who was much despised by Lambert, who described him in his report as 'selfish, arrogant, disloyal'. The reality is probably rather different. Not much is known about the SDS man, other than he left the unit for a life as a successful hotelier.

The trip to Scotland to seek advice from this exiled SDS officer was, in Lambert's view, another sign that Chitty was going off the rails. He confronted Chitty about his decision to ask for help from the former SDS man and recorded his reaction in the report. 'When challenged as to the propriety of seeking such counsel, he countered colourfully: "Who the hell else am I supposed to talk to when the whole fucking organisation is out to screw my arse to the floor?"'

A month later, the alarm was raised when Chitty's Ford Sierra crashed by the promenade in Worthing. Chitty was missing. Despite the considerable operation to find him, there was no sign of him on the beach or in the sea. He was found, alive and well, later that night, in the town.

Lambert was left with a vivid memory of Chitty sitting in an interview room in Worthing police station: 'Distracted, almost haunted, a broken man obsessed by persecution and his own professional guilt (not the guilt of betrayal of animal activists but of letting down the SDS). As the wise old duty officer observed, "He's not a well man, is he?"'

Chitty had undoubtedly reached a low point, but it is important to remember that Lambert had a stake in the rival spy's tragedy. Lambert must have known that if Chitty went over the edge, and talked to the newspapers, the future of his own career was in doubt. And for all his vulnerability, Chitty still conjured the strength to take on his bosses at Special Branch.

Facing disciplinary action, and with a dawning realisation that Lambert and others now knew about his second life, Chitty threatened to press the nuclear button. He wrote a letter to Sir Paul Condon, the commissioner of the Metropolitan Police, complaining about his treatment by the SDS and threatening to spill the beans on the whole operation.

The contents of his five-page letter were read by Lambert and later summarised in his report. 'His letter to the Commissioner is well written and, in parts, persuasive in its agenda,' Lambert said. The thrust of Chitty's argument was that he received no psychological counselling at the end of his deployment and was unable to deal with feelings of guilt at having betrayed the animal rights activists.

Chitty argued he should be diagnosed as being mentally unfit to continue in the police force, paving the way for his departure with a pension to compensate for his ill-health. Lambert, who would not have wanted to annoy senior managers at the SDS by suggesting they were culpable, showed little tolerance for that view. However, he did concede a small amount of ground. 'Yes, he is right,' Lambert noted at one point. 'SDS managers do need to encourage a healthy environment in which field officers feel safe to talk about inevitable emotional ties to their target groups.' Reading between the lines of Chitty's letter to the commissioner, Lambert was alive to the potential threat of the rogue officer going public. 'Implicit is the message: does Special Branch really want my secret, dirty washing aired in an open forum?' Lambert wrote. 'Equally, the letter contains a barely veiled threat along the lines: if I go down, I'll take as many people as possible with me, SDS in particular.'

For a squad cloaked in absolute secrecy, the spectre of public scrutiny was a terrifying menace. Lambert was at pains to spell out quite how catastrophic it would be for the SDS programme of long-term infiltration if it was ever discovered by the public: 'It would put at risk the safety of former (and possibly current) field officers and their families.' He estimated that it would take no more than 10 minutes to prove that 'certain former highly regarded activists had in fact been undercover police officers who were responsible for the imprisonment of close comrades and the disruption of large-scale [animal rights] criminal activity'. Those spies and their families could expect at 'the very least' postal bombs at their homes, Lambert claimed.

This warning should also be read with caution. It was in Lambert's interest to exaggerate the danger of Chitty going public. Lambert, more than many other SDS officers, had a huge amount to lose if there was a series of revelations about the SDS and its activities, particularly if they related to his own conduct undercover.

In one telling section, Lambert warns there was one 'true story' that Chitty could make public that would 'answer a lot of questions the [animal rights] hierarchy has been asking about infiltration for several years'. Exactly what that true story was is not explained, but it would seem likely that Lambert was referring to his own role in the arson attacks on Debenhams. There was of course another 'true story' that he was desperate to keep quiet: by then the son he had fathered with the activist named Charlotte was nine years old. Lambert had not seen the child since he vanished from his life years earlier and probably hoped he would never have to.

Lambert was careful not to make his reasoning appear too personal. He wrote in his report that 'there are of course a hundred and one facts' about SDS operations that 'sympathetic lawyers and friendly investigative journalists would be delighted to hear about'. Lambert believed everything had to be done to ensure those uncomfortable truths were concealed from the public. 'Such disclosure would be seriously damaging to the safe and secure running of the current operation,' he said. Revelations in the newspapers would place a burden on the fleet of spies who were currently deployed and had 'enough to worry about without the fear of a rogue former SDS officer queering their pitch'.

The risks were high, but Lambert calibrated that the chances of Chitty following through with his threats were relatively low. He believed that Chitty lacked the courage to bring down the squad by going public. A more likely, but no less worrying, scenario painted by Lambert was that Chitty might 'inadvertently open his heart out' to the woman he once wanted to marry 'over several bottles of Stella and under the added influence of cannabis'.

April 1994 was not a good month for Chitty. He had been on sick leave for nearly two years. It was just weeks after the dramatic crash in Worthing and he was still facing an internal disciplinary inquiry over his expenses. What was going on in his mind at that point was difficult to discern. Lambert suggested that Chitty was becoming increasingly unstable, his behaviour 'confrontational, highly volatile'. Some evidence about his mental state comes from a visit he made to a doctor.

Lambert, who was either present during the consultation or had access to Chitty's medical notes, said he offered the doctor 'a slightly sanitised view of his secret double life'. It seems Chitty was advised he was suffering from a psychological phenomenon evident when hostages develop feelings of loyalty toward their captors. By the tone of his report, it did not seem Lambert thought much of Chitty's claims about his psychological well being. 'Disarmingly, he told the doctor, "My psychiatrist tells me I'm not mentally ill, I know I'm not, I've just got a syndrome, Stockholm syndrome."'

Whether he was suffering from a psychological condition or not, Chitty continued to socialise with his old friends in the animal rights movement. Perhaps he had given up hope of extricating himself from the mess and was reaching out to people he believed cared for him. Maybe his loyalties had shifted entirely, from the SDS to the 'wearies'.

Lambert on the other hand believed that there was an element of calculation in Chitty's behaviour. If senior officers believed he might defect, they could be more likely to meet his demands, drop the disciplinary action and pay out in compensation. Indeed, Lambert even suggested that Chitty had rekindled one particular friendship – based 'on a common interest in illegal herbal substances and heavy metal music' – because he knew the activist in question would be under heavy surveillance. If Chitty was deliberately trying to get spotted among his activists, it worked. Reports were quickly relayed back to Special Branch that a former SDS man on sick leave was in contact with a well-known campaigner.

One afternoon that month, Chitty joined a group of friends who attended a leaving party for an activist who was returning to Canada. It was a boozy affair, and Chitty, after seeming somewhat tense, appeared to relax as the drink flowed. He was spotted flirting with one woman, asking her if she fancied going on a date with a racing driver. She laughed indulgently, encouraging his approach. By the end of the meal, Chitty was in such a good mood he offered to pay half of the bill for all 10 of the diners. The group then retired to a nearby house to smoke some dope.

It was by pure chance that, unbeknown to Chitty, the party was witnessed by a serving SDS officer. The following Monday, at one of the squad's regular meetings, he retold the whole, incredible story to astonished colleagues. The SDS spy said 'it was clear that no one present had any idea' of Chitty's real identity. To the activists, he was still Mike Blake, the jovial animal rights campaigner who had been around, on and off, for more than a decade.

Four days later, Chitty's predicament took a turn for the worse. He was en route to another doctor's appointment when he used an invalid travel pass at Victoria Station. An altercation with guards escalated and police were called, arresting Chitty on the platform. He did not have his warrant card on him. But he told officers that he was an undercover police officer on a mission and gave the names of colleagues who could back up his claim.

Chitty was eventually released, but was abusive towards the transport police, who lodged a formal complaint with the Special Branch. Lambert, silver-tongued as ever, was called in to smooth things over. He explained that Chitty was on sick leave and 'probably not intentionally rude'. Apology accepted, the transport police dropped the complaint. But the episode underscored how precarious Chitty's situation was – he was still an officer in the Special Branch, but seemingly out of their control.

The police officer's confrontation with his managers was descending into something of a Mexican standoff. In 1995, he began legal action against Scotland Yard on the grounds that he had suffered psychiatric damage from the stress of his covert work. Claiming damages totalling £50,000, he accused the police of negligence and failing to 'monitor, support, counsel, and care for him' between 1982 and 1994.

Shortly afterwards, he seems to have dropped the lawsuit, and was awarded an ill-health pension. There is no information about how the dispute was reconciled, but it seems likely that the rogue officer won out. Chitty has never spoken about his undercover life. Not long after the legal action was suspended, he disappeared. He is currently living in South Africa and has not responded to requests to comment.

Chitty was probably never given the contents of the SDS report into his conduct, nor informed about the lengths the unit was going to, behind his back, to try to work out the reason for his discontent. It is reasonable to assume that he would be particularly shocked if he knew the role played by Lambert, who was pretending to be on his side while he was on sick leave. It was a clever move by Lambert, who helped dissuade Chitty from going public, which would have been a disaster for the SDS.

It was a close shave for the close-knit squad of 'hairies'. Crisis had been averted, but the Chitty episode underlined how quickly unpopular members of the unit could be isolated and become a liability. Even Lambert perceived danger in this collective lack of empathy for SDS men who went off the rails. 'There seems to be a prevailing attitude within Special Branch that association with colleagues under investigation is some sort of contamination,' he wrote in his report. 'Such an unenlightened view ill becomes an intelligent and sophisticated workforce.'

Lambert had good reason to want to improve pastoral care in the SDS. Chitty was not the only colleague who had gone wayward and fallen out with his police spymasters, and he would not be the last. The exploits of the more erratic and sometimes even uncontrollable undercover police officers were well known in the SDS. Some of the behaviour counted as low-level misdemeanour. Two SDS officers, for example, were arrested for driving while under the influence of alcohol while on covert duties. Both were taken to a police station, where they volunteered they were undercover cops. One even had on him official documents revealing his true identity. Colleagues 'were appalled at this seemingly wanton disregard for professionalism, and in consequence, team morale suffered, and the officers lost their "street" credibility,' Lambert noted.

Other cases were more serious. The first SDS deployment to go seriously awry involved an operative who, just like Chitty, appears to have enjoyed the company of his undercover friends more than his colleagues. According to a Special Branch officer, when this particular spy was told in the early days of the squad that his deployment needed to come to an end, he refused to come out of the field, quitting the police and returning to his life as a radical leftist campaigner. Astonishingly, this SDS officer seems to have turned completely 'native', making a permanent transition from cop to activist. He may well still be living the life of a protester, albeit now a pensioner, using the same fake identity given to him by the SDS many years ago.

A second, mutinous spy infuriated the command of the SDS for a different reason. He completed his undercover tour in 1983, but was dismissed from the Met police two years later over an alleged assault. Like Chitty, he wrote a letter to senior officers, threatening to run to the papers and expose the squad's dirty secrets unless his dismissal was reversed. He too said he suffered psychological difficulties as a result of the covert work. His appeal over the disciplinary inquiry for assault was upheld. This was the officer who relocated to Scotland, and who had consoled Chitty during his breakdown, much to the annoyance of Lambert.

A third spy was recruited to the SDS despite suffering from some kind of personality disorder. Needless to say, his operation did not go well and was abruptly terminated in 1988. His handlers judged the mission to be 'unsound', although the details of what went wrong are not widely known. But when SDS managers looked into his history they realised that their vetting procedures had failed badly. Years earlier, when he joined the police, the officer had used a false identity on his application form.

When the detective constable was removed from SDS duties he reacted badly. Missing for some time from his home, he was later found wandering around York. He was put into the care of a police psychiatrist. Yet again, this SDS man threatened to expose the secrets of the unit to the media. This time police chiefs played hardball, threatening him with a prosecution under the Official Secrets Act. The tactic worked. The officer never went through with his threat of public disclosure. He retired from the Met with an ill-health pension for the same disorder he suffered from when he joined the SDS.

In the history of the SDS, the history of closely averted calamities is surprisingly long. It was as though the unit was constantly on the edge, just one crisis away from its operations being subject to the unseemly glare of publicity. A fourth ex-SDS spy, for example, was arrested for gross indecency in St James's Park, near Buckingham Palace. When he was approached by police in a public toilet, he ran away, trying to evade arrest, but was caught.

The officer had not worked for the SDS for around 10 years, but when he was brought before a disciplinary board in 1991, he argued that his attempt to evade the police was a 'reflex response' linked to his past undercover work. Medical evidence, supported by at least one former colleague, corroborated his argument that he had been psychologically scarred by his years working as a covert agent. The officer, who had by then risen to the senior rank of detective superintendent, also left the police with an ill-health pension.

Unlike the others, he refrained from making a direct threat

to expose the SDS operation. But Lambert and the other senior men at the SDS were well aware of quite how potent a weapon the threat of exposure was. An SDS officer who fell out with the unit had the power to bring it crashing down. They could call the shots in the knowledge that the squad had enough embarrassing secrets that it could never risk the British public finding out what it was up to. Within the walled garden of the SDS, there was even a name given to the technique of threatening to blow the whistle unless one demand or another was met: 'playing the SDS card'.

Somehow, those in charge of the SDS managed to negotiate their way out of a crisis each time the card was played. Either by agreeing to the demands of their wayward employees, or threatening to make their life a misery, they always avoided the very worst-case scenario: the truth coming out.

But the inevitable was always going to happen. By the late 1990s, SDS managers were contemplating how to handle one particularly headstrong spy. They would, initially, manage to keep his mouth shut. But he would eventually break ranks completely, spilling more secrets than any other officer in the history of the SDS. He became the whistleblower who shone a light on almost half a century of clandestine police espionage. His name was Pete Black.

CHAPTER 7
Enter Mr Black

Orange smoke swirled around thousands of protesters and police. Bottles, sticks and bricks hurtled in every direction while the crowd roared. For a few brief moments, the silhouettes of police on horseback appeared out of the clouds of coloured smoke. The confrontation in suburban Welling, beneath blue autumnal skies, had a dramatic, almost revolutionary air. There was a crush of bodies, pressing against lines of police shields as they tried to force their way to the headquarters of the far-right British National Party.

Among the swirling ruck of bodies trying to push through the police barrier was a determined-looking man with a long brown ponytail called Pete Black. Barely weeks after he had been sent to infiltrate the anti-racism movement, this SDS officer was already on the frontline of his first big operation. Sooner than anyone could have anticipated, Black had been transformed into a hard-core street-fighting activist, and he was relishing the brutal excitement of it all. It was like a part of his personality that had remained hidden for all of his adult life was set free. Now this dimension of his character was shouting and punching its way into the middle of a riotous battle with the cops. 'It is a high, an adrenaline high, you can't even begin to get there,' he says. 'It was a very intense thing within such a short time of being deployed.'

It was not just the intoxicating spell of the violent crowd that was making Black's veins pulsate. He was 'already on a high' after penetrating the group he had been tasked with spying on faster than he thought was feasible. And the novelty of his undercover deployment had still not worn off – he was still excited by the thrill of knowing he was pretending to be another person. As he muscled his way through the crowd, dodging missiles and baton swipes, he was conscious that one small error could blow his cover.

Black had another reason to feel pleased with himself. This was the first major protest he had been asked to forecast for SDS managers, and his predictions had proved spot on. Black was among seven SDS undercover operatives at the demon-stration that day. All were asked for their thoughts ahead of the demonstration, to allow senior commanders to prepare a suitable response. Despite his limited experience, Black told his superiors there would be a massive turnout of activists, determined to get to the BNP building. As he put it, 'all shit was going to kick off'. Having pushed himself to the front of the march, Black watched the protest descend into 'exactly' the kind of sustained clashes he and his fellow SDS colleagues had anticipated.

From his point of view, the violence in south-east London was turning into an unmitigated success. Even if police were overrun by the crowd, Black would be safe in the knowledge he had warned his senior officers to prepare for the worst. 'I could not give a shit – if they get through and burn the fucking building down, I am totally covered because I told them it was going to happen,' he says. The crowd was large and angry, but Black knew there would be reinforced lines of police ready to stop them from getting through. He remembers looking at the police barricade and thinking: 'As long as [the protestors] have a hole in their arse, they are not going to get through this. I know that there are waves and waves of rozzers behind it.' Black was an SDS man now. He had the privilege of that unique vantage point: a glimpse behind the scenes of two opposing worlds.

That eventful day in Welling was a crowning moment for Black. He had proved to his superiors within the SDS that he could gain the trust of activists and gather intelligence ahead of a major protest. At the same time, he had established his credibility among protesters, whom he had been warned would be hostile to outsiders. Black felt he was being tested in battle, watched as he fought shoulder to shoulder with activists for hours in Welling. 'My role on that day was to be a street activist and to show them that no matter how much bottle they have got, I would be with them,' he says. He recalls 'a lot of exchanges' with police – 'a lot of pushing with the shields, a hell of a lot of running … as soon as they ran a little bit forward, we would run back, then the horses came down'.

Black wanted to be at the front of the demonstration, earning his spurs with other activists and getting a measure of how far these left-wing activists would go in their confrontations with riot officers. He was impressed. 'I was pleasantly surprised by the balls they had, considering that some of them were injured. I thought our lot would run away as soon as the riot shields and horses came out. I thought it would be over,' he says. 'We were right where the clown let off the orange smoke bomb. The police horses went through it.'

The undercover officer got whacked by a police baton in the mayhem, but escaped serious injury. He was fortunate. By the end of day, 41 demonstrators and 19 police officers were injured and 31 arrests had been made. Black knew that one way he could avoid getting hurt as a protester was to draw on his training as a cop.

Riot police use long shields to protect themselves from head to toe, often forming defensive lines. Shorter, round shields, clasped to their left arms, have a different function: they tend to be used when police are about to go on the offensive against rioters. The smaller shields are easier to wield, enabling police to swing batons over the top. Police sometimes use the hard edge of the shield as a weapon, although it is officially discouraged.

'Now I found myself on the other side of the shield,' Black says. 'The only advantage it gave me was that I could see the tactics being used whereas my targets [the protesters] could not. I knew that when the long shields were out, that was fine because all they could do was push. But when the short shields came out you knew that it was trouble. You can go right up to one of the long shields and all they can do is jab you from around the side. They can't get you from over the top. With the short shields, you really have to get out of the way. That was the time to run. And if the dogs came out, it's a bad day for mankind.'

Of course, Black had to act on his inside knowledge with caution. If he suddenly warned fellow demonstrators about an imminent police charge, he might raise suspicions. 'You end up trying to find a way to tell them [to run away] without making it sound like you've done this sort of thing before,' he says.

In the days after the Welling demonstration, Black joined the other SDS officers for the routine postmortem. The Special Branch officers sifted through police long-lens photographs of the protest, identifying known activists involved in the clashes. Flicking through hundreds of images, Black was suddenly taken aback by one particular photograph. It was an image of him, standing in the middle of the crowd. It was the first time he had seen a photograph of his alter ego surrounded by anti-racist campaigners.

On the surface, Black is a forbidding character – intense, blunt and hard. One of his police managers, with whom he clashed, described him as 'one of most direct and forthright officers I have ever encountered'. Nowadays he is shaven-headed. He almost always dresses head to toe in black. He does not want to reveal his real name – doing so, he believes, could put him at risk of physical retribution.

Black has deep-set, staring eyes and a thick jaw. At around 5ft 9in, he is short for a police officer, but stocky and strong with long arms. He admits to a 'very aggressive' dimension to his personality, one he kept suppressed 'within the normal bounds of society' for many years. However, his predilection for confrontation was unleashed when he went undercover. He confesses to enjoying the 'totally feral environment' of protests that turn violent. He is, he admits, a 'natural fighter'.

But beneath the bulldozer-like surface is a more complex character. For someone who claims to have a short temper, Black is often stone-cold calm. He can be adventurous, thoughtful and funny; when recounting the more absurd aspects of his deployment, his sombre stare usually gives way to a broad smile.

Black also has something that some of his former police colleagues lack – the ability to form solid opinions about ethical issues, regardless of what his seniors in the SDS might believe. In some ways, he is unlike many other cops. An independent thinker, Black is unafraid to voice his views, even if that means a battle with the hierarchy. And once his mind is made up, he does not take kindly to anyone who attempts to persuade him he is wrong.

That may be a trait acquired through childhood. Black was born in London in 1965 and moved to Norfolk, but by the time he was 12, his German mother and New Zealand father had divorced. His mother did not adapt well to life in a small village, and turned to drink. She struggled to bring up her three children. 'It wasn't the easiest of childhoods. I was angry a lot of the time, a lot of suppressed rage at the world,' he says. 'I did not stray too much and I realise there are plenty of people out there with far bigger problems. [But] I was pretty much the only kid in my school whose parents were divorced. Also the fact that my mother was German caused a few problems and issues,' he says.

A turning point came at the age of 13, when he confronted a school bully. He recalls the moment as a realisation that he had the ability to achieve what he wanted. He became head boy of his school – to the headmaster's surprise – and secured nine O-levels and, later, three A-levels. Interested in the law and public affairs, he harboured an ambition to join the security services. It was an idea he dropped after an A-level teacher advised him that, realistically, MI5 'only recruited from the Oxbridge set, posh kids with public-school backgrounds'. But the teacher offered an alternative.

'He said what I had a good chance of getting into was Special Branch,' Black says. 'He explained what it was and it sounded absolutely perfect. A chance to do some of the same work as the Security Service without having to be a part of it.' Turning down a university place to study law, he enrolled in the police, determined to join the Metropolitan police's elite squad of officers. He got there in 1990, after a short spell in uniform.

Black's first Special Branch posting was to Heathrow, monitoring suspected dissidents travelling to and from Ireland. He was then in B Squad, which was investigating Irish republican and loyalist terrorists. 'It was a great time to be working in the field,' he says. 'It was such a small unit that everyone was involved in everything. I would say that between 1990 and 1993, I had a part in the case of every single terrorist arrested in London. I was either involved in interviewing them or following them or gathering other intelligence on them,' he says. Later, Black began working in C Squad, the department that had the remit of monitoring 'subversives'. 'Interestingly, I didn't really know what a subversive was until I started working for Special Branch,' he adds.

His route into the SDS, the 'unit within a unit' in Special Branch, was the result of what Black calls 'several twists of fate'. One day he got a call from an officer in Bromley, south London, where he had worked while he was a uniformed constable. Local borough police had picked up a man who was found to be carrying 'a vast amount of left-wing literature'.

'They asked if I wanted to go down and have a look. It turned out he was a major activist with the Socialist Workers Party. I went down and looked through everything from his bags, copied the lot and cross-referenced every name that was mentioned in his papers and his diaries.' Black then wrote a report that he says attracted 'a huge amount of interest' from the SDS, which already had the activist with the offending literature on its radar. An SDS manager met with Black to thank him personally, but also, he later found out, to gauge whether he was suitable for a transfer to the unit.

A few weeks later, Black got into a row with an inspector who he claims 'lost control of an operation and was treating his men like shit and ordering them around'. He believes his dispute with his boss told the SDS something about his character. 'That actually made me stand out a bit. The branch was looking for people to go into the SDS who were capable of making that kind of a stand. It was a little flash of individuality.'

Soon afterwards, Black was partnered with a former SDS officer in a long surveillance operation. 'We ended up giving each other our whole life stories during the course of the operation, although he never mentioned the SDS,' he says. Looking back, Black believes this job was no coincidence either. 'All the things I had been doing had, unbeknown to me, marked my card as someone who might be able to fit in with the unit.'

Black eventually attended an interview at a secret SDS office. 'I remember being there and saying that, until the day before, I had not even heard of them. They did not give much away during the interview. They told me that they worked for the Metropolitan police and also directly for the security services. That for me was all I needed to hear. I felt that I'd finally arrived and that after all this work I was on the cusp of my whole life's dream of actually working for the Security Service.'

The job was not initially as adventurous as Black might have expected. In January 1993, he arrived at the cramped headquarters of the SDS in Cundy Street, central London. There was nothing to give away it was the base for a fleet of police spies. It was just a converted flat, in Johnson House, a block usually used for newly married police officers. Black was made the 'back-office boy' to four superiors who ran the operation.

Part of his job was to provide the administrative support to the squad's 10 undercover operatives then 'in the field'. At the time, three police officers were embedded in left-wing groups, two in the animal rights movement, two in right-wing groups and others in campaigns supporting causes such as Irish republicanism. Black's main job involved handling the undercover officers' 'blue bags', in which they delivered reports to the squad. These files also contained requests, from undercover operatives or their seniors, for specific pieces of information held elsewhere in Special Branch. 'There might be a request to check a number plate or phone number or to identify a particular person in a photograph. As the back-office boy, you take that information and provide the answers,' he says.

Mornings were taken up with paperwork, but afternoons were generally more practical. The whole routine was part of an SDS ritual. The 'back-office boy' would always spend months doing menial work and preparing their alias, ready to replace one of the 10 when their mission ended. It was a revolving system, and each time a 'back-office boy' graduated, another was recruited to start learning the ropes. 'What I didn't realise until I got there was that not everyone who goes into the back office actually makes it out into the field,' he says. 'About a fifth of the recruits never make it out of the back office at all. They get watched closely and it is decided that they simply don't have what it takes to make it any further.'

The first challenge for all new recruits involved constructing their fake identity, or 'legend'. It was not just a name they were searching for, but a whole life story that would provide a plausible explanation for their interest in activism. The SDS had protocol for the creation of these legends: they would search out the identity of a suitable dead child, steal it, and claim it as their own, without ever informing the parents.

The process of acquiring these dead children's identities was as bizarre as it was gruesome. SDS officers would visit St Catherine's House, a prosaic government building near Aldwych in central London, which until 1997 housed the lists of Britain's births, marriages and deaths going back more than 150 years. For years, legions of amateur historians pored laboriously over the huge ledgers containing clues to their ancestors. But among their number were SDS men who, like Black, had a more sinister purpose.

'You go to St Catherine's House and you are looking for someone of a similar age to you who died, starting at age three or four and up to age 14 or 15,' he explains. Wherever possible, spies were required to find someone who shared their first name. This was important: it was notoriously difficult to suddenly adopt a completely different first name. 'It doesn't matter how good you think you are,' Black says. 'If you are undercover as "David" and you're walking down the road and someone behind you starts shouting out "David", there's no way in the world you're ever going to turn around, so you don't change your first name.'

He adds: 'Surnames always have to be general. You don't want something which is going to stand out too much or be too memorable, like Aardvark. You don't want to draw any unnecessary attention to yourself. Green and Black are good. But you don't want something like Smith. No matter what your first name is, that surname will always sound fake.'

Searching through death records for a child who had died years ago had a ghoulish quality. Black remembers a 'real moment of discomfort' when he came across the boy whose identity he was about to take. He was a four-year-old. 'I looked and saw the little chap's death certificate. It might have been to do with the age of my son at the time – a very similar age to the age this boy died. A part of me was thinking about how I would feel if someone was taking the name and details of my dead son for something like this. For me that was a little pang going on. And that was the first of many moments I ended up having. You have to use people. You end up using a lot of people.'

The strange ritual undergone by undercover police officers had a purpose. The idea was that by pretending to be a real person – albeit one who had died decades ago – the SDS officers were protecting themselves. If anyone they infiltrated became suspicious of them, and researched their background behind their back, they would most likely come across a real person's birth certificate. 'What you are always gearing up for is someone saying: "I'm suspicious. I don't like him, I'm going down to St Catherine's House in order to check him out."' By resurrecting the identities of real people, the SDS felt they had a stronger cover story.

It was not a technique that was unique to the SDS. The trick had been used by fraudsters and serious criminals for many years and was fictionalised in Frederick Forsyth's 1971 novel *Day of the Jackal*; the professional assassin who was paid to kill French president Charles de Gaulle resorted to the same ruse of assuming a dead person's identity. In recognition of the book, the SDS came up with a nickname for the process of searching for suitable dead children: they called it 'The Jackal Run'. Black was not the only SDS officer to feel a little uneasy about the morality of the identity fraud.

A second SDS officer, who chose an infant killed in a road accident, said he did so in the knowledge that his parents would 'still be grief-stricken'. 'I thought: what would his family think if their son's name was being used for the greater good, how would they feel about it, and should they be consulted?' he says. 'There were dilemmas that went through my head.' He adds: 'Your choice of name was of fundamental importance because on that would rest your whole identity, sense of security, confidence and ability to do the job. You are feeling vulnerable right from the first day. All the work you did before you started the job you felt paid off because you felt more comfortable, more confident and stronger within that identity.' He believed the tactic was probably justified 'because we had this mission to accomplish and this was the only way of doing it'.

Black did not feel the same way. 'For me that was the first marker,' he says. 'In many ways those first feelings of discomfort were a sign of the problems that I would end up having later on.' The boy Black chose had a 'totally English' surname. His father served in the Royal Marines and was initially stationed in the Far East; his son had died around the age of four in his next posting in the Middle East. The birth certificate was therefore kept in a more obscure overseas registry and would have been almost impossible to find. 'I made it so hard – I could only just about find myself afterwards.'

Choosing a child who had died overseas was the kind of ruse SDS officers liked to use. Undercover officers never wanted the birth certificates of the dead children to be too easily located. The more hoops activists had to go through to find the birth certificate, the more time the SDS would have to respond. Black felt his difficult-to-find birth certificate might one day help him if he ever came under suspicion. He figured he would have time to accuse activists of not trusting him and act enraged, secure in the knowledge that he could eventually tell them he was born abroad. If they looked hard enough, activists would find evidence he really existed.

'You want to prolong their pain and make as big a scene as possible,' he says. Of course, if it ever got to the stage of activists hunting through the birth certificate registry to work out if he was a real person, Black knew his deployment would be over. 'If someone has checked you out that much, you need to go anyway, your time is up,' he says. 'The operation is important, but not as important as my life.'

Another similar SDS trick was not to go for a precisely matching name, but to choose a child with a middle name they shared. That would also make it initially harder for activists to track down the documentation. John Dines, the SDS officer who posed as John Barker, for example, did not opt for a child whose first name was John. Instead he used the identity Philip John Barker, an eight-year-old boy who died of leukaemia in 1968.

The same ploy appears to have been used by Bob Lambert, whose undercover alias was Bob Robinson. He seems to have used the identity of Mark Robert Robinson, who was born in Plumstead, south-east London, on February 28 1952. SDS officers always looked for children who were born around the same time as them, and Lambert's choice was ideal – born just 16 days before Lambert's real date of birth. He died of acute congestive cardiac failure at the age of seven after being born with a malformed heart. The child's headstone was a sculpture of the boy stood guard above the grave in Branksome cemetery near Poole. The engraving said: 'Safe in the arms of Jesus'.

It seems likely that Lambert visited the boy's gravestone. SDS officers often did. They were not just using the names of deceased people – they were assuming their entire identities, so they made sure they familiarised themselves with the lives of the people they were pretending to be. That usually meant a visit to the house where the child was born and spent the first few years of their life, to get to know the surroundings. 'It's those little details that really matter – the weird smell coming out of the drain that's been broken for years, the location of the corner Post Office, the number of the bus you get to go from one place to another,' Black says.

SDS officers memorised the names of the dead child's mother, father and siblings, as well as other relatives, and found ways to work small details into their own back-story. Black for example used his fake father's job in the armed forces to integrate a 'violent' streak to his persona. 'I actually built into my identity the fact that my father was a trained Royal Marine and he used to beat me up,' he says. The fact he was pretending to be a dead person would always linger at the back of Black's mind, particularly during the awkward moments of his deployment when he celebrated his acquired birthday. He knew that was a day when the boy's parents were 'thinking about their son and missing him'. 'I used to get this really odd feeling – I wish I had not done it,' he says. 'It was almost like stomping on the grave.'

Aside from the ethical problem, there was also one very obvious risk to using a real person's identity. There were flaws in the formula: activists could always get hold of the dead child's birth certificate and then try to track down their real family. 'They could go and find the mother listed in the birth certificate and turn up on their doorstep,' Black says. 'They could knock on her door and say, "Where is your son, I want to hurt him because he is an infiltrator." And all she will be able to say is, "What are you talking about? My son died." These are the kind of things you start to imagine. You worry about all the random hurt being dished out to people who don't deserve it, all because of what you are doing.'

The other risk the SDS ran was even more serious. There was always a possibility that activists would not stop looking after discovering the birth certificate. What if they somehow managed to root out the death certificate, too?

Black knew of one such case. It concerned an SDS officer who infiltrated a left-wing group in the 1970s. One day, the SDS officer was invited by some campaigners to a drinking session at a pub followed by what was supposed to be a party at a friend's house. The spy realised something was not quite right as soon as he walked into the flat, located in a tower block. The atmosphere changed. His friends were looking at him strangely.

One activist blocked the door; others lined up around the room. Then the campaigners produced a piece of paper and handed it to the SDS officer. It was his death certificate, suggesting he had died, decades ago, as a young boy. So what was he doing, alive and well, attending their meetings?

Put on the spot, the SDS officer blustered. He began to panic. Fearing the situation was not going to end well, he glanced around the room for an escape route. His eyes settled on an open window and, acting on impulse, he ran and jumped through, forgetting he was two storeys up. The officer hit the ground, breaking a bone in his ankle, and was last seen hobbling away in agony. To this day, the former SDS spy still walks with a limp.

The activists were never able to work out he was a police officer, although they presumed he was some kind of imposter. By this point, the SDS decided it was too risky for him to continue undercover. When he was released from hospital, the SDS operative's managers told him his deployment was effectively terminated.

Many years later, Black was sitting around at a party with an old left-wing activist who began telling the very same story, from the perspective of the campaigners who had outed the infiltrator. The tale came out of the blue when the activist suddenly announced: 'I caught a spy once.' He went on to retell the story: the trip to the pub, the interrogation at the flat, the look on the man's face when he realised the game was up and jumped out of the window.

As he heard the story, Black's heart began racing. He wondered if the anecdote was a prelude to him being confronted. Were these activists about to produce his death certificate? 'You never know,' he said. 'When you first go undercover, you start off being extremely paranoid. Lots of activists think that there are spies left, right and centre.' As it turned out, it was an innocent, light-hearted conversation.

Black has never disclosed the full details of the dead boy whose identity he used. The name 'Pete Black' was one of several he used when he was undercover and it was not that of a dead child. Other times he called himself Pete Daley. It was not unusual for activists to have several different names. But the dead child's name was the most important one. It was printed on the fake passport, driving licence, bank account and national insurance card he was issued by the SDS. Once he had those documents, his transformation was almost complete.

Undercover officers who are deployed to infiltrate serious criminal conspiracies are sent on formal training courses beforehand, but that was not the SDS way. Black was told he was to learn his spycraft through osmosis, taking his lead from more senior SDS spies, who were considered the real experts. 'As the back-office person, you watch these people and that is how you learn the way to behave in order to do the job,' he says. 'You realise that if you arrested a group of people from the BNP and then you sat them down in a room to watch them all and tried to work out which one the undercover policeman was, you would not be able to do it.'

The squad had an oral culture in which knowledge, experience and tricks were handed down to the new recruits by old hands. Black was assigned a mentor for his first year. A former SDS officer who had infiltrated the Anti-Nazi League and the Socialist Workers Party in the 1970s, he was 'very professional and regarded with a lot of esteem', Black says. To use the jargon of the squad, his mentor was 'a very deep swimmer'.

As Black prepared to start his covert mission, senior officers in the SDS were deciding on his future undercover role. They were constantly working out which political groups needed infiltrating and which officers would make suitable spies. Initially, Black was lined up to become an anarchist. At least three SDS officers had already been embedded in anarchist groups in the early 1990s. One was in a small anarchist group called the Direct Action Movement (DAM), which had existed since 1979. Its associates believed capitalism should be abolished by workers organising themselves at the grassroots level, a political philosophy known as anarcho-syndicalism dating back to the late 1890s. One confidential Special Branch document states that a detective constable who worked as an SDS spy 'successfully' infiltrated DAM between 1990 and 1993.

Another group of interest to the SDS was the better-known Class War, which achieved some notoriety after it was set up in the 1980s. Anarchists linked with Class War produced a newspaper of the same name, styling it Britain's most unruly tabloid. At its zenith, it was reputedly selling 15,000 copies per week. It provoked a lather of indignation from the right-wing tabloid press, which was enraged by the publication's tongue-in-cheek promotion of violence against the wealthy. One front-page headline suggested that the newly married Duke and Duchess of York were 'Better Dead Than Wed', while the birth of Prince William was greeted with 'Another Fucking Royal Parasite'. A third showed the then prime minister Margaret Thatcher with a hatchet buried in her head.

A regular feature was the 'hospitalised copper' page – a photograph of a police officer being assaulted. 'We loved that. But it was done with humour, so even though it was violent, it didn't come across as psychotic violence,' says Ian Bone, Class War's loudest advocate. There was an element of pantomime about the group – in their 'Bash the Rich' demonstrations, supporters were invited to march into affluent areas of London such as Kensington and Hampstead.

Bone, a wiry sociology graduate with small round glasses who was once dubbed 'Britain's most dangerous man' by the press, said later that no rich people were actually 'bashed' – 'but it felt good walking down there. We gave a lot of abuse and shouts and they did cower, a few of them, behind their curtains.' The SDS viewed Bone and his friends as considerably more sinister. The unit posted at least two undercover police into the group.

One was in place in February 1992 when he had a meeting in a London safe house with David Shayler, the MI5 officer later jailed for breaking the Official Secrets Act after leaking details of alleged incompetence in the secret services. Shayler had at that time been assigned to investigate whether Class War posed a threat to British democracy. The SDS officer supplied intelligence to the Security Service, and had become an official MI5 informant, designated the code number M2589.

According to Shayler, the 'peculiar arrangement' in which the SDS officer lived the life of an anarchist for six days a week, returning only occasionally to his friends and family, had 'affected the agent psychologically'. Shayler recounts: 'After around four years of pretending to be an anarchist, he had clearly become one. To use the service jargon, he had gone native. He drank about six cans of Special Brew during the debrief, and regaled us with stories about beating up uniformed officers as part of his "cover". Partly as a result, he was "terminated" after the 1992 general election. Without his organisational skills, Class War fell apart.'

According to Black, the true story was a little different. He says the SDS officer in question was a 'top end' operative who served the unit well. During the encounter with the MI5 officer, he acted the part of a coarse anarchist because he had little time for Shayler, who was perceived to be a 'desk wanker' – though Black concedes that 'some MI5 desk officers who came out to talk to us were superb and we had a very, very good relationship with them'. A second SDS officer was later sent into Class War, but it became apparent the group was fading out. Rather ignominiously for the anarchists who wanted to tear down the state, the SDS concluded they could no longer justify spending money to infiltrate them.

Hence, in 1993, when Black was due to begin his life as an anarchist protester, the plan was suddenly changed. Black was disappointed; he had spent months perfecting his persona as an anarchist. 'It was all based around the fact that I was a half-German anarchist with tenuous connections to the Baader-Meinhof group. It sounds ridiculous when you say it and it's hard to imagine that it would stand up to scrutiny, but it would have,' he says. 'I used lots of elements of my own life to ensure it came across realistically.'

Instead, weeks before he was due to be deployed, he was called into the office by the head of the SDS. 'The boss pulled me in and said: "This anarchist work you've been doing, absolutely spot on.

I don't think I've ever seen anybody work so hard on their cover. First class. Now you can fucking forget all about it because you are not going into the anarchists. We've got something else in mind."'

At short notice, Black was plunged into another world – the bitter and at times violent conflict between the far right and their adversaries in the anti-racist movement. The far right was spreading its neo-Nazi message across the country, leading to a surge in racially motivated attacks and murders. They were also attacking the left at demonstrations, using iron bars, hammers and bottles as weapons.

The anti-fascists could be similarly violent in their retaliation. Some felt they needed to crush the resurgent far-right movement, using force if necessary, before it had a chance to take hold. The approach had a historical tradition – famously, thousands of Jews, socialists, anarchists, Irish Catholic dockers and others successfully blocked fascists led by Oswald Mosley from marching through east London in 1936. Of course, there were many other anti-racist groups who did not agree with using violence, deriding the tactic of 'bashing the fash' as immature and unjustified.

Still, there had been a string of bruising encounters between neo-Nazis and their opponents in London. Some of the most ferocious clashes occurred one Saturday afternoon in September 1992 when there were running battles between hundreds of anti-fascists and racists for hours in and around London's Waterloo station. More than 40 were arrested during the fighting which closed the station for 45 minutes and trapped passengers on platforms, as fighting spilled onto the concourse. Sixteen people were injured as anti-fascists sought to stop the racists from assembling and then travelling to see a concert organised by a neo-Nazi group called Blood and Honour.

Inevitably, the clashes came under the scrutiny of the SDS, which felt it needed to get a hold on what was happening. Black was redirected into the anti-racist movement. The detail of his mission was set out in a classified report, headed 'Targeting Strategy'. It was produced by the head of the SDS in September 1993. 'The continuing major threat to public order caused by the confrontations between right- and left-wing adherents continues to be a priority target for the SDS,' he wrote. 'Recent events show this is likely to be the dominant issue for street protests for the foreseeable future.'

The key group the SDS believed was involved in confronting the far right was called Anti-Fascist Action (AFA). Formed in the mid-1980s through a loose alliance of anarchists and left-wingers, the SDS said it was now subject to a political rift. In a trait painfully familiar to radical politics over the decades, there was an alphabet soup of competing organisations campaigning against racists. To make matters more complicated, each group was often just a front, controlled by another political faction.

Black was told he should penetrate Youth Against Racism in Europe, better known by its acronym YRE. It was a front for the revolutionary left-wing group, Militant. The head of the SDS believed there was a new anti-fascist alliance forming 'within the loose confederation' of the YRE, a second Trotskyist group and 'sundry ad-hoc student and Asian youth groups'. The SDS boss identified an obscure anti-fascist group at a further education college in Camden, north London, as a possible stepping stone into the YRE.

The SDS technique was to identify a key individual within a political group and get close to them. In Black's case, the target was an anti-fascist campaigner at Kingsway College. Black was instructed to attend the college and befriend this particular individual, who had connections with the YRE. 'This allows an entry into the YRE and possibly AFA,' his boss wrote. If this failed, there was a plan B: Black could penetrate 'an autonomous group of anarchists' based in Hackney, east London who had been previously infiltrated by the SDS.

Tensions on the streets were rapidly rising. They were brought to the boil on September 16 1993, when the BNP won its first-ever council seat: Derek Beackon was elected on to Tower Hamlets council, a deprived working-class area in east London. His election followed a number of racist attacks in the area – the previous week, for instance, a gang of eight white men had beaten a 17-year-old Asian boy called Quddus Ali and left him in a four-month-long coma, resulting in permanent brain damage. The election triggered further demonstrations, some of them violent.

One flashpoint was Brick Lane, the heartland of the Bangladeshi community. For many years, the fascists had been selling their newspapers on the street on Sundays. Their anti-fascist adversaries made several attempts to physically drive them away.

The weekend after Beackon's election, the anti-fascists pulled off what they believed was a small but important victory. As usual, the BNP were standing around selling their paper when they were joined by a group of 20 skinheads dressed in fascist uniform: bomber jackets, jeans and Dr Martens boots. They were chanting 'Rule Britannia' and giving Nazi salutes. The police allowed these apparent sympathisers to stand next to the BNP. Seconds later, the small group of skinheads turned on the BNP, attacking them and chasing them down the street.

The YRE activists who had disguised themselves as racists felt victorious. One told the *Guardian* newspaper: 'The damage we did to the Nazis that day was very effective. They have been taken out of the streets and neutralised in the Brick Lane area. Our prime aim is to build a mass-based anti-racist movement, but we also believe in tackling the Nazis head on. It gives the community confidence and helps them to help themselves.'

That same month, Black started his undercover role in college, taking his first tentative steps en route to the YRE. He had few clues to guide him. Intelligence about the Kingsway group was virtually non-existent. 'The SDS didn't have a clue about exactly what the group was up to. Nothing at all,' Black says. He recalls one superior telling him: 'There is no pre-intelligence, but we know that you know how to look after yourself, so best of luck to you.'

The deployment did not start well. 'The SDS did not realise that the Kingsway college was split across four different sites,' Black says. 'All I had was a name and a group so I enrolled at the college only to find that I had actually joined the wrong part. I wasn't where I needed to be at all.' Where he needed to be was at the college's site in Gray's Inn Road. Black was feeling vulnerable. The last-minute change to his deployment meant he did not have much time to 'put together my new character'.

'I knew the key to getting alongside my targets would be to not be too keen,' he says. 'You can't get into a situation like that already believing whatever particular brand of politics it is that they are spouting. You need to let them convert you, or at least think they have converted you. My attitude at the beginning was "Fuck off with your poxy student politics" and letting them come and try to prove me wrong. You have to allow them to come to you. If you go in and you say, "Oh, I love the left wing, I think you are all wonderful," then you might as well put a sign on your head.'

Within days Black had what he considered a lucky break, allowing him to get close to the Kingsway student he was told was a key figure. It happened in the college canteen. 'I was in a queue for lunch and there was some sort of altercation between a couple of people in front of me and the lady who was serving,' he says. 'I didn't hear the beginning of it but it actually then took on a really racist undertone. I've never liked bullies or racism. It was nothing to do with being a police officer because at that moment the last thing I wanted to do was break my cover. I was just intervening because it was the kind of thing I would have done in my personal life. I barged forward and said to the person who was causing this trouble that this woman does not deserve this. She is just doing her job. It's irrelevant if she's fucking black or white or whatever, you shouldn't be giving her a hard time. He then turned round and had a swing at me. And that was that, it was all over in a second and he was on the floor.'

The fracas was seen by a student who was friendly with Black's target, the Kingsway anti-fascist campaigner. A few days later, the two of them tried to persuade Black to join a demonstration against the BNP.

'I went into my full spiel: "I'm not going along to do anything with a bunch of student wankers",' he recalls. '"It's a student wanker demonstration and I'm not interested." He tried to explain that it wasn't like that at all and that by going along I'd be making a stand against racism, something I clearly believed in because of the way I had reacted in the canteen. I told him that was nothing to do with racism; it was just a mouthy git who got what he deserved. He shook his head and told me that whether I realised it or not, I had been making a stand. I knew I couldn't be seen to be keen and I thought that I seemed to have played it just right.'

After initially appearing reluctant, Black agreed to take part in the demo that weekend. The following day, he reported everything back to the head of the SDS. His boss commended Black for befriending his target so quickly, but warned him not to seem too hungry. 'If I got burned, they explained, then my tour was going to be the shortest in the history of the SDS,' he says.

As it transpired, the Kingsway anti-fascist students never suspected that their new recruit was a police spy. Why would they? They had no reason to believe police would plant a spy in their ranks; they were students, in a tiny, mundane group which was barely noticed in the wider anti-racist movement. However, it was common practice in the SDS to first target marginal groups such as the Kingsway anti-fascists, so that the spies could gradually build up their credibility and wheedle their way into the centre of a movement.

Within weeks, Black was gathering intelligence on a large demonstration that was planned to take place to protest against the BNP at Welling on October 16. The presence of the BNP in Welling had been a febrile political issue for some time. The extreme right-wing party occupied a building that was ostensibly a bookshop. On the outside, 154 Upper Wickham Lane looked innocuous. But behind the locked and bolted doors, the building was the headquarters of the party.

The location of the BNP building was considered incendiary. South-east London had become notorious for racial attacks and murders. In the previous two years, there had been three racist killings in the area, including the shocking murder of 18-year-old Stephen Lawrence in April 1993. Anti-racist campaigners said that racial attacks there had sharply increased after the BNP arrived in 1989, a statement backed up by Home Office figures which record that the number of racial attacks increased from 292 in 1988 to 811 in 1992. Richard Edmonds, the BNP's national activities organiser, and a convicted criminal, openly said that the party was '100 per cent racist'.

Campaigners had persistently called on the local council, police and government ministers to close down the building. But the BNP headquarters remained open, and campaigners resorted to increasingly confrontational tactics. There were angry demonstrations outside the building in May that year, including one attended by Duwayne Brooks, Stephen Lawrence's friend who was with him on the night he was murdered just a few weeks earlier. Declassified Home Office documents show that the prime minister John Major was personally briefed on the disorder, as Sir Paul Condon, the Met commissioner, came under pressure to stop the escalating confrontations.

By the autumn, it became clear protesters were planning a major demonstration at Welling. The date was set for October 16. This was going to be the big one. Organisers informed police that up to 50,000 campaigners were going to march, one of the biggest protests against fascism since the 1930s. It fell to the SDS to work out whether that prediction was accurate and, if so, whether the march would turn violent.

It was at times such as these that the SDS was under pressure to justify its existence. Their forecasts would inform senior commanders, enabling them to deploy the right police resources on the streets. Ever since the days of Conrad Dixon, this was considered to be the main purpose of the SDS, and it was essential that its spies delivered the goods. If the undercover officers failed to anticipate the level of conflict, police might be overrun. Then again, if they exaggerated the threat, police might waste resources preparing for a damp squib of a demo. 'At the end of the day, that was what the SDS was there for – when Condon or the Met commissioner really does get the big cheque book out, it's not wasted,' says Black. 'If he has to spend so many millions, it's totally justifiable.'

The SDS was fortunate that seven out of the 10 spies in the squad were sufficiently embedded in the right political groups to supply intelligence in advance of the demonstration. Some of them of course were only on the periphery. But one SDS officer was masquerading as an activist in the Anti-Nazi League, one of the main groups organising the march. The ANL, which was previously infiltrated by the SDS in the 1970s, had been relaunched after a decade's dormancy. It was supported by trade unions and some Labour MPs, but widely viewed as a 'front' for the Socialist Workers Party, the Trotskyite revolutionary group.

Another well-placed spy was Black, newly enrolled at Kingsway College and quickly making the right friends. He and the other operatives formally submitted their predictions for the October 16 demonstration. The collective wisdom among the spies was that the march would be bigger than previous protests and that serious disorder was likely to break out. Scotland Yard responded with a huge show of force. Police leave was cancelled and more than 5,000 riot officers and 84 horses were deployed to control the demonstration along the narrow streets of Welling.

On the eve of the march, Condon told the public to stay away, warning of 'mob violence'. He said his commanders would allow the march to go ahead but had banned it going past the BNP headquarters, which he feared would be the scene of violent attacks. Organisers of the demonstration accused Condon of making inflammatory remarks. They said they planned a 'peaceful but determined' march and knew of no plans for violence, insisting they wanted to walk past the BNP headquarters because it was a symbol of racism. It was a delicate, potentially explosive mix.

On October 16, Black was on one of 550 coaches that transported campaigners down to Welling for the demonstration. He was preparing himself for 'biggest ruck since the poll tax riots' three years earlier. He says he readied himself to behave with 'the same dumbshit mentality' as campaigners, during any tough, physical confrontations with police.

The very idea of trying to take on lines of riot police struck Black as futile. 'How are you going to fight the rozzers with all their shields and everything else? You are dumb as a fucking loo-brush. But if this lot want to give it a go, my role is to be as dumb as a loo-brush with them as well.'

The likely flashpoint had been obvious to many for some time. It was a fork in the road: to the left was the police-designated route the demonstrators were being ordered to follow; the right side was the road that took them directly to the BNP bookshop.

That route was blocked by row upon row of police in riot gear, with instructions to corral marchers away. After a standoff, the inevitable fighting broke out. Black recalls seeing his SDS colleague in the fray who was trying to dissuade others from heading toward the BNP building. 'There was a moment when I am an SDS officer going forward with my group, and there's another SDS officer in the Anti-Nazi League running backwards, calling on the crowds to go with him away, trying to get people to follow him.' The ANL did not have the same reputation for street confrontations. It would have been out of character – and frowned upon – for Black's SDS colleague to do anything other than try to lead his friends away from the violence.

They were not the only police spies on duty that day. On the other side of the police line, an SDS officer infiltrating a vicious right-wing group called Combat 18 was patrolling the outskirts of the demonstration, in the company of hard-core Nazis. They were beating up any anti-racists unlucky enough to stray from the march and find themselves isolated.

A fourth SDS spy was actually inside the BNP bookshop. For some time, he had been a trusted member of the party. He and others were expected to defend their headquarters in the event the crowd broke through the police lines and started attacking the building. 'He was bricking it,' Black says. 'We had to protect the bookshop that day as Condon knew that there was an undercover police officer in there.'

True to predictions, Welling was the worst public disorder since the poll tax demonstrations, although the police lines held together. Afterwards, away from the public row about who was at fault for the violent clashes, Britain's most senior police officer paid a visit to a quiet residential flat in Balcombe Street in Marylebone. As commissioner of the Met, Condon felt indebted to the intelligence the men of the SDS had provided and he had gone to the squad's safe house to thank them in person.

It was a rare visit from Condon. Every commissioner since 1968 had known about the work of the SDS, but its existence was barely mentioned, and of course never admitted, outside of a close circle of top cops and Whitehall mandarins. Black recalls the visit from the VIP as a 'good moment' for him and the rest of the unit. Condon gave them a bottle of whisky. 'We had done what we were there for,' he says.

For his troubles, Black was rewarded with a smaller, private meeting with the commissioner, who asked him about his undercover work and what happened on the day of the demonstration. But Black detected a slight discomfort on the part of the police chief.

The sight that confronted Condon that afternoon was a world away from the police control rooms and borough stations he routinely visited. In the flat in the Georgian block of Brunswick House were 10 scruffily dressed people who looked nothing like police officers. They were in ripped jeans and bomber jackets, many sporting beards and long hair. With his earrings and long, bushy ponytail, draped over his shoulder, Black could not look less like a cop if he tried.

But as he burrowed deeper into the anti-racist movement, Black realised that it was not just his appearance that had changed. He would soon find himself questioning the ethics of his entire mission.

CHAPTER 8

Changing Course

For the seventh night in a row, Pete Black felt alone and isolated in the middle of the Bavarian forest. It was the summer of 1995, and one of the most stressful experiences of his life. Normally his nerves were pretty resilient. But camping in a giant, thick spruce forest, surrounded by more than 1,500 anti-racist activists from 18 different countries, he was gripped by a fear that he would be found out. Part of the reason for his paranoia was the knowledge that if anything were to go wrong, there was no effective back-up for miles around. He had no mobile telephone or tracking technology. He was on his own and the fear of what might happen if he attracted suspicion was terrifying.

Black was in Germany for a summer camp organised by the YRE. By now, he was heavily involved in their campaign, a key London organiser. The camp, in a big clearing in the forest, was designed partly to be a holiday for European anti-racist campaigners, a place they could meet each other, socialise and let their hair down. There was a disco tent, a chill-out area and a marquee where attendees could be entertained by some German rock bands.

But this was also a political gathering, a meeting of minds where ideas could be swapped between anti-racist activists from across the continent. The location of the camp deep in this particular forest was no coincidence. It was a two-fingered salute to neo-Nazis, who claimed this part of Germany as their heartland. The camp was protected around the clock against attacks from fascists, with regular patrols around the perimeter. 'I had to do night-time patrols as well,' Black recalls.

One corner of the campsite was taken over by the Black Bloc, hard-core anarchists who, Black says, had brought firearms with them. They were notoriously frosty to outsiders. One night, the activists were woken by gunshots. The next day, the anarchists insisted it must have been hunters shooting wild boar – or Nazis firing bullets into the night sky to scare the campers. Whoever was responsible for the shots, they only added to the anxiety gripping the undercover police officer.

'It was scary, an absolute nightmare – I can't begin to explain it,' he says. Black's fear was compounded because he had made a crucial error that made it far more likely he would be exposed as a police infiltrator. He had failed to anticipate that he and the other activists would be sleeping beside each other in a large tent. Black feared he would talk in his sleep, and he was terrified he would inadvertently mutter something about being a police officer when dreaming.

Back in England, when campaigners stayed at his flat, Black had a technique to stop himself from blurting out something incriminating in his sleep. 'No matter how many bedrooms you had they would always – bar the occasional female – camp in the lounge, so when I went into the bedroom, I could slam a chair under the door handle and sleep.' In the depths of the Bavarian forest, that was not an option.

'I could not sleep properly for a week,' he says. 'Your weakness is always when you're asleep. With the benefit of hindsight, I should have brought my own tent. But I had never built into my cover story anything about a tent. If you brought your own tent, but did not know how to use it, it would have looked like you had deliberately brought a tent to be by yourself.' He had no choice but to bed down with five other activists, bury his head in his sleeping bag and hope for the best. 'I thought, "Fuck it, go with the flow,"' he says.

Black says that week in Bavaria 'was the most intense pressure' over a sustained period of time he had experienced on the job. 'You are undercover trying to pretend you are enjoying yourself, in this huge drinking environment,' he says. If activists had been harbouring suspicions about Black, he knew the remote camp was the ideal opportunity to confront him. The camp organisers had taken and photocopied everyone's identity documents. 'I thought: if it really did go tits up, my identity had to be perfect. I could not get out of the camp as they had my passport.'

Underneath his calm exterior, Black was riddled with paranoia. He worried about the most improbable of scenarios. For example, when he was much younger, Black spent a few years living in a German village. Now he was worried that someone from his younger days might by sheer coincidence attend the camp and recognise him. He kept rehearsing this and other unlikely scenarios in his head, preparing himself for the unexpected. 'What you do in the SDS is you hope, if not pray for the best,' he says. 'But you always plan for the worst.'

Black had himself to blame for finding himself in the German forest. He had insisted the SDS should let him travel to the camp, even though the squad had until then never dispatched one of its spies abroad. He had gone through 'a world of pain' to get special approval from Special Branch and the German police authorities. By then he had risen to become the secretary of a branch in the YRE and he thought it would have been deeply suspicious not to attend the camp.

'Everyone knew that I had German connections, with my mother being German,' he says. 'It was beyond belief that I would not go.' For the SDS, the experiment in foreign espionage was a gamble. Special Branch bosses stipulated that another officer had to travel with Black and meet with him regularly, but it turned out to be too risky for Black to slip out to speak with his handler.

'We had no contact during the week,' he says. Instead, Black's handler spent the week relaxing on the SDS expense account in a nearby hotel.

Given this was the first foreign mission for the SDS, the unit decided Black should be accompanied by a particularly senior officer – a man who had recently rejoined the squad. And so it was that as Black was sleeping fitfully through the night, terrified at the prospect of being exposed, Bob Lambert was taking in the scenery at a safe distance. 'I was – I kid you not – in the middle of an isolated Bavarian forest; he was holed up in a hotel a few miles away enjoying himself,' says Black. Even though Lambert was some distance away, he was a reassuring presence for Black. The older man's reputation preceded him. 'He did what is hands down regarded as the best SDS tour of duty ever,' Black says.

Under the deal Lambert struck with German authorities, Black was required to provide an extensive report on the country's home-grown activists – in addition to his routine work for the SDS. He was under pressure to record everything that was happening around him but felt unable to resort to writing down notes.

'Where are going to hide them – in your underpants or something?' he says. 'You can't stick a report in your underpants, you are in a tent sharing it with people. You do it from memory, you remember absolutely everything. That's old tradecraft – you never write things down. They would rather you lose intelligence.'

Once his adventure in the forest was over, Black spent days downloading everything he could recollect from the camp. He compiled and delivered a series of reports on the YRE campaign and their connections on the continent. He says that because he spoke German, and could converse with native activists, he managed to provide the host country with high-grade intelligence. The Germans felt the SDS had done them a 'huge favour', he says.

Lambert and the rest of the senior command felt the trip was a success. It paved the way for other undercover officers to travel abroad. One went to France with the Anti-Nazi League, while the following year Black travelled to another summer camp (this time, with his own tent) in Greece. It was the start of a trend. Within a decade, there would be an almost constant exchange of undercover police officers across Europe posing as activists.

Back in London, Black had moved on from the small Kingsway anti-fascist group. He was now secretary of the Hackney and Islington branch in London of the YRE, with access to much of the group's paperwork and the revolutionary party that pulled its strings. For Black, membership of Militant Labour, which controlled the anti-racist group, was crucial.

'There is no way on God's earth that I could become a branch secretary of the YRE without becoming a member of Militant,' said Black. Militant's heyday had been in the 1980s, when it was a household name. Its Trotskyist supporters infiltrated the Labour Party, running a covert 'party within a party' as part of a strategy to radicalise Labour. Then known as the Militant Tendency, it was most well known for taking control of Liverpool Council and making a defiant stance against Margaret Thatcher's policy of cutting public funding. During the course of the decade, Labour leaders gradually expelled Militant operatives from the party until, in the early 1990s, they were forced to come out into the open to establish an overt political group, Militant Labour. By then its influence was fading. When in 1997 it changed its name to the Socialist Party, Black remained embedded.

Once inside Militant, Black turned himself into an 'intelligence-gathering machine' for the SDS. He continuously cultivated his activist fake persona, which he rightly believed would be crucial to his success. Black's alias was a mixture of 'Mr Angry' and 'Mr Hard', a tough guy who could handle himself in a fight. He wanted to be known as a character who 'was angry with the whole world'. 'I could bristle with anger,' he says. Hannah Sell, a YRE leader, remembers Black as 'a bit hot-headed and macho'. She says the newcomer 'tended to argue for brawling' with the far right. 'We explained that defeating racist and fascist groups is a political task which required patient campaigning in working-class communities, rather than street fighting.'

Like all SDS officers, Black tried to anchor his constructed personality in life experiences from before he was deployed. 'You use things from your real life to incorporate into your fake life, but you don't use something that hurts or is too personal,' he says. 'The only thing I found all too close to home was the idea of making my mum an alcoholic. Instead I made my fake dad an alcoholic and gave that as the reason he had been beating me up. I needed that because I knew that at some point I was going to have to explain how it was that I could fight so well. The answer was a simple one. I told people that if they had a father who beat them up every day, they would learn to fight pretty quickly too.'

Every aspect of an SDS officer's legend had a purpose. For example, Black pretended to be dyslexic, even though he was perfectly capable of reading and writing. He even made sure to deliberately skew a test before his deployment, to give the impression that he had the disability. 'It's something you can teach yourself,' he says. 'In about half an hour I can turn it on.' The main reason for the faked dyslexia was that Black needed an excuse to attend Kingsway College as a mature student. 'My story was that I was going back in order to get my first ever GCSE and to make my German mother proud,' he says. 'That gave my cover a real emotional pull to it. I said I'd grown up thinking I was stupid and not doing very well at school, but had come to realise that this wasn't the case.'

Black's purported dyslexia had other advantages, too. SDS officers liked to emphasise their vulnerabilities, generating sympathy from people they met. Black wanted activists to be taken in by the sad story of a man held back by his disability, despite an innate intelligence. He wanted to come across as a frustrated soul who needed nurturing politically. He was soon being invited to workshops to be taught about Trotskyism.

'I used to go to educational classes every second Sunday unless there was a demo,' he says. 'These were one-on-one sessions where you would be taught by people, sometimes from the top of Militant. You would go round to their houses and talk about Marx or Engels. It was a complete nightmare because I was not interested in that stuff at all, yet I still had to learn it and show that I was willing to be educated to some degree. That was important in order to gain their trust and respect.'

He adds: 'But for me the dyslexia was a huge bonus. It meant I could refuse to be given the large books on theory. It meant that I had a good reason to stay at the level where I was. They'd asked me how I was getting on with a book and I'd say that I had only made it up to page three so far and there was not a lot they could say about it. It was a very effective way of fending people off.'

Black also took care to maintain the appearance of a revolutionary leftist. To activists, the combination of a ponytail down his back and balding patch made Black stand out – one would go as far as to say he looked 'like a loser'. There was a sense in Militant circles that Black was eager to please – a reputation the operative wanted. He knew that his best chance of gaining the trust of the group was to do many of the boring jobs other campaigners always wriggled out of.

Sell remembers how Black did a 'lot of the donkey work' and never turned down a request for a favour. Like almost all SDS officers, Black owned a van – it was the signature prop for the squad, allowing its operatives to make themselves useful by ferrying activists around. 'The van was good cover,' Black says. 'I did a lot of photocopying for the campaigners and I carried things around in the van. All the groups we targeted were poor and never had any transport so having a van made me instantly valuable.'

The SDS had provided Black with a basement flat in Furlong Road, a quiet residential street in Islington. He chose that location – rather than an apartment in Hackney, where Militant's headquarters were located – to minimise the likelihood activists would pop around unannounced. During the two years he lived there, Black tried to keep the place 'clean and tidy' and fill it with sufficient furniture to avoid it looking empty. The leftist campaigners appear to have been unimpressed. One activist recalls Black's flat as being 'a bit tacky, like a student flat', while another, Greg Randall, says it looked 'grotty'.

For a job, Black called in a favour from someone he knew who worked in a local school for children with special needs. 'I said to her that I would like to volunteer to work at the school. I said I didn't want to lie to her, and that I would be using it as cover of sorts.' The woman knew Black was a police officer, but not much else.

The friend agreed, and Black was told he could help out around the school, and receive free dyslexia lessons in return. The school authorities had no idea about his true role. 'They didn't know that I was an undercover police officer and they didn't know that I didn't have dyslexia either,' he says. With regular access to the school, Black contrived a somewhat different explanation for his friends in left-wing campaigns. Instead of telling them he occasionally volunteered at the school, he

claimed to be its handyman. The two sides – the school authorities and his activist friends – had a different concept of what he
was doing there.

'As long as the two never met up for a longer interrogation,
it worked,' he says. 'You need to have a job so that people don't
wonder why you have enough money to do things they might not
be able to do. But it can't be a regular job. Somehow you have
to be flexible enough to be able to take time off at short notice
whenever there is a demonstration or a meeting and that kind of
thing. You need to be able to move things around.'

The SDS always stressed the importance of a watertight
cover story. From its long experience in political espionage, the
unit knew that campaigners had their own, often sophisticated,
methods of counter-surveillance. Suspicious individuals would
be followed home or subjected to minor interrogations. Some
activists even had access to the tools of the state to research the
backgrounds of newcomers who did not seem quite right. Many
Militant campaigners, for example, worked in the public sector,
and could quietly run checks on government databases to verify
whether people were who they claimed to be.

Managers in the SDS arranged for fake national insurance
numbers and tax records to be drawn up and inserted into the
official bureaucracy for each of their undercover officers. 'This is
not Mickey Mouse cover,' Black says. 'You have perfect Inland
Revenue records stretching back, usually involving some kind of
manual labour so that there are no bank transfers and so on. If
you were to look at it, you would not see anything wrong.'

And in this particular battle, police had the upper hand.
Unbeknown to public-sector employees who were running database checks on the sly, there was a silent trigger on all official
records belonging to SDS officers. It meant that the moment an
activist pulled up a file belonging to an SDS officer, an automatic

alert was sent to the unit. This was how Black discovered that secret background checks were being conducted on him, around the time he was being considered for the post of a YRE branch secretary.

This particular incident was not too concerning. Campaign groups routinely looked into people they did not know too well, and Militant was especially paranoid. 'They had infiltrated the Labour Party and expected to be infiltrated themselves,' Black says. He also felt he had taken sufficient precautions. The rent for his flat, for example, was paid in cash, and later recouped from the police. His van was registered to the school, so nothing suspicious would pop up in a search of records at the Driving Vehicle Licensing Agency. Believing that activists could even get access to the Police National Computer, the SDS had ensured that its spies had fabricated files listing some past misbehaviour. A false criminal record was created on Black's undercover identity and inserted into the national database. 'You have to have a PNC record with some violence on it. Not too much, but a little bit,' he says.

These safeguards were all useful, but Black knew what really mattered was his ability to make friends. He threw himself into socialising, determined to persuade them that his fake persona 'was the real thing'. The social life was 'pretty unrelenting', Black says; often activists went to the pub after a meeting or demonstration and carried on drinking in one of their flats until the small hours.

'I had a really good time with my targets and enjoyed their company enormously – there was a genuine bond,' he says. 'There's a sense of comradeship in what you have done together, the battles you've had, your battle scars and what you have been through.' But deep down, Black knew that these were not the sort of people he would associate with in his real life and he always remembered his 'overarching loyalty' was to the SDS. 'Would I have been friends with any of these people, would I wish to be friends with any of them? Not a single one of them.' When Black felt himself becoming close to an activist, he tried to remind himself he was just 'pretending'; that the bond, however strong, had a strictly utilitarian function.

But it was not always easy for Black to maintain his ruthless detachment. There were times when he realised his friends were genuinely good people. One day, Black needed to take some time off. His wife was giving birth to his child and so he needed an excuse to spend fewer days living undercover. In his real life, when he was a child, Black's parents had divorced and his mother took to drinking heavily. In the end, his grandmother had helped bring him up as a sort of surrogate mother. Around a decade earlier she had fallen ill with cancer.

It was a biographical detail that Black integrated into his cover story – with a twist. In order to manufacture a reason for his time away from London, Black told friends that his mother in Germany had cancer. It was a lie, but it enabled Black to draw on the genuine emotions he felt when his grandmother had fallen ill. By resurrecting the illness that had ravaged his grandmother 10 years earlier, and pretending it was now affecting his mother, Black could speak convincingly about the physical and emotional toll the disease was taking on him.

Every time Black needed a break from undercover life, he reused the fabricated tale about his mother's cancer. The fiction lasted around two years. His friends became more concerned for Black, who they believed was going through a hard time. He still has the sympathy cards, signed by more than a dozen activists, that he received whenever he told them he was off to Germany to visit his gravely ill mother. One of his friends wrote: 'Peter, just a thought from the branch. We heard about your mum and this is just a note to say we're thinking about you and hope she's doing OK.'

By the middle of his deployment in 1995, Black had settled into the weekly routine of an undercover SDS officer. Early on a Monday morning, he woke up in the Furlong Road flat and drove through rush-hour traffic to the home of his real family, outside London. Once there, he went into the study to write up a report into what the activists had been doing over the weekend. Once it was finished he drove back into London, made his way to one of the unit's safe houses in the afternoon and hooked up with the rest of the squad for one of their regular weekly meetings.

'The work of the day was to give a debriefing on the weekend,' he says. After the meeting, Black often went for a drink with the squad and then returned home to be with his wife and kids. It was often a long journey; SDS officers took circuitous routes every-where to ensure they were not being followed, a process known as 'dry-cleaning'. Once home, he says, 'you would be lucky if you could stay into Tuesday afternoon or evening'. It was the briefest of respites: a quick, sobering dip into his old identity – that of a police officer, father and husband – before driving back into town to reassume the identity of an unwavering Militant campaigner and bachelor.

Black liked to be back at his Furlong Road flat by the late afternoon, giving the impression he had spent a day doing odd jobs at the school. He was in the school for two days a week. 'It's a real role – if the activists came to the school, you would be there,' he says. The rest of the week was spent with the activists, trying to pick up intelligence about forthcoming protests, either that weekend or in the future. On Thursday afternoons, Black attended the second regular SDS meeting of the week, at which the undercover officers were expected to brief their bosses on any protests coming up that weekend.

Black tried to be at his Furlong Road flat on Friday nights, too, in case activists came round. He spent the weekends involved in political activity, attending protests, selling Militant's paper on street corners or socialising with campaigners. His boss Lambert placed great emphasis on making friends and going out. It made for more reliable cover. Of course Black also knew that SDS officers regularly slept with women activists to build the credibility of their persona.

Unlike the likes of Lambert and Chitty, he never developed any long-term relationships with women when undercover, but he did have sex with two activists. It is a subject he talks about in a matter-of-fact way. He argues it would have been virtually impossible to do his job without occasionally sleeping with women.

The unofficial motto of the SDS was 'By Any Means Necessary', and all operatives knew that sex was one tactic in their repertoire. 'Basically it's just regarded as part of the job,' he says. 'It'd be highly unlikely that you were not having sex.' It was so widespread that out of the 10 SDS officers undercover when Black was deployed, only one did not sleep with campaigners. That included the small number of women in the squad, who had sex with male activists.

There was no specific rule against having sexual partners. It was so commonplace that, he says, it was barely remarked on. 'Among fellow undercover officers, there is not really any kudos in the fact that you are shagging other people while deployed,' he says. Having sex with campaigners was something that – either implicitly or explicitly – had the blessing of those running the SDS. They knew it was going on and did nothing to stop it. Indeed, Black says that while sex was considered acceptable, one unofficial rule was that operatives should 'never fall in love' with their targets.

'When you are using the tool of sex to maintain your cover or maybe to glean more intelligence – because they certainly talk a lot more, pillow talk – you would be ready to move on if you felt an attachment growing,' he says. 'The best way of stopping any liaison getting too heavy was to shag somebody else,' he says. 'It's amazing how women don't like you going to bed with someone else.'

But there were occasions when the undercover officers strayed too far. When Black was undercover, he was not aware that anyone in the unit knew that Lambert had secretly fathered a child. However, they did know of another former SDS officer who fathered another child during a short-lived relationship. Like Lambert, he vanished from the lives of mother and child when his deployment ended. The mother brought up the child on her own, while the SDS officer continued his career in the Special Branch. The woman remained politically active, enabling the former SDS spy to periodically check up on her by reading confidential reports about her campaigning.

The spy watched from afar as the child grew up. He was reputed to have been agonised by the separation from his child. The story was recounted by Lambert to new recruits like Black without even hinting that he too had fathered a child undercover. Lambert even had the gall to criticise the officer for behaving unprofessionally. He told Black that the moral of the story was that he should always use contraception when sleeping with political campaigners.

Black's wife knew that he was undercover, but was unaware of the details of his work and certainly had no idea he was sleeping with other women. His long absences and unforgiving schedule left virtually no time for his wife and two children. For more than four years, he was away for six days a week. Sometimes, during school holidays, he found a way to spend more time back at home in the real world. But it was never enough. Black paid a personal price for 'trying to be the best SDS officer I could ever be'. He admits his wife had a 'very difficult time'. 'The fact I was working so much eventually caused the break-up of my marriage,' he says.

The top brass at the SDS, however, valued his dedication to the job. Lambert said in an early appraisal that Black was self-motivated and a hard worker who 'demonstrated an innate professionalism'. The next year Lambert offered yet more praise: 'Operating in a hostile environment where one slip can have serious implications for the officer and the team, [Black] has again demonstrated essential qualities of sound judgment and ingenuity. Combining, as he does, these qualities with a single-minded determination to succeed, it is a pleasure, and no real surprise, to report that his efforts have again been rewarded with excellent results.'

The results that Lambert was referring to included regular updates on what was going on in anti-racist groups across London, as well as the inner workings of the YRE and Militant. Black calculates that Special Branch was keeping files on around 100 members of the YRE, Militant and other anti-racist campaigners at the time. The files on individuals would contain reports of their activities at protests, other more general intelligence and information from sources such as newspaper articles. It would include, for instance, where they lived, where they worked, and whom they were friendly with in the campaign. Black himself opened up new files on around 25 campaigners he believed needed to be monitored.

Each file on an individual required an up-to-date photograph and Special Branch had an uncanny ability to acquire photographs when it needed them. Official images were available to the squad – from driving licences, passports and suspect mugshots taken inside police stations. Upon request, Special Branch could also deploy sniper-like photographers with long lenses. Black recalls arranging for one such snapper to be hidden in a van outside Conway Hall in London to capture images of everyone who attended one of Militant's conferences. The SDS also had access to the network of CCTV cameras that in the mid-1990s were proliferating across the capital. When Black travelled on the Tube with activists, Special Branch acquired footage from London Underground, enabling the officer to identify who he was with.

While Black's job was primarily to hoover up intelligence, there were opportunities for him to broaden his mandate. On one occasion this enabled him to realise a schoolboy dream. For decades, surveillance of radical left-wing groups had been a staple feature of MI5's work. Government ministers had, since the 1950s, ordained that the Security Service could spy on any individual who might undermine parliamentary democracy, national security or the economic wellbeing of the country. Critics complained that MI5 was effectively spying on individuals for having opinions that the government disliked, using a definition of subversion that was so loose that it included anyone who was exercising their democratic right to protest.

The point is made by Annie Machon, a one-time MI5 officer who resigned in protest at its activities. She says that from 1952: 'MI5 and subsequent governments used to argue that all members of certain parties – such as the Communist Party of Great Britain or later the bewildering array of Trotskyists, with names like the International Marxist Group, Workers Revolutionary Party, Revolutionary Communist Group, anarchists and the extreme left – were threats to the security of the state or our democratic system. This in itself is a contentious proposition. None of these Trotskyist groups was cultivating Eastern bloc finance or building bombs in smoky back rooms but were instead using legitimate democratic methods to make their case, such as standing in elections, organising demonstrations and "educating" the workers.'

During the cold war, MI5 devoted huge resources to spying on left-wingers; tapping phones, opening mail and running agents within organisations. For a long time, Militant was a prime focus, because of the threat it posed to the Labour Party. But by the early 1990s, MI5 was becoming less interested in domestic political threats. It was becoming harder for the spooks to justify spying on groups that, by any objective view, posed little or no threat to the foundations of the state. Militant, whose membership was in any case beginning to dwindle, was operating as an open political party. According to Machon, MI5 began to downgrade its work spying on revolutionary left-wing groups around 1993. By late 1995, according to one account, MI5 was allocating only one of its officers to monitoring so-called subversives.

Lambert and others in command of the SDS spotted an opportunity. As MI5 retreated, the SDS could occupy the ground the security services were vacating. In one confidential briefing memo, Lambert noted how MI5 was winding down its 'active role in respect of domestic subversion'. The SDS offered to channel intelligence about Militant to MI5, keeping them abreast of what was going on in the group.

The offer was accepted and, in 1995, Black began a dual role, working partly under the command of the SDS but also as an official informant for MI5, with his own code number: M2672. Lambert, who believed Militant was 'one of the most insular groups ever penetrated by the SDS', was impressed that one of his spies was providing intelligence for the Security Service. Black was raising the stock of the squad in official circles and allowing senior officers like Lambert to punch above their weight. When Black produced a report on a large number of Militant activists, and handed it over to MI5, Lambert complimented his efforts. 'This performance, both in terms of content and presentation, was of the highest calibre and brought considerable kudos to the team,' he wrote. In another Special Branch document, Lambert noted how the Security Service was 'an appreciative consumer of the unique high-grade intelligence' provided by Black.

The spooks were genuinely grateful for SDS assistance. MI5 gleaned most of its intelligence not from undercover officers, but informants, many of them paid. These individuals, known as agents, were given a rudimentary instruction into espionage tradecraft by MI5, which then cultivated them as sources. According to one account, MI5 recruited around 30 Militant members to inform on their comrades over a 30-year period during the cold war, although by the early 1990s there were only a handful of snitches left. As with all informants, their reliability varied wildly.

When Black noticed that MI5 was holding erroneous intelligence about Militant, he assumed the Security Service must have been fed by a dodgy agent. 'I started to realise that there was a spy in our midst,' he recalls. 'I decided I was going to try and spot their agent. In the event, it did not take very long.' Rather worryingly, Black says the MI5 agent stood out like a sore thumb.

'He was doing things like only turning up to meetings when something really interesting was being talked about. Those sort of things made him stand out,' he adds. Acting on his instincts, Black decided to confront MI5 and ask them: 'Is he one of yours?' The question sparked an immediate reaction from the MI5 officer in charge of running agents. The agent handler left Thames House, MI5's imposing headquarters on the bank of the River Thames, for a hasty meeting with Black, Lambert and other Special Branch officers in the safe house in Beaumont Court, Chiswick.

It felt like a showdown. At first, the MI5 officer refused to give anything away about the suspected agent. 'They tried to bluff me and said they could not confirm it, but they would take [my suspicions] on board,' Black says. But the SDS officer was characteristically stubborn, insisting he had the right man. Eventually, Lambert and the other officers were asked to leave the room. Black and the man from MI5 remained, for a 'frank discussion' about the Militant activist identified as an agent.

'I said to him that I knew it was him, and if he did not agree that the man was an agent, I would expose him at the next Militant meeting. The handler replied, "OK, he is ours – don't blow him out of the water but we will get rid of him."' The MI5 agent was withdrawn a couple of months later. Black felt the move was long overdue; if he had managed to work out the informant's true motives, then so too could other members of Militant. They might easily have fed the agent faulty information, knowing it would be passed on to MI5.

'The biggest problem was that his intelligence reports were shit,' Black says. 'He was giving information that was inaccurate about people, which meant he might well have been giving out inaccurate information about me as well.' Later, Black's managers told him he was the first SDS officer in history to catch out an MI5 agent. 'So it was big kudos for the team,' he says. 'The Security Service was grateful.' Later M15 came over and presented Black with a shield on a wooden block. It was engraved with MI5's crest, and the service's motto – 'Regnum Defende', Latin for 'Defend the Realm' – at the bottom. Black was told he was the only SDS officer to receive such an accolade. It was a moment to remember, a standout episode that Black hoped would make it into the annals of SDS folklore – the kind of success that would have made Conrad Dixon proud.

Sitting in the Chiswick safe house with Lambert and his other SDS colleagues, Black soaked up the convivial atmosphere. 'I felt proud at the time. It was some sort of recognition because the Special Branch does not really recognise the work you do that much,' he says. It was an especially satisfying moment for Black, who always wanted to work for MI5. The shield still hangs on his wall in his study at home.

Things were going well for Black. His career was on a high and he should have been proud of his achievements. But in fact he had begun to experience deep misgivings about his deployment. His final mandate as a spy would leave the normally decisive officer grappling to discern right from wrong.

CHAPTER 9

Exit Mr Angry

Towards the end of Black's deployment, the tide changed. The focus of anti-racist campaigning in London was starting to shift, and police chiefs were worried. Large numbers of people in the movement were becoming animated by a series of perceived injustices. The names of the victims, and their stories, were well known. There was Joy Gardner, a 40-year-old Jamaican who was bound and gagged with 13ft of black tape in her flat in Crouch End, north London, in 1993. The following year, Shiji Lapite, a 34-year-old Nigerian asylum seeker, received 36 injuries, including a kick to the head, and was asphyxiated in a neck-hold in the back of a police van in east London. In 1995, Brian Douglas, a 33-year-old music and boxing promoter, died after his skull was fractured. In March 1996, Gambian asylum seeker Ibrahima Sey, aged 29, was forced to the ground, sprayed repeatedly with gas and then held face down for 15 minutes. He went totally limp and stopped breathing.

All of the victims had two things in common. They were black. And they were believed to have died as a result of police brutality.

For many in the 'black justice' campaigns, it was not only the disturbing circumstances of the deaths that caused concern, but also the apparent impunity that allowed police to escape punishment. In the case of Gardner, who was being deported, the police who wrapped her in tape, while her five-year-old son was in the flat, were acquitted of her manslaughter. The circumstances of Lapite's death in 1994 were heard by an inquest, which concluded he had been unlawfully killed. However, prosecutors decided not to bring charges against the officers who caused his injuries in the back of a police van. Another inquest concluded that Sey had been unlawfully killed when he was restrained by police and sprayed with CS gas but, again, prosecutors decided not to charge the police officers responsible.

These were just the more high-profile cases. In the first seven years of the 1990s, a total of 484 people died following some form of contact with police. Often these were categorised as deaths in 'custody', meaning the individuals died in prison cells or police vans. Figures showed that deaths of this kind were rapidly increasing, and disproportionately affected black people. Against this backdrop, anti-racist groups, which had long been focusing on combating the far right, now turned their attention to racism in the police.

The campaigns revolved around supporting grieving families in their quest for truth and justice, attending silent vigils outside police stations or political rallies. Black found himself helping to organise these anti-police protests, while at the same time passing information back to his handlers at the SDS. He was finding it harder to justify his work. He was taking part in one of these protests, standing outside Kennington police station, when he started to doubt his actions.

'I found myself questioning the morality of my actions for the first time. To some extent, these campaigns had been taken over by extremists, but at their heart were families who had lost their loved ones and simply wanted justice,' he says. 'By targeting the groups, I was convinced that I was robbing them of the chance to ever find that justice.'

Black, via the YRE, was particularly involved in the protests over the death of Brian Douglas. It was a long-running campaign.

In May 1995, a week after Douglas died, 400 people came out on to the streets to protest outside Vauxhall police station. His relatives and friends called for the two police officers involved in arresting him to be suspended. A year later, prosecutors announced that no police officers would be prosecuted. The inquest, which recorded a verdict of misadventure, heard that Douglas and a friend had been stopped near Clapham High Street by police who believed that they possessed a CS gas canister, a lock-knife and cannabis. His friend testified that police hit Douglas twice on the head with their batons. He died from his injuries five days later. Scotland Yard said its officers acted to ensure their own safety and decided against disciplining them.

On a personal level, Black grew uncomfortable about what he believed was the failure to hold police to account and the attempts to stifle protests over the deaths. 'I did not feel like a proud member of the Metropolitan police,' he says. It was a view that Black – perhaps unwisely – expressed to Lambert and others in the SDS. He told them he was worried that unless the police took deaths in custody more seriously, and disciplined officers who were at fault, there would be an escalation of violent protests. In December 1995, the death in custody of a 25-year-old black man triggered a peaceful protest outside Brixton police station which suddenly descended into disorder. Several hundred youths rioted, ransacking shops and setting fire to cars. It was a flashback to the riots of the 1980s, and a warning of what might happen in the future if police did not get a hold of this issue.

In the end it was not a death in custody, but the appalling failures by police to properly investigate a racist killing of a black teenager that became the darkest episode in the history of the Metropolitan police. Among anti-racist campaigners, there was no case more important than the murder of Stephen Lawrence, the 18-year-old stabbed by a gang of white youths as he waited for a bus in Eltham. His death in April 1993, and its long, drawn-out aftermath, shocked the nation and proved to be a seminal moment for British race relations.

The campaign for justice over Lawrence's death was led by his mother, Doreen, and father, Neville. In July 1997, the then home secretary Jack Straw bowed to mounting public pressure and announced he was setting up a judge-led inquiry into the police investigation of Lawrence's murder. The inquiry would also examine the police's handling of racist murders and attacks in general.

Led by the high court judge Sir William Macpherson, the inquiry eventually concluded that, as the Lawrences had said during years of being disbelieved and ignored, police had failed to catch his killers because of their own racial prejudice and incompetence. Macpherson's famous conclusion, in 1999, that London's police were 'institutionally racist' was a terrible indictment of Britain's largest and most powerful force. It took 18 years, a failed private prosecution, and the emergence of new evidence before the Lawrence family finally had some justice, when two of Stephen's suspected killers, Gary Dobson and David Norris, were convicted for his murder in 2012.

Back in 1997, however, in the weeks following the announcement of a public inquiry, the Met was in a state of trepidation. The tide of public opinion was turning against the force, a shift represented by the decision by the *Daily Mail*, historically a reliable supporter of the establishment, to back the Lawrence campaign. Behind the scenes, police chiefs were consulting lawyers as they grappled with delicate questions about how much information they should disclose to the inquiry. Most of the evidence they were considering handing over related to the investigation into Lawrence's death, but Macpherson had cast a wide net. Black felt strongly that this was the time for the force to admit it had been spying on the black justice campaigns. He even wanted his bosses to disclose the details of his personal deployment in the anti-racist movement.

Black knew there were some disturbing skeletons in the SDS cupboard that should have had a direct bearing on Macpherson's deliberations. Specifically, there had once been a secret order from the top of Scotland Yard, he says, requiring the SDS to place the Lawrence campaign under surveillance. The order was given at a time when the commissioner of the Metropolitan police, Sir Paul Condon, was coming under persistent pressure from the Lawrences over the failures by the police to mount a proper investigation into the murder of their son. Black says that the controversy over the Lawrence murder 'became a huge thing for Condon'. 'It changed my deployment,' he says. 'I had to get any information on what was happening in the Stephen Lawrence campaign. There was huge pressure from the commissioner downwards.'

The former spy compares the pressure to obtain intelligence about the Lawrence campaign with 'a bomb going off'. He says commanders were concerned public anger would spiral into disorder on the streets and had 'visions of Rodney King', whose beating at the hands of police eventually led to the LA riots in 1992. 'It was huge, monumental,' he says. 'They wanted the campaign to stop. It was felt it was going to turn into an elephant.' Black says there were three SDS officers tasked with obtaining intelligence about the Lawrence family and their campaign for justice. But with his access to anti-racist groups, Black was considered to be in a key position. 'Lawrence was a constant pressure. Throughout my deployment there was an almost constant pressure on me personally to find out anything I could that would discredit these campaigns.' He adds: 'I didn't feel qualms about that. It was a public order giant and our responsibility was to quell it.'

Finding out inside information about the Lawrence campaign was not easy. The grieving family were focused on getting justice for their son and distanced themselves from the assorted campaigns of the anti-racist movement. Much of their campaign work was co-ordinated by the moderate Anti-Racist Alliance and they showed little interest in the patchwork of campaigning groups that, according to Lawrence's mother, Doreen, 'were tearing each other apart and were in danger of destroying our campaign'. None of the groups that Black or the other SDS officers were infiltrating were close enough to the family to find out much useful information.

However, they did, according to Black, resort to some appalling dirty tricks to undermine the Lawrence family. Black says he reported back any snippets of rumour that might discredit the Lawrences. 'It wasn't for me to work out what someone else might be able to do with the intelligence,' he says. He and other SDS officers were 'hunting for disinformation' about the family that could be used against them, at a time when the Met should have been concentrating on catching the killers of their son. 'Anything you could get. I put total conjecture into reports,' he says. Black says that part of the problem for police was that the murdered teenager did not conform to stereotype. 'Stephen Lawrence wanted to be an architect and he was totally clean,' the spy adds. 'He was almost like white, middle-class. He was not your usual black kid, he had never been in trouble.'

As Lawrence and his family could not be undermined, Black says police found a way to discredit him by association. On the night Lawrence was killed, he was with Duwayne Brooks, a friend, who was also the main witness to the murder. Black recalls a concerted effort to find dirt on Brooks, who was becoming involved in anti-racist campaigning. When Brooks visited Kingsway College, Black paid close attention. 'I remember I was watching him all the time,' he says. 'Because if you watch somebody really carefully, you get a feel for somebody.'

Later, Black and another SDS officer embedded in the anti-racist movement trawled through 'hours upon hours' of footage from one of the protests against the BNP which had turned unruly. The police were desperate to find any evidence that Brooks himself participated in the violence. Senior officers, Black says, wanted to 'smear' the Lawrence family's campaign. 'They were trying to tar Stephen Lawrence,' he adds. 'If we could come up with anything like that, that was genius. We were trying to stop the campaign in its tracks.'

Duwayne Brooks was captured on video in the mêlée at a demonstration in Welling in May and later admitted to being caught up in the frenzied anger over the death of Lawrence, who had been murdered just weeks before. Brooks was pictured holding a stick, and was part of a crowd of youths who pushed over a car, although he did not himself damage the vehicle. He was arrested in October that year, after the Lawrence suspects were released, and charged with criminal damage. The Crown Prosecution Service appeared desperate to prosecute him, despite protestations from a judge, who eventually stayed the proceedings. Brooks has repeatedly asked why he was targeted by the authorities during the failed prosecution, saying he feared they had a vendetta against him.

When the Macpherson inquiry was eventually announced, Black says he argued strongly that the role played by the SDS in obtaining intelligence about the Lawrence campaign should be disclosed. 'I was convinced that the SDS should come clean,' he says. 'The inquiry was an investigation into all aspects of the police, to reassure the public. I was overruled.' He believes the decision to keep the spying operation secret from Macpherson was taken at the top of Special Branch. 'The remit of the SDS was to prevent disorder. The overall consensus was that if my role had been made public, the streets of London would have erupted all over again,' he says.

By then, a decision had been taken to remove Black from the field, bringing a premature end to what should have been a five-year tour. Black wanted to remain undercover, believing that he was well placed to monitor the impact the Macpherson inquiry would have on the anti-racist movement. But his managers insisted he should come out, to be replaced by another SDS officer at a later date.

Black began preparing his exit. In one sense, it was the worst time for someone to say that they were leaving anti-racist campaigns out of disillusionment. They were reaching a high point: a public inquiry into endemic racism in the police. There was a buzz of excitement, a sense that objectives were being achieved. Still, Black was told by his bosses it was time to go. He put into place an elaborate subterfuge for what the SDS called an 'off-plan' – the process through which he planned to disappear quietly, without raising alarm bells.

Every undercover officer will have a different explanation for their disappearance, although the SDS had a few set pieces. Most commonly its officers pretended to have a mental breakdown or go on the run from police. But there will always be slight differences – personalised adaptations that suit each officer. Black says that a good undercover operative starts planting the idea of their eventual exit among activists almost as soon as their deployment begins. They will then have a ready-made excuse, which can be used at short notice whenever they need to leave.

In the summer of 1997, Black started to draw together various threads from his cover story in order to weave together his excuse for leaving. Throughout his deployment, Black often talked about wanting to go travelling abroad, spreading the idea that he had always yearned to go wandering. Now, he told his friends, the time had come. He pretended that his mother had finally lost her long battle with cancer. He also claimed that this had coincided with more bad news: he had been sacked from his job at the school. This did not come as a surprise to his friends. Preparing the ground, Black had spent months complaining about his work as a handyman, saying he was being paid pennies to work long hours.

To his friends, the confluence of events must have seemed like bad luck. In quick succession, his mother had died and he had lost his job. It was no wonder that he seemed to be going through a personal crisis and contemplating going abroad.

All Black needed now was a reason not to return. He confided in friends that he was so angry at his treatment by the school authorities that he had stolen the van, televisions, videos and other equipment from the grounds. Black was about to flee the country, avoiding any interview with the detectives who were investigating the theft at the school.

It was a stupid thing to have done, but in keeping with the headstrong activist his friends had come to know. What must have seemed to them to be the height of irrationality was, in fact, a meticulously planned deception, laid out in detail in a confidential Special Branch document headed 'Withdrawal Strategy'. The 1997 report is written by Lambert, who clinically unravels what he calls Black's 'web of deception'. Lambert praised Black for 'winning the complete confidence of senior activists at the very heart of a committed and insular group'. But now the 'overriding objective' was to 'ensure the ongoing credibility of a departing activist who has formed close relationships within a security-conscious group.'

The plan, according to Lambert, needed to take into account the 'close trust' Black had built with his friends, ensuring that even after his departure 'his political comrades have every reason to believe in the authenticity of his alter ego'. Lambert reflected on the work Black had put into convincing his friends that he wanted a fresh start in life and concluded: 'It appears entirely understandable to them that he should, notwithstanding his commitment to their shared revolutionary political ideals, be contemplating a dramatic change of lifestyle.'

Black sold the contents of his flat and gave the proceeds to Militant. He then went on a six-week trip on his own. He drove the stolen school van through Normandy, Brittany and along the French coast and then on to Barcelona. He slept in the van, picking up odd bits of bar work and manual labour for a few days at a time. Then he sold the van and flew to Greece. Although he was abroad, Black had to maintain the deception. He phoned the activists from call boxes and sent them postcards, with the all-important postmarks to show that he was abroad. To make the deception more persuasive, Black travelled back to Greece just before Christmas to post another set of postcards. The correspondence left hanging a suggestion that Black was unsure where he was going next, hinting they might not hear from him for some time.

By creating the illusion of constant movement, it made it far less likely his friends would suggest linking up with him on a holiday abroad. He wanted to leave a paper trail that could be used as proof of his foreign journey, using a credit card stolen from the school to pay for petrol and hotels. However improbable it might seem, Black felt it was not beyond the realms of possibility that activists would gain access to bank records to check where he had been. 'It's a golden rule – don't underestimate your opponents,' he says. Lambert was kept abreast of every move and the SDS quietly reimbursed the school for the stolen credit card, van and equipment.

The deception worked. Many years later, the activists Black infiltrated still remember the totally believable circumstances of his departure from London in search of a new life abroad. No one questioned it. Sell says that no one in the YRE 'remotely suspected him' of being a policeman, during his deployment or in the years after.

For Black, the trip abroad was an opportunity to rediscover his former self. The weeks and months when SDS officers are made to travel to distant places abroad can be the most testing times. They are alone, without the visual prompts or surroundings to remind them which identity they are supposed to be adopting – police officer or political activist. They have time to reflect on the years they spent living as someone else and decide who they now want to be.

Black spent six weeks on his own, contemplating his past and future. He was frustrated that his deployment had come to a premature end. 'I was not happy about coming off, not by a long fucking way,' he says. 'I wanted to get my head together. After what you have been through, you want to be alone. You need time to think of what you have been doing, what's happened and what the activists mean to you.' He repeated to himself the SDS mantra, drilled into spies to ensure they do not get too close to activists: 'They are not your friends, they are your targets.'

Not long after his extended holiday under the Mediterranean sun, Black returned to London to say another set of goodbyes, this time to fellow 'hairies' in the 27 Club. Formally, Black left the SDS on September 27 1997, a valued member of the team.

As part of his au revoirs, the SDS went paintballing outside London, a typical day out for the SDS and a chance to – quite literally, in their case – let their hair down. He was given a leaving card, on the theme of *Star Wars* and Darth Vader. The card shows the esteem Black was held in and gives an insight into SDS camaraderie. Lambert, as befitting of the boss, used a football manager analogy to compliment Black's professionalism: 'Congratulations on a truly fantastic performance – Premier Division – no question,' wrote Lambert, a keen Chelsea supporter. 'Welcome to that early retirement feeling.' Another SDS manager praised Black for a 'job really well done ... in your inimitable style'. A quiet, shy-looking colleague called Jim Boyling, who was in the middle of a deployment that would eventually prove as morally fraught as Lambert's, wrote simply: 'Can I have your van and regimental ponytail?'

Others made a play on Black's reputation as an angry man. Squad member Chris joked 'Calm down', while another, Trevor, wrote: 'To Mr Angry, well it's all over, four years of blood guts and cheers.' Another member, going by the name of 'Sauce', perhaps best summed up the attitude the squad had toward political activists, with a short poem: 'Whenever the comrades see *Reservoir Dogs* / They will think of you Pete and ask "Why was he such an angry sod?" / We know the reason, the answer why. They're weary fuckers and they deserve to die.'

Life after the SDS was not easy for Black. After a six-month break, he was reassigned to other duties in Special Branch. It was far less exciting stuff. He was looking after covert recording devices used to pick up conversations and film suspects. His old boss acknowledged that Black was struggling to adjust.

In a note written in January 1998, after a debriefing over 'a nice lunch at a nearby tandoori', Lambert wrote that Black was 'missing the activity or stimulation of the job ... This is natural, particularly after such a consuming role or alter ego as the one he adopted.' The truth was actually far worse for Black. In his words, he was 'not a well teddy'.

The psychological damage from his undercover work took a while to manifest itself, but when it did, Black was in a bad mental state. Part of the problem was that his undercover life had placed a nerve-wracking strain on Black, who felt on edge throughout his four-year deployment. 'It's too much to be able to deal with,' he says. 'I never had any respite when I was back at home. I simply couldn't relax. The respite for me was being back in my undercover flat because that was where I was supposed to be.'

His bosses admitted in an assessment in 1998 that Black had been 'engaged for four years on dangerous and demanding specialist operational duties', and 'not unnaturally, such pressure took its toll, and he undoubtedly experienced extreme stress, which affected both him and his family'.

It was only looking back that Black realised the strain he was under during his undercover life. He was constantly worried he would be found out by his friends, or worse still targeted by any number of far-right groups who made a pastime out of hunting down lefties and beating them up. As a well-known face on anti-fascist demonstrations, Black had always worried he might be cornered one day by a group of Nazis. The SDS had ways of minimising the likelihood one of their own was attacked in this way. SDS officers who had infiltrated neo-Nazi groups could, for example, go through the photo collections that Nazis kept of prominent left-wingers they wanted to target, surreptitiously removing images of those who were fellow undercover police. But there was still a risk an SDS officer like Black could be targeted. In his Furlong Road flat, he had always slept with a heavy torch, baseball bat and a knife beside his bed.

'I used to have a hell of a lot of nightmares, all the time I was undercover. Everything you were doing in your SDS life was perfect, but in your nightmares, you fuck it up constantly.' Now these same nightmares were continuing, and would do for years: flashbacks to the orange smoke and cavalry charges at the Welling demonstration, his terrifying week in the Bavarian forest, or his fights with the Nazis or the police.

These anxiety-inducing memories only partly explained Black's mental deterioration. He was also unable to cope with the realisation that his deployment had changed him permanently. He was now irrevocably different to the keen young constable who had gone undercover years earlier.

When his deployment began, Black had a clear sense of who he actually was. Now he could not shake the feeling that part of his inner core was the person he had been pretending to be for four years. As he puts it: 'I was a different person when I went in to what I came out. You have created an identity so well for the purpose of survival, you then end up getting rid of whatever else you had.'

When he tried to resume normal police work, he found it difficult, as he puts it, to get 'out of his role' as a revolutionary, hard-headed activist. He likens it to some of the Method actors such as Daniel Day-Lewis who immerse themselves so much in a character that they continue to live in that role, even off-stage or when the cameras are turned off.

'I had spent years hating the police and then suddenly I was one of them again. I just couldn't deal with it. You can be easily traumatised [when undercover] in the SDS because the police are chasing you with their horses and their sticks,' he says. 'It was a total head-bender. I was a police officer, but in my undercover role I hated the police with a vengeance. They were the enemy. I had been in too deep and for too long. I had real sympathy for the "black justice" campaigns. I also witnessed numerous acts of appalling police brutality on protesters. I genuinely became anti-police.'

Black had come close up to families who had lost loved ones at the hands of police, and personally had a series of bruising encounters with riot officers himself. Black is adamant that he did not develop 'Stockholm syndrome', the psychological phenomenon that Mike Chitty claimed to have been suffering a few years earlier. Instead, Black felt his changed state of mind was a rational response to what he saw as the routine misbehaviour by his uniformed colleagues: 'It was the simple reality that they were repeatedly in the wrong.'

After clashes with police management, and time off sick suffering from post-traumatic stress disorder (PTSD), his managers decided that Black was unfit to continue as a police officer. In April 2001, the Met retired him and gave him a pension. He was 36.

Black was angry at his treatment and not in the mood to 'take any shit'. He contacted lawyers and launched legal action against the Met for damages, arguing that his mental health had been damaged as a direct result of his covert work. He is believed to have been the first SDS officer ever to sue the squad over a failure to look after its spies. A few years previously, Mike Chitty had threatened legal action, but had apparently dropped it. Many officers in the squad, according to Black, had suffered mental problems, but they had all coped on their own and not made a fuss.

Black insisted that the SDS was at fault and said he was not going to back down. He argued that police chiefs should have had safeguards in place to protect the mental welfare of their operatives and paid closer attention to the long-term psychological consequences of spending half a decade living a double life. It is a view privately supported by other SDS officers, including one who says that when he was deployed in the 1970s, operatives who complained were considered wimps and risked being thrown off the squad. The solution to mentally unwell officers was invariably a good drink with the lads down at the pub.

Two decades later, when Black was recruited, not much had changed. In the archives of Scotland Yard one document reveals how the SDS sought out advice on how to deal with long-term infiltration. The head of the squad flew to America to consult the FBI on how they handled prolonged espionage.

When he returned, the senior officer issued a guidance document, which essentially put the onus on undercover officers to
monitor their levels of stress. The guidance listed some common
symptoms of stress for spies, such as 'development of a "short
fuse" or uncharacteristic anger and resentment' and 'significant
increase in alcohol consumption'. The guidance was greeted
with amusement. SDS officers deployed at the time joked that,
between them, the squad exhibited every symptom on the list.

In his legal action, Black argued that, with the exception
of this flawed guidance for stress monitoring, the unit had no
substantial procedures in place to care for their operatives. There
was no profiling to check the psychological make-up of recruits,
for example, before they were sent undercover, to see if they
could handle the pressure. Black felt his headstrong personality
was unsuited to undercover work. 'I should never have done
this work in the first place, because I can't do anything half-
arsed,' he says.

When word went around that Black was suing the SDS, he
was joined by another former undercover officer, who had also
developed PTSD. This second officer infiltrated the left wing
slightly later than Black. Indeed, Black estimated that of the 10
SDS officers he served alongside, six experienced psychological
issues. The SDS dismissed this claim, saying the fact that the
other officers had returned to work after their deployment proved
there was no wider problem. Not long after, three more former
SDS officers left the Met. One retrained as a teacher, another
emigrated to Canada to work as a lumberjack, while a third transferred to a force outside London, hoping for a quieter life.

Black's legal battle with police lasted five years. He accuses
police of using dirty tricks to discourage him from pursuing his
claim. He says he received anonymous calls asking to speak to
his children, and he presumed it was the police attempting to

frighten the family. The calls stopped, Black claims, after he told police that if anything happened to his children, he would publicly name every single SDS officer. As his dispute with police became more bitter, Black lost contact with other SDS officers. With the exception of his co-claimant, none of his former colleagues gave him any support.

In June 2006, on the eve of the hearing in London's high Court, Black and his SDS colleague accepted an offer from the Met to settle the case out of court. Black was characteristically reluctant to give in and wanted to turn down the offer so he could have his day in court. But his co-claimant was by then worn down and wanted the case to end.

The Met police admitted that undercover work in the SDS had caused the pair psychiatric injury and paid them an undisclosed sum in compensation. Black says he wanted to force the Met to implement better care for future SDS spies. After his lawsuit, the SDS brought in new rules so that their undercover officers would be sent for compulsory examinations by a psychologist before, during and after their deployments.

Even after reaching the legal settlement, Black felt he had unfinished business with his employers. One memory in particular rankled. Back in 1997, Lambert had decided that Black's undercover mission deserved a commendation from the Special Branch for his 'outstanding initiative and investigative skills in a prolonged sensitive operation over a four-year period'. Only a few SDS operatives were given such accolades. It was a tribute to the outstanding constable who took part in the squad's very first overseas mission and succeeded in snuffing out a lacklustre MI5 agent. To Black's frustration, the commendation had never actually been presented to him.

On September 27 2007, exactly a decade after Black left the SDS, he visited Scotland Yard, passed his jacket through the airport-style security and was escorted in the lift to one of the top floors. Three men were waiting to present him with a certificate, a bottle of whisky and a Special Branch commemorative shield. One was the then head of the Yard's counter-terrorism intelligence command. Another was the man who in many ways came to personify all that the SDS stood for: his former friend, Bob Lambert.

Black took hold of his framed commendation. It congratulated the former spy for having 'exhibited tradecraft of the highest order'. 'There is little doubt that the stresses of the SDS work did disrupt his family life, almost inevitable in this kind of work, but he never relaxed his professionalism in favour of cutting corners – he is to be congratulated for this,' it said.

Lambert apologised to Black for not doing more to look after his mental welfare when he was undercover. It seemed old wounds were being healed. He was promised an invite to celebrate 40 years of the SDS, an anniversary that was going to be celebrated on October 27 2008.

In the end, no invite arrived in the post. Black felt cheated again. He was told by Lambert that other members of the SDS had deemed Black too disloyal. In the grand tradition of the secret ballot in institutions such as the Freemasons, Lambert said the black balls had outweighed the white balls.

Years after his own deployment, Lambert was, it seems, toying with Black's feelings. After presenting Black with a formal tribute, praising his professionalism and apologising for not treating him well, Lambert had raised his hopes that he would once again be accepted in the club. Now he was telling Black that his perceived disloyalty meant that he would never truly be part of the 27 Club.

For Black, it was the last straw. It was after that call that he decided to contact a journalist.

CHAPTER 10
Nothing But the Truth?

When defendants and witnesses give evidence in a court in England or Wales, they are duty-bound to take an oath that dates back to Anglo-Saxon times. It is a promise to Almighty God that a person will speak only 'the truth, the whole truth and nothing but the truth'. There is perhaps no commitment more important to the judicial process than honesty.

For the men of the Special Demonstration Squad, this posed a problem. How could spies maintain their cover if they were called to give evidence in a trial? There was no apparent legal fix to this quandary, no get-out clause for undercover police. The solution the SDS came up with was unsurprising for a unit that had become accustomed to believing it had a licence to operate outside the normal rules. Rather than risk being found out, SDS officers would place their hands on a Bible and swear solemnly and sincerely that they would tell the truth. Then they would lie.

The first known case of an SDS officer appearing to conceal his identity from a court involved Bob Lambert. When the spy was posing as an animal rights campaigner in London, he organised a demonstration outside a Brixton butcher, known as Murray's Meat Market. He was joined by Steve Curtis, an activist who considered himself to be a close friend of Lambert. Their group designed what Curtis says was a provocative leaflet – two babies hanging from butchers' hooks. When they arrived and started handing out the leaflets, the butcher's staff were furious. Words were exchanged and amid the commotion police were called. Lambert was arrested – the only one in the group to be taken in by police, since he appeared to be the ringleader.

Soon after, in January 1986, Lambert wrote to another campaigner, Martyn Lowe, and mentioned he was 'backwards and forwards to Camberwell Green magistrates court for distributing "insulting" leaflets outside a butchers' shop'. According to Curtis, Lambert said he went to court once over the arrest, for what seems to have been a preliminary hearing to set the date and venue for a trial. If this was the case, Lambert would have used his fake identity of 'Bob Robinson'. A few weeks afterwards, Lambert said the charges had been suddenly dropped.

At the time, Curtis was surprised that prosecutors had not taken the chance to bring the case to court; protesters were often prosecuted over far more petty issues and Lambert was the kind of troublemaker police would want to see convicted. The reality is the charges were probably quietly dropped after whispered discussions between the SDS and prosecutors about the case.

The second time Lambert appeared in court under his fictitious identity was as a witness. In the same year, Curtis was arrested on a demonstration to protest against the US president Ronald Reagan's decision to send US jets to bomb Libya. Curtis was stood outside the US embassy in Grosvenor Square, talking casually to Lambert, when police suddenly swooped and arrested him for public disorder. He says he was not doing anything wrong and was astonished when magistrates sentenced him to 28 days in jail.

Curtis lodged an appeal, which was held at Southwark Crown Court in July 1986. He recalls how Lambert appeared as a witness in court, swearing under oath that he was Bob Robinson, before he was cross-examined for 10 to 15 minutes. Lambert was one of a handful of witnesses who were called by defence lawyers to support Curtis's version of events. The appeal failed, but the episode helped Lambert improve his standing among the activists, especially Curtis, a 21-year-old in need of legal support.

The SDS believed that breaking the law was a kind of a rite of passage in some activist circles. It might only be trespass or vandalism, but those campaigners who were willing to undertake illegal activity were thought of as more serious players. 'Being arrested increases your credibility among the wearies [protesters], going to court would increase your credibility,' says Pete Black. There was always a risk. 'The nightmare for us was being recognised by someone – you are sitting in the back of the van, surrounded by three rozzers, and one of them knows you and winks at you, then it's over.'

Every now and then senior Special Branch managers authorised the operatives to be prosecuted in court using their undercover aliases. There is of course a standard protocol that allows covert officers to give evidence in court during prosecutions of serious criminals. They will usually be granted anonymity by a judge and then appear behind a screen to protect their identity. The process is transparent – all sides are aware that the evidence is being provided by a covert officer. This was not an option the SDS was ever willing to contemplate for its long-term deployments.

It would have meant prematurely ending operations each time a spy was charged or asked to give testimony in a criminal trial. And the moment one activist was exposed as a police operative, political campaigners would know the lengths police were going to gain intelligence, instantly compromising future surveillance.

An unofficial rule of thumb therefore emerged for the SDS. Police could be prosecuted for relatively minor crimes if it was necessary for the continuation of their deployment. For example, conviction resulting in a fine or an order to do unpaid work for the community was acceptable. 'It did not matter if you were arrested. It happened regularly. That was the easy bit. What you were worried about was what you would be charged with,' says Black. Senior officers would not allow their spies to be prosecuted for anything serious enough to result in a jail term. 'If there was any chance of the SDS officer going to prison, they would not go.'

On the few occasions when SDS operatives were caught committing more serious crime, the matter was quickly escalated and dealt with behind the scenes. In such circumstances, police would lobby the Crown Prosecution Service to quietly drop the case against their spy. 'Bob Lambert would ring up and say, "Look, we need a chat, he's one of ours,"' Black says. So as not to raise suspicions, that ordinarily meant charges were dropped against other protesters who might have been arrested around the same time. 'I know of cases that were pulled because the SDS officer would have been charged with something serious,' says Black.

If that was not possible, the SDS had a final card it could play. Any SDS officer really worried about facing a stretch in jail could jump bail, tell their friends they were going on the run and then vanish for good. It was a deft solution: the SDS officer would have a perfect excuse to disappear at the end of their deployment. The court case against all the other activists, on the other hand, could continue.

The most well-documented case of an SDS officer misleading a court involved a doe-eyed, skinny police officer called Jim Boyling. He was one of Lambert's juniors, working under the veteran SDS man when he was running the squad in the 1990s. Activists remember Boyling as a quiet, reticent man who seemed uncomfortable in the company of other people. His edgy demeanour was reinforced by a strange affliction that caused one of his hands to occasionally shake.

'He was not a big conversationalist,' one friend recalls. Another describes him as 'nervous'. He had a tendency to become exasperated, even crabby, with fellow campaigners, earning the sobriquet 'Grumpy Jim' among friends. Activists say he was a voracious smoker of dope, smoking cannabis on a habitual, some say even daily basis. He would later dispute the claims, saying that he was 'creating the appearance of regular drug use so as to preserve [his] undercover status.'

His undercover alias Jim Sutton first appeared in 1995 among 'hunt sabs', protesters who disrupted – or 'sabotaged' – fox hunts. In the standard tradition of the SDS, Boyling grew a luxuriant, shaggy brown beard for the start of his covert duties. Within a year he shaved off his facial hair, making him look rather straight. The taciturn operative was then mainly tasked with infiltrating a raucous collective known as Reclaim the Streets, notorious for occupying roads and hosting impromptu street parties. It was an anti-capitalist, green movement against the dominance of cars. Its exuberant, rowdy street occupations became synonymous with the free party scene of the era.

It was such a protest, the kind of demonstration that infuriated the capital's taxi drivers, that Boyling joined on August 7 1996. On a cool, slightly cloudy morning, Boyling was among 500 activists who cycled slowly around Trafalgar Square in London, bringing the rush-hour traffic to a halt. Motorists sat helplessly in their cars as the shoal of cyclists pedalled from the historic square through Whitehall to Parliament Square and then back again.

Car horns were honked and abuse shouted out of windows, to no avail. The cyclists, many wearing high-visibility jackets, waved, whooped and rang their tinny bells in defiance. Some precariously held up a banner across the road: 'Don't Squeeze the

Tube'. They were on a solidarity protest, in support of workers on the London Underground who had gone on strike over pay and the length of their working week.

As the demonstration wound down, a splinter group of around 20 cyclists separated off and headed to a building not far from Trafalgar Square where the managers of the Tube were based. They burst through the reception, evaded the security guards, rushed up to the seventh floor and made a beeline for the office of the chairman, Peter Ford.

Not unusually for this kind of activist occupation, there was some light-hearted banter. 'One of them started throwing my papers around. I asked them to leave my family photographs alone, which they did,' Ford said. 'I asked them what the problem was and one said they were in favour of bicycles, so I told them I was a keen cyclist.'

Boyling hung a huge pink and white banner out of the window. In the words of one activist present that day, Sutton was 'totally part of the crew', one of the last two cyclists to be arrested by police and escorted from the chairman's office.

He was taken to Charing Cross police station where the custody sergeant locked him in a cell and inserted him into the bureaucracy as prisoner CX/5011/96 under the name of 'Peter James Sutton'. He told police he was a cleaner living in Vicarage Road in Leyton, east London, and that he had been born on April 24 1967. Six weeks later, Sutton and the other protesters were charged with threatening and abusing London Tube staff. Once again, he signed the official custody record to verify that he was 'Peter James Sutton'.

Over the next few months, on four separate occasions, Sutton and the other protesters made their way to Westminster magistrates court, near the River Thames. Once there, the activists stepped into one of the shabby courtrooms and waited while their lawyers and prosecutors discussed the arrangements for their trial. Throughout these months, Mike Schwarz, a lawyer at Bindmans solicitors, prepared the defence strategy for his clients, diligently scrutinising the police's evidence as the trial approached. As would be expected, Boyling, still posing as Sutton, was part of those private discussions about the tactics.

In January 1997, all the activists were back at the magistrates court in Horseferry Road for their three-day trial. Boyling's evidence to the court was recorded in notes taken by the court clerk: after he swore under oath to tell the truth, the spy testified that he was 'Peter James Sutton' and, under questioning, supported the account of the arrests which had been given by fellow activists. He rebutted claims by prosecutors that protesters had been 'shouting and screaming'. Boyling and his comrades must have come across as honest and sincere witnesses because by the end of the trial, the court sided with them and against the prosecution. Boyling and all but one of the protesters were cleared of the charges.

What few people at the time knew was that what had appeared to be an ordinary prosecution was anything but. The truth was concealed and only pieced together from long-forgotten archives years later by Schwarz, the activists' lawyer. His client, the man who had sworn he was 'Peter James Sutton', did not, in fact, exist. He was not called Sutton and he was not born on April 24 1967. The signature that adorned official documents was a forgery. Indeed, the only accurate declaration in the documentation was his height: 5ft 8in.

The spy had gone through the entire prosecution process from arrest to acquittal under a false identity. Lawyers, clerks, witnesses, members of the public in the gallery, the judge, and by extension the British judiciary itself, had been hoodwinked by the SDS.

Shocking though this is, at least in this case no one was hurt by the deception, though no doubt court officials would have taken a dim view of the situation if they had known the truth. However, it is an arguably more serious problem when innocent people are caught up in someone else's lie, and suffer direct harm to their own lives as a result. Jim Boyling discovered this for himself when he met a young woman towards the end of his deployment. That much was routine for the SDS. But what happened next was a historic first.

CHAPTER 11
Invisible Men

If there was one tactic that was the signature of the Special Demonstration Squad, it was the use of long-term relationships with women activists who could help give undercover operatives the credibility they needed. In fiction, the likes of Ian Fleming base entire storylines around spies sleeping with the enemy. But in the real world, the use of intimate relationships is considered dangerous and even poor tradecraft. Irrespective of the morality of agents of the state having sex with citizens, how can operatives remain detached or provide objective intelligence if they are romantically involved with their targets? The SDS had a few rules to prevent their officers from becoming too emotionally tied to the opposite sex. For a long time, the squad only recruited men who were married or had stable relationships, assuming they would be less inclined to develop strong connections with the women they slept with. There was informal advice that they should use contraception. And they were told to avoid falling in love.

Intimate relationships with political activists undoubtedly gave covert officers superb cover. But it was also their Achilles heel. To put it harshly, there was always the tricky question of what to do with their girlfriends when their time in the field came to an end.

*

John Dines, aka John Barker, the tough-looking, mullet-haired SDS man who had been deployed in London Greenpeace between 1987 and 1992, was one such officer who faced this question. In large part his success in infiltrating the group and its McLibel campaign was down to his relationship with Helen Steel, one of the two defendants in the long-running trial. She had the courage to take on the might of McDonald's. Dines started courting Steel in 1990.

'He engaged me in quite a few deep conversations about personal subjects. He asked me out a couple of times. He sent me a Valentine's card, a birthday card, expressing love for me,' she says. One day, he asked to borrow money from Steel so he could fly to New Zealand for his mother's funeral. 'The night before he got the flight to go there, he stayed at my place and kind of poured his heart out,' she says. 'We became emotionally close. When he got back, we got together.' There was no funeral in New Zealand and Dines had no need to borrow money. But Steel had known Dines as a fellow protester for three years and had no reason to suspect him. The couple ended up in an intimate relationship for two years.

'He said he wanted to spend the rest of his life with me,' she says. 'In a short space of time I fell absolutely madly in love with him in a way that I had never fallen in love with anyone before or since. He said he wanted us to have kids. He used to say he had once seen an elderly Greek couple sitting on a veranda gazing into the sunset, and that he pictured us growing old like that.' By the summer of 1991, as part of an exit strategy, Dines began exhibiting symptoms of a mental breakdown. 'He kept talking about how he had nobody left apart from me,' Steel said. 'His parents had both died. He had no brothers and sisters. The only woman that he had ever loved before me, a woman called Debbie, had left him. He said he was convinced I was going to do the same to him.'

Dines gave the impression he wanted to run away to escape his inner demons. 'I saw him crying loads,' Steel says. 'He told me that he had thrown all of his mother's jewellery into a river because he thought she never loved him. He told me his parents had abused him.' In March 1992 he left a message for Steel saying that he had put a letter in the post to her. Four days later she received it, saying that he had been at Heathrow Airport about to fly to South Africa as he could not handle things any more. After that, Steel received two letters with South African postmarks. Then her boyfriend vanished altogether. 'I was very worried about his mental state,' she said. 'I was also sick with worry that he might kill himself. After he left, I was on a complete rollercoaster of emotions. I did not know whether he was alive or dead.' Steel contacted the British consulate in South Africa and frantically phoned hostels in Johannesburg where she thought he might have stayed. She eventually hired a private investigator, who could find no trace of her partner.

For some of the time that Steel thought her boyfriend was missing abroad, he was actually working in the same city as her. Dines had lost the mullet, and returned to a desk job at the Met headquarters in Scotland Yard. A Special Branch officer who came across Dines around this time recalls him looking 'a moody, miserable fucker' who 'seemed to be carrying a lot'. 'He looked like he was always going to kick off,' the Special Branch officer said. Dines left the police by 1994 and was given a pension to compensate for his ill-health. He later returned to New Zealand, where he had said he had spent some of his teenage years.

In her search for clues to find him, one of the first things Steel did was locate a copy of what she assumed was her boyfriend's birth certificate. The document confirmed the details he had always given her: he was born in Derby in January 1960. She had no idea that the identity was a forgery, or that the real John Barker had died of leukaemia aged eight.

In April 1993, desperate after a year of searching, Steel decided to visit Barker's family home in Derby in the hope of finding any surviving relatives, but when she knocked on the door of the terraced house there was no answer. The boy's parents, Thomas and Nora, had conceived another boy and moved to a house around the corner, but Steel was unable to find them. Looking back, Steel wonders what would have occurred if the dead child's parents had opened the door. 'It would have been horrendous,' she says. 'It would have completely freaked them out to have someone asking after a child who died 24 years earlier.'

It was another 18 months before Steel decided to inspect the national death records. She was walking past St Catherine's House, the government office that contained the birth, marriage and death certificates. 'I just suddenly got this instinct to go in there and look through the death records.' She was astonished to find the real John Barker was dead. 'It sent a chill down my spine,' she says. 'When I got the certificate itself, it was so clear. The same person. The same parents. The same address. But he had died as an eight-year-old boy.'

The discovery turned Steel's world upside down. 'It was like a bereavement but it was not something I could talk to people about. Now suddenly he didn't exist. This was a man I had known for five years, who I had lived with for two years. How could I trust anybody again? I don't even know the name of the person I had been in a relationship with. This person who I'd spent so much of my life with, and who I really loved, and who I lived with, and I don't even know his name. All the photographs I've got, all the memories I've got are of a nameless stranger. What do you do with that?'

Steel now knew her boyfriend had lied about his identity, and the idea he might have been a police spy crossed her mind, but he could also have worked in corporate espionage or had some hidden criminal past.

Steel had two clues to go on. One was the name of a woman in New Zealand who Dines had told her was an aunt. The other was a letter in which he had made a curious reference to his biological father being a man he had never met, called Jim Dines. The woman in New Zealand was not his aunt but, bizarrely, the mother of Dines's real wife. Stranger still, Jim Dines was, in fact, the police officer's real father and had brought him up in London. Steel has no idea why the undercover police officer chose to compromise his deployment by giving her cryptic references to people in his real life. Perhaps he was psychologically traumatised by his dual identities and wanted to leave a trail that would allow Steel to find him.

Whatever his reason, the clues led Steel to a public archive in New Zealand. It was there, in 2002, that she made a crucial connection: a document that linked Dines with the woman he married, Debbie. Steel instantly realised they must have been a married couple. Back in London, she ordered the couple's wedding certificate. She immediately recognised her boyfriend's handwriting. 'What hit me like a ton of bricks is that he listed his occupation as a police officer,' she said. 'When I read that, I felt utterly sick and really violated. It ripped me apart basically, just reading that.'

Steel was now agonisingly close to the truth. She knew that Dines was a police officer when he married his wife in 1977. But there was still a possibility that he gave up his job before becoming a political activist. She shared the evidence with friends and family. Some cautioned her against concluding Dines had been a police spy. 'I remember my dad and others said: "You're being paranoid – that would never happen in this country."'

Over the course of a decade, through ingenuity and perseverance, Steel had all but worked out the true identity of her boyfriend. It had been an accomplished feat of detective work, and one that did not go unnoticed in Scotland Yard. Senior managers at the SDS had been watching Steel, tracking her moves as she found new pieces of the jigsaw.

In 2002, when they feared that Steel was getting close to Dines in New Zealand, they took a remarkable decision. At considerable cost to the British taxpayer, they decided to uproot and relocate their former spy to another country.

She was not the only woman searching for an invisible man. Around the time that Steel was being drawn to New Zealand, a woman named Alison was searching for her boyfriend, a burly Scouser named Mark Cassidy. The couple had lived together for four years. Alison, a secondary school teacher, first met Cassidy when he appeared on London's left-wing political scene in late 1994. It did not take long for her to feel drawn to him. He was friendly and up for a laugh. Cassidy could be coarse – his jokes bordered on the politically incorrect – but he was also irreverent and funny. A touch over six feet tall, he had a broad neck, large shoulders and big thighs; he had a tough, working-class quality.

Cassidy told friends he had come to London to find work. He said he was born in Dublin 27 years earlier and brought up in Birkenhead in Merseyside. He drove around in a red postman's van that had been converted into a cosy home-from-home, complete with curtains. After meetings, he often ferried activists around, dropping them off one by one around the capital. He once collected left-wing comedian Mark Thomas and delivered him to a concert to raise money for a political cause.

By the spring of 1995, Alison, a peaceful anti-racist campaigner, had started a relationship with Cassidy. He was living in a tiny bedsit in the deprived borough of Hackney; rent was paid in cash to a landlord who went by the name of Wally Pocket. The flat in Osbaldeston Road, Stoke Newington, was bare, even grotty, very much a single man's abode. He did not have sheets on his bed, just a sleeping bag. He dressed like he did not care about clothes – a free spirit who eschewed the superficial world of consumerism.

By the start of 1996, Cassidy was hardly spending any time in his bedsit, so he moved permanently into Alison's flat. Their friends recall how Cassidy spent almost every night in the apartment for the next four years. 'We lived together as what I would describe as man and wife,' says Alison. They had affectionate nicknames for each other. He met her relatives, who trusted him as her long-term partner. A photograph has recorded him at Alison's mother's second wedding. Family videos of her nephew's and niece's birthdays show Cassidy teasing his girlfriend fondly. Other videos record him telling Alison's grandmother, before she died, about his own, fictionalised family background.

Cassidy claimed a drunken driver had killed his father when he was eight years old. His mother remarried, but to a man he did not get on with, and so he had ceased contact with his family. He had a half-brother, whom he barely saw because he lived in Rome, and a grandmother who had died. Cassidy said his grandfather was still alive, but the one time they went to visit him he was out on a church outing. It was a typical back-story for an SDS officer; a hard-luck tale designed to generate sympathy.

With Alison as his girlfriend, Cassidy delved into radical politics. He had a particularly dubious mission: keeping an eye on campaigners exposing police wrongdoing. Cassidy became a key member of a group called the Colin Roach Centre, which was helping to uncover allegations of police corruption in Hackney. The allegations included gratuitous violence, faking evidence, planting drugs, perjury, racism, false imprisonment, fraternising with criminals, and drug dealing, and led the MP, Brian Sedgemore, to label his local constabulary 'nasty, vile and corrupt'. The campaigners also helped people who had been assaulted, fitted up or wrongly arrested by the police to sue Scotland Yard.

The police always liked to keep on top of campaigns against them. In the neighbouring London borough of Newham, there was a respected local organisation which since 1980 had been campaigning against police harassment and racial attacks. The SDS did not have an undercover officer in the Newham Monitoring Project at the time, but made sure to receive regular reports about its activities. 'Every single event they were organising was being reported back to SDS,' says Pete Black. 'We knew everything that was going on in the NMP.'

While monitoring the Colin Roach Centre and a campaign to improve safety on construction sites, Cassidy turned his attentions to another small left-wing group. Cassidy's bulky demeanour made him suitable for Red Action, which sought out confrontations – and often hand-to-hand combat – with far-right groups to stop them meeting or promoting their propaganda. Red Action members admitted their group had been 'associated with violent, semi-clandestine conspiratorial activities' since its formation in 1981. The group's support for the IRA's paramilitary methods, unusual on the left, also allowed Cassidy to burrow himself into the campaigns that championed the political cause of a united Ireland.

Early on his deployment, he went on a week-long trip to Belfast with a small group of English activists who wanted to show their solidarity with the republicans. He was not the first SDS to show an interest in republicanism; its officers had been dabbling in espionage across the border as far back as the 1970s.

But this was in the late 1990s, when the IRA had declared a cease-fire, edging towards agreeing a deal to lay down its arms. Special Branch sources believe Cassidy was asked to gauge the appetite among hard-core republicans for an end to violence.

The fact he was trusted to spy in Ireland was testament to his reputation. Among other SDS officers, Cassidy was considered a top operator. His relationship with Alison – one of the most enduring of any police spy – was crucial to his success, but it came at a cost. During the occasional spells when he was not undercover, Cassidy would be trying to live a normal, off-duty life with his wife. It is hard to conceive how he managed that. Unlike other SDS officers, who tried to take at least one or two days out of the field, Cassidy was living permanently with Alison. The couple repeatedly went abroad on holiday together – once for three weeks.

Within the squad, it soon became known that Cassidy was having marital problems. That was not unusual for an SDS officer. What made his duplicity so astonishing was his way of coping. It shocked some within the squad. As his relationships with his wife deteriorated, Cassidy attended counselling sessions to repair their marriage. Around the same time, he was also seeing a second relationship counsellor with Alison. 'I met him when I was 29 … It was the time when I wanted to have children, and for the last 18 months of our relationship he went to relationship counselling with me about the fact that I wanted children and he did not,' says Alison. The SDS officer had two separate, and totally different lives, with two strained relationships, and two counsellors.

The end of his deployment, and his chance to disentangle himself from the mess, came toward the end of 1999. His departure was put in motion with what appears to be a typically elaborate SDS plot. The day before Christmas Eve, Cassidy told his girlfriend he had received an enigmatic message on his pager: 'Call Father Kelly.' He said his grandfather in Birkenhead had had a stroke. 'I said I would go with him, and he said, "No, no, I've got to do it myself" and he was very odd,' recalls Alison. It was their first Christmas apart since they had started living together.

When he returned shortly after Christmas, Cassidy was, according to Alison, 'a very different man'. He claimed to have had a row with his stepfather and said he punched him in the stomach. In the following weeks, Cassidy seemed on a downward spiral. He stopped smiling and looked withdrawn. He spent hours staring silently out of their kitchen window. One day in March 2000, he left.

The note Cassidy left for Alison made painful reading. It said: 'We want different things. I can't cope. When I said I loved you, I meant it but I can't do it.' He claimed he needed time to get his head together. He returned the following weekend and said that he would stay. But most of his possessions had gone – he only had a few clothes in a kitbag. The tool bag he claimed to have used for his work as a joiner was gone. Ten days later, leaving another note, Cassidy vanished for good.

He said he was going to Germany to look for work. Soon afterwards, Alison received a letter – a postcard sent from Germany. Cassidy wrote: 'Don't want a holiday in the sun.' It was an elliptical reference to a song by the Sex Pistols, inspired by the punk band's trips to Berlin and Jersey. The last line of the song was: 'Please don't be waiting for me.'

According to her friends, Alison looked numb the week after he left. She functioned like an automaton – getting up, showering, making cups of tea, buying a newspaper, and staring into space. As Cassidy's disappearance sank in, Alison became confused and snappy. She started to feel paranoid and fear she was going mad. She felt abandoned without explanation. 'I was stuck. I had no grieving process. It was like someone was lost at sea. I had no answers.' She examined the only things that Cassidy had left behind – a receipt from a cash card, a piece of paper with the registration number of his van, and a prescription for two asthma inhalers.

Cassidy had executed the standard operating procedure for departing SDS spies. It was a formula: the breakdown, the love notes and the sudden and unexplained disappearance, followed by the letter from abroad. Then silence. John Dines had done exactly the same to his girlfriend Helen Steel nearly 10 years earlier. And just as Steel was unable to stop searching for her boyfriend, arriving, eventually, in New Zealand, Alison felt compelled to find her man.

This time round, the girlfriend had reason to suspect her partner early on. Weeks after Cassidy had vanished, Alison was contacted by an activist who wanted to speak to him. After explaining that he had left her without trace, she agreed to meet to talk through his disappearance. She left this meeting thinking he might be some kind of spy. As it dawned on her that Cassidy was not coming back, she began researching his background. It was a journey that, like Steel's, began in the archives of birth and death certificates. Alison recalled the date Cassidy claimed his father had died in a car crash. She opened up the bound volumes and started to run her finger down the lists of deaths for that year. When she discovered there was no trace of the death, she broke down.

Alison eventually decided her boyfriend had probably been a spy, and that she had inadvertently provided him with 'an excellent cover story … The level to which he was integrated into my family life meant that people trusted me, people knew that I was who I said I was, and people believed, therefore, that he must be who he said he was because he was so welcomed into my family, so much part of it.'

Just as Steel had done before her, she hired a private detective, who managed to access Cassidy's tax, welfare benefits and national insurance records. Once again, the covert triggers attached to the files would have flashed an alert silently back to the SDS headquarters. They would have revealed once more to the SDS managers that someone was searching for one of their spies.

A year after his disappearance, the detective's findings showed that her boyfriend was a fake, but she had to dig further for his real identity. She was left raking over the past. It was only in retrospect that aspects of his behaviour did not fit. He supposedly had a favourite football team, Tranmere Rovers, but he was never recognised by anyone among the small band of followers. And then there was the kitchen he installed in their flat. It was not built very neatly for a man claiming to be a professional joiner. But the most incriminating incident had occurred about a year and a half into their relationship. Intuition had told Alison there was something not quite right with her partner. When he was out at the shops, she rifled through his jacket. She discovered a credit card in the name of M. Jenner. When he returned to their flat, Alison confronted her boyfriend. His hands clasped the sides of his head in shock. She had never seen him do that. 'He told me he bought it off a man in a pub and he had never used it. He asked me to promise to never tell anyone, which is what I did. I never told anyone until after he disappeared.'

Ten years later, in 2011, Alison was informed by the authors of this book that Mark Cassidy was an SDS officer. His real name was Mark Jenner. He is believed to be still in the police, working in London.

His disappearance and the resulting trauma has had an 'enormous impact' on her, she says. 'The experience has left me with many, many unanswered questions, and one of those that comes back is: how much of the relationship was real? I have, for the last 13 years, questioned my own judgment and it has impacted seriously on my ability to trust, and that has impacted on my current relationship and other subsequent relationships. It has also distorted my perceptions of love and my perceptions of sex.'

The 'betrayal and the humiliation' she experienced was 'beyond any normal experience', she adds. 'This is not about just a lying boyfriend or a boyfriend who has cheated on you. It is about a fictional character who was created by the state and funded by taxpayers' money.'

The stories of Alison and Steel have one thing in common. Despite their extensive efforts, and clues that put them on the right path, they never actually managed to track down their boyfriends. The SDS officers got away. They nearly always did. Jim Boyling was the exception. The story of Laura, an environmental activist who managed to track him down, must count among the most tragic in the history of the SDS. Boyling says that the story she tells is mainly 'incorrect', although he declines to elaborate.

The pair met toward the end of his undercover deployment, in the summer of 1999, when they attended a meeting of the Reclaim the Streets environmental group in a traditional Irish pub, the Cock Tavern, near to London's Euston station. 'He would rub his shaved head in meetings with a supposed coy but friendly shyness, but he was also known for not suffering fools gladly,' Laura says of the man she knew as Jim Sutton. To many, he was 'Grumpy Jim', the Reclaim the Streets campaigner who had once been prosecuted for occupying the headquarters of London Transport. The ice broke some time later, when she was cooking a meal for fellow activists and he initiated a discussion about the merits of using fresh coriander.

The relationship developed quickly. In November, they started going out and, by February of the following year, Boyling had invited her to move in to his rented flat in Dulwich, a gentrifying part of south London. He had decorated the apartment with simple, hippyish items – Celtic and African patterned throws. Through a window, they could look out onto a yard where Laura grew herbs. Laura says her boyfriend looked after himself and would often go for a run to keep fit. 'He ate very well – he bought ingredients I wouldn't have been able to afford. He regularly bought specific ingredients such as papayas and sauces to add flavours. He took for granted that it was part of his regular shopping – speciality green leaves for stir fries and salads. He never cooked up a cheap, nutritious and simple stew.'

During the early part of their relationship, Laura felt she was experiencing the deepest love she had ever known. She was oblivious that he was being paid to spend time with her. 'The public was paying him for the lengthy time we spent courting, spending time in the park, and even sleeping together,' she says. The romance was almost overwhelming. 'In the beginning I nearly broke it off because it felt too strong. It was as if he was a perfect blueprint for something I didn't even know I was looking for.' There was only one moment when Laura questioned the background of the man she thought was her soulmate. It was the briefest flicker of doubt. 'It was the way he was cleaning his walking boots. I suddenly thought, "Who the hell is in my kitchen?" and then I came to and suddenly he was Jim again. It was such a brief moment and it made such little sense that I blanked it.'

In May 2000, conscious that Boyling had shown some interest in gardening, Laura returned home with some strawberry plants and ceramic pots. 'Out of the blue, he told me that he had to leave me. He seemed quite shocked and it made no sense. It was completely out of character. He said he had to go alone; that there were things in his head that he had to sort out.'

The next few months were agonising for Laura. Boyling's moods 'swung violently'. He kept breaking down and crying in her arms, saying: 'I never want to lose you'. He told her that he had been adopted and had had a disturbed childhood. He showed Laura a photograph of what he said was him climbing out of a cardboard box on the lawn at his adoptive parents' house.

In September of that year, Boyling left, saying he was going to travel to Turkey and South Africa. A postcard from Turkey arrived soon afterwards, and it was followed by a phone call. 'I told him I loved him and he sobbed his heart out. He said he thought he had messed everything up,' she says. 'He was supposed to call me again when he was hitchhiking through Syria. When he didn't, I became worried and called the Foreign Office to ask what was going on. They told me he hadn't left Istanbul and they were instigating a missing persons search.'

News of this development would have been sent over to Scotland Yard where Boyling's supervisors would have looked on disapprovingly. Operatives were expected to be skilful enough to vanish without loose ends. A little anguish over the disappearance of a loved one was useful; it cemented the idea among activists that the spy had gone for good and made the exit seem real. But too much, and people left behind would try to track down the missing person. Laura was a case in point. Hers was an extraordinary and single-minded quest to find the man she loved.

She began looking into his background. She was worried that he may be at risk in some way. She had also become increasingly distressed and confused by his behaviour, and needed counselling for her depression and panic attacks. 'I tried to locate his parents because I was worried, but I couldn't find them, or his brother, who he said was an independent travel agent in Nottingham. I wanted someone to know to contact me if something happened to him,' she says. 'If Jim was a nice guy,

I wanted to help him. If he wasn't a nice guy, I needed to know that so I could move on.'

Unable to find any trace of Boyling, she began to consider the possible explanations. 'I was suspicious, but I kept thinking there was some explanation,' she says. 'I kept trying to turn to something solid to base the truth on but I couldn't find it – each time it crumbled.' She discovered from official records that he was not adopted and neither was he born on the day he claimed. 'When I found a hopeful lead, I felt that there was hope that life would start to make sense, that life was going to be OK, but when it didn't come through, I would be sat on the floor in an empty hall feeling overwhelmed, my head spinning. He no longer existed in physical presence or on paper. I didn't know what to think or what to do. I felt like I was trying to climb out of a black hole with my fingertips.'

Tenaciously, Laura pressed on. Boyling had emailed her to say that he still loved her, but had been forced to leave her against his wishes. He claimed that he was not coping very well, but hoped that he could go back to her. Another email led her to believe that he was working in a vineyard in South Africa. In the summer of 2001, she travelled there and spent three months searching for him. As months passed by, Laura became exhausted and the strain was showing. She returned to London, but with nowhere to live. 'I used all my savings trying to find him and I was very thin, down to 6 stone 12 lb. I stayed for a while in a backpackers' hostel on Gray's Inn Road and on a stranger's sofa.'

What happened next was extraordinary. Although enfeebled, Laura managed to track down one of the squad's secret safe houses. The trail began some months before with a list of all the phone numbers Boyling had rung while he was living with her. Laura sifted through the list of telephone numbers for clues, and found two she did not recognise. She dialled the first number and said she wanted to speak to Jim Sutton. The man who answered sounded panicked and demanded to know how she had got the number. Later she called the second number; another voice answered and said he did not know anyone called Jim Sutton, but offered to help and took down all of Laura's details. He never called back.

With the help of a private detective, Laura traced the two numbers to a rundown office block on Camberwell New Road in south London. In November 2001, more than a year after Boyling had melted away, Laura sat in a pub opposite the block and watched who came in and out. She noted down the registration numbers of the cars parked nearby. She could not have known that she was conducting surveillance on what was at the time the clandestine headquarters of the SDS, situated above the nondescript City Office Superstore stationers.

She had however previously discovered that the phone numbers belonged to a government agency. By now she was 'very, very scared' that she had stumbled upon some sort of malevolent secret state. She did not know if Boyling was part of this state or running away from it.

It was a low point in her search but, two days later, she saw him again. Her detective work had yielded several leads about his real identity. Part of this information had come by tracing the locations of the computers he had used to send his recent emails. She believed that she had found out his real name, his relatives and the school he had attended. In one of his emails, he had appeared to encourage her to believe that he was in England. She had come to suspect that he was living in Kingston in Surrey and had started to spend a lot of time in the area. She took a job in a local bookshop. 'I remember thinking it was the kind of place Jim would go,' she says.

On the first day in her new job, Boyling walked in. It was more than a year since he had disappeared. 'He said: "Don't be angry," and I said I wasn't,' Laura recalls. 'He asked for a hug, and he smelt the same, which was weird.' She urgently needed him to explain what he had been doing. 'I needed answers,' she says.

Later that day, in a café near Kingston Bridge, Boyling made a confession of sorts. He admitted he had been a police spy and disclosed his real name, but claimed that his experience under-cover had changed him. He said he regretted what he had done. 'He said he'd got involved when he was young, and had no idea about politics, that he'd been sucked in, that he had always cared about Friends of the Earth and done his recycling,' says Laura. He told her that he was very much in love with her and wanted to continue the relationship.

She has come to believe that he was fabricating a story to make her forgive his betrayal and entrap her deeper into a rela-tionship that she would never have started in the first place if she had known the truth. At the time she was desperately vulnerable, fearful and traumatised – a state of mind, she believes, that he exploited. She believes that he manipulated her as her long search had left her unable to work out what was real and what was not.

She says Boyling repeatedly promised her that he would leave the police and start a new life, saying that he was opposed to the work of the spies. But he claimed that he was worried about the consequences if he left the police and cited another case in which an undercover operative was 'hounded' after abandoning the squad.

In hindsight Laura no longer believes Boyling's justification for staying in the police. 'He just morphs for his own self-interest with no moral basis or grounding,' she says. 'He has no loyalty to anyone or anything – not to the police, not to activists, not to his own family. He finds out what people psychologically want and then he gives it to them. He's exceptionally talented at portraying compassion in himself. You genuinely feel that you're looking into a man's soul.'

Soon there was another factor to consider. Within two weeks of the meeting in the bookshop, she became pregnant with his child. They had started living together. However, Laura believes that he deliberately began to isolate her from her life in the environmental movement. Now living in a gated community in Surrey, he insisted that she get rid of the telephone numbers of her political friends. He encouraged her, she says, to believe the police were able to monitor everything that was going on and would spot her if she tried to contact other activists.

Boyling also appeared to be desperate to conceal their relationship from his police bosses. Laura says he even made her change her name by deed poll to diminish the chances of anyone discovering their relationship before they could start their new life. It is a claim he disputes, saying that she made the change 'out of her own volition'. The change of name took place in January 2002 – after, Laura says, her boyfriend told her that there was a danger their address could be discovered and their child – then unborn – put at risk.

Boyling was far less risk-averse when it came to preserving the secrets of the Met police, she says. Some time after coming off his undercover deployment, he was transferred to the Muslim Contact Unit, which was run by his old SDS boss, Bob Lambert. Laura says her boyfriend boasted about his access to confidential information and sometimes divulged secrets. 'He would oscillate between being open about his activities and those of his colleagues in the police,' she says. 'He only told me things when they were unsolicited by me.'

She says her boyfriend told her that spies were permitted to have sex with activists because it was considered a 'necessary tool'. 'Jim complained one day that his superiors said there was to be no more sexual relations with activists – the implicit suggestion was that they were fully aware of this before and that it had not been restricted in the past,' she says. 'He was scoffing at it, saying that it was impossible not to expect people to have sexual relations. He said people going in had "needs" and I felt really insulted.' He is known to have had relationships with at least three activists while he was undercover.

Boyling also revealed classified details from confidential police files on activists, according to Laura. He told her about phone messages her old activist friends were receiving and the contents of Helen Steel's luggage when it was searched at the airport. He even gave his girlfriend a glimpse into the modus operandi of trained SDS men, which she found repugnant. 'He said the trick was to have a whole and detailed story but not tell too much of it. He said if you're lying, it's tempting to tell too much of your cover story, but that's the mistake.' Laura recalls her boyfriend saying he missed his covert work. 'He said it was great because it was like being God. He knew everyone's secrets on both sides and got to decide what to tell who and decide upon people's fate.'

However, the worst breach of security was the way in which Laura describes her boyfriend disclosing the identities of other SDS spies. In an ordinary relationship, it might not be considered problematic for a police officer to share details of his confidential work with a partner. But Laura was an activist, one of the very people he had been spying on. Still, he talked to her about Lambert, the legendary SDS spy and his mentor, as well as John Dines, the SDS officer who had a relationship with Steel. On another occasion, during a local fair to promote sustainable living, they nearly bumped into a bearded, stocky man with black wavy hair in a ponytail. Boyling insisted she hid. He told Laura that the man was a police officer, and the spy who replaced him in the SDS. Previously, Boyling had told Laura that he had been the last SDS officer to infiltrate environmental protesters. Boyling feared his SDS replacement might recognise them and report their relationship to senior officers at Scotland Yard. The SDS officer who replaced Boyling appears to have had a relatively uneventful deployment before disappearing to Holland around 2005.

That was the year that Laura and Boyling married and shortly afterwards moved out of London with their two children. Laura says she wed at a time when he was volatile. She hoped that marriage would bring him stability and the courage to leave the police. But it did not work. Soon after, the relationship entered a period of what Laura calls 'darkness and destruction'; she says Boyling was 'increasingly controlling, erratic and abusive'. In February 2007, she entered a women's refuge, after receiving help from the organisation for more than eight months. 'I was concentrating on looking after my two children and getting us through day to day in a situation of emotional and psychological trauma,' she says. 'I was in a state of post-traumatic stress – I remember gripping my own face in the mirror because I couldn't recognise my own reflection – it never worked.' Eventually, after periods living apart, the couple divorced in 2008.

Laura was left alone and in an unenviable position. Boyling was still a police officer, despite what she says were his many promises to leave the force. She desperately wanted to reach out to her old friends in environmental groups, to tell them what had happened. But she had no way of knowing who she could trust. If her own boyfriend turned out to be a police officer, how could she know who was a real protester and who was an informer? Boyling had left her deeply fearful about the power of the police.

In total, Laura and Boyling's time together had spanned nearly a decade, with a gap of around a year when he vanished. She now feels she was treated 'like an unknowing and unpaid prostitute'.

'You don't expect the one person you trust most in the world not to exist,' she says. 'You don't expect it, especially when you are really not that important. I don't think the Metropolitan police consider us at all. The abuse of people in this way is just seen as realistic cover to get what they want, to win other people's trust because they are having a relationship. To make them more credible. You are a head to be trodden on, on the way up the ladder of credibility.'

For his part, Boyling says that he 'never behaved abusively' towards Laura. He says they were 'no longer together as a couple' when she went to the refuge. He adds: 'Not withstanding our separation, I have always tried to support her. I have always supported the children financially and continue to do so. Despite everything I don't wish to be critical of Laura, who has always been a loving mother to our children. Life has been difficult enough.'

Two years after her divorce, when still seeking help for the trauma of the relationship, Laura plucked up the courage to contact one of her activist friends. She sent a message to Helen Steel, asking to meet her. When they met, Laura told Steel that Jim Boyling had been a spy. She also revealed how Boyling had claimed he felt sorry for Steel as the London Greenpeace campaigner had been spied on by three undercover officers – himself, Lambert and John Dines.

Steel had been waiting more than 18 years for confirmation. Dealing with it has been an emotional ordeal. 'Although it was massively painful, there was a sense of relief that I finally knew the truth. I didn't have to keep wondering,' she says.

For nearly two decades, Steel hoped that, despite his betrayal, Dines may have genuinely loved her. It was only recently that she decided his love was also fake. 'I got out all the old letters that he sent me and read them again, with the knowledge he was an undercover police officer and that his parents were still alive,' she says. 'What had once seemed like heart-wrenching stories in these letters, disclosures that made me really worried about his well-being, were completely false. That is manipulation. It is abuse.'

CHAPTER 12

Things Can Only Get Better

At the turn of the century, three years after Tony Blair's New Labour government came to power, there was an unprecedented increase in the undercover infiltration of political activists. There was no apparent rise in the threat from radical politics to explain the change in gear. The nature of protest was, as ever, changing. The kind of confrontational street demonstrations that Pete Black and Mark Jenner had taken part in were giving way to more imaginative direct action protests, increasingly facilitated by the use of the internet. The 1990s had seen the emergence of the anti-road protests, in which activists organised bold civil resistance – climbing trees and digging tunnels – to oppose road expansion plans. There was a growing international trend toward organising large anti-capitalist mobilisations against summits of global leaders. But protest was no more or less threatening than it had been in previous years.

The Special Demonstration Squad was still going strong. The unit created by Conrad Dixon 30 years previously had proved to be a durable beast. There had been a few occasions when it looked like it would come apart. Mike Chitty, who had been found wandering around Worthing, very nearly blew the lid on the whole spy programme. Others had also threatened to expose the operation. But the Special Demonstration Squad had survived these and other scrapes and it was continuing to plant undercover cops at the heart of protest groups. Police chiefs, however, thought it was time for more. In 1999, a second squad of police spies came into existence that would rival and eventually replace the SDS. It went by the unwieldy name of the National Public Order Intelligence Unit.

Undercover police officers working for the NPOIU had much the same job as their counterparts in the SDS. For nearly a decade, the two squads would run in tandem. Effectively, senior officers doubled their spying resources. The spies were occasionally deployed in the same groups and would come across each other in the field – there were some supervisors who worked for both units. But for the most part they were separate and independent teams of officers with their own distinct identities, until the SDS was quietly disbanded in 2008.

For the nine years the units were working alongside each other they had had separate turfs. The SDS belonged to Special Branch, the elite department in the Metropolitan police. When the branch in the capital merged with another unit to form the Counter Terrorism Command, or SO15, in 2006, the SDS remained a London-based squad, although by then, with the war on terror consuming most senior police resources, its days were numbered. But for the four decades the SDS was in existence its spies were almost always deployed in London.

Undercover operatives working for the NPOIU, in contrast, were peppered in towns and cities across England and Wales. Operatives were often seconded to the unit from regional police forces. They had some previous experience in covert policing and were granted permission to do other kinds of undercover work, such as catching drug dealers. Successful NPOIU recruits were placed on nationally accredited training schemes and given a short introduction into the world of protest. One former NPOIU spy describes one such course, which lasted five days, involving

role-play at an abandoned warehouse tha
look like an anarchist squat.

It was a quite a different set-up to th
give the impression its officers were cut fr
Just as it had done in 1968, the squad still o
boys' club. Recruits had rarely applied to join the SDS – it ...
privilege that came by invitation only, and the squad prided itself
on only ever selecting from the cream of Special Branch. Its operatives had little contact with other parts of the police services and
were trained exclusively in-house, often learning first-hand from
seasoned mentors such as Bob Lambert. They saw themselves as
an elite who were considerably more professional than the young
pretenders in the NPOIU. One former SDS man disparagingly
calls the rival squad a 'Mickey Mouse' unit.

The reality was more complex. Certainly, the NPOIU did
not have the benefit of the tradecraft perfected by the SDS
over decades, and there is evidence to suggest its spies were less
convincing in their undercover roles. But it appears that the
NPOIU could draw on far more resources and successfully saw
its reach expand over the years. Part of the funding for the newly
formed NPOIU was supplied by the Home Office under the then
home secretary, Jack Straw. Over time, more than £30m of public
money would be channelled into the NPOIU. The unit would
eventually expand to a staff of 70, dwarfing their counterparts in
the SDS.

The two units also had subtly different mandates. From its
inception, the SDS had always been about monitoring political
'subversives'. By the late 1990s, 'subversion' was considered an
archaic term, unsuitable for the targets of the NPOIU. Police chiefs
such as the unit's first head, Barry Moss, went about inventing a
whole new vernacular at secret meetings in hotels including the
Miskin Manor outside Cardiff and the Blunsdon country house

shire. They eventually settled on a new mission statement definition of the people they would be spying upon.

It was an Orwellian phrase, as meaningless as it was useful to police who advocated a catch-all term: 'domestic extremism'. With no legal basis or agreed definition, the phrase could be applied to anyone police wanted to keep an eye on. In the most general terms it was taken to refer to political activity involving 'criminal acts of direct action in furtherance of a single issue campaign', but would not be restricted to criminal conduct. Domestic extremists, police decided, were those who wanted to 'prevent something from happening or to change legislation or domestic policy', often doing so 'outside of the normal democratic process'.

It is a natural tendency of state bureaucracies to expand their empire. And the domestic extremism apparatus that grew under the Labour government was no different. In the first decade of the 21st century, funding for policing domestic extremists doubled. The breadth of activity being targeted by police also expanded. Documents that chronicle the birth of the NPOIU reveal it was initially intended to focus upon two groups: hard-core animal rights activists behind sometimes nasty campaigns against vivisectionists and a group defined as 'environmental extremists', taken to be a loose reference to the anti-roads movement.

The animal rights surveillance took the lion's share of resources. Some police chiefs argued they had fought and won a covert war against sinister and often violent protest campaigns targeting, for instance, universities involved in animal experimentation. But they also claimed it made sense to now broaden the scope, applying the same methods to the green movement and widening the remit of the NPOIU. The unit's targets multiplied to encompass groups of every political hue, from socialists through to far-right activists, covering the turf traditionally occupied by the SDS. Domestic extremists now included campaigners against war, nuclear weapons, racism, genetically modified crops, globalisation, tax evasion, airport expansion and asylum law, as well as those calling for reform of prisons and peace in the Middle East.

By widening the surveillance net, police found themselves having to justify some unusual catches. There was one defining case that underlined quite how wide the trawl for domestic extremists had become. A 69-year-old retired physicist, Peter Harbour, discovered his name listed as a domestic extremist in legal papers published by police online. Dr Harbour had never been convicted of any offence and had always passed the security checks when he worked in government laboratories. He was stunned. It turned out his 'crime' stemmed from his involvement in a campaign to protect a beauty spot – Thrupp Lake – where locals used to walk, swim and picnic and watch otters dive into the water. RWE npower, which owns the nearby Didcot power station, wanted to empty the lake and fill it with ash. Wildlife enthusiasts marched, wrote letters and signed petitions. A small number stood in the way of the company when it tried to cut down some trees. The campaign was never anything other than entirely peaceful.

With domestic extremism defined widely enough to include the likes of Dr Harbour, it was necessary to build an even larger apparatus of surveillance. The NPOIU was the first, and largest, unit to be created. A second branch was set up in 2004 following lobbying by big corporations. The National Extremism Tactical Co-ordination Unit, based in Cambridgeshire, was tasked with giving security advice to hundreds of companies in aviation, energy, research and retail who were the targets of protest. Its one-time head, superintendent Steve Pearl, said the unit was established by the Home Office after ministers were 'getting really pressurised by big business – pharmaceuticals in particular, and the banks – that they were not able to go about their lawful business because of the extreme criminal behaviour of some people within the animal rights movement'. Many if not most of the companies it advised, however, turned out to be the targets of very different forms of protest.

The third part in the triumvirate of units was the National Domestic Extremism Team, formed in 2005 to co-ordinate investigations conducted by forces across the country. The following year all three units were merged and brought under the auspices of one particular body that would mean their covert activities would escape proper scrutiny. To many people, the Association of Chief Police Officers will sound like a club of top cops. It used to be exactly that. But in recent decades ACPO has morphed into something new, taking a leading role in influencing government policy in policing. It has no statutory power, is not accountable to parliament and for a long time was not subject to freedom of information laws. ACPO is a company, with an annual income of £18m, and a surprising amount of power.

When it took responsibility for the management of domestic extremism – including the NPOIU and its spies – the company found itself at the helm of a national police operation. There was no public consultation before the power grab, which effectively placed the NPOIU in a place it could not be held properly to account. It all happened in secret.

The result was that ACPO was empowered to manage a national database of domestic extremists, housed in an office block near Westminster. In effect, the SDS paper files on subversives, still locked in an archive, were being replaced with a digital library of modern-day campaigners. If the SDS was a unit suited to an analogue age, the NPOIU and its sister organisations now exploit the vast possibilities of digital surveillance. According to the most recent figure, the database contains confidential details of 8,931 political campaigners.

Names, pseudonyms, photographs and dates of birth are kept on the database, as well as information about telephone calls and email activity. The files record CCTV video and, if an activist has a car registration number, can detail logs of their journeys via number plate reading traffic cameras. Particular attention is paid to any political activity: attendance at demonstrations and meetings, political pamphlets, comments on blogposts. In at least two lawsuits, police have been found by judges to have been storing information illegally and forced to remove certain files. Yet they have continued the process of accumulation unperturbed.

Senior police admit many protesters they keep files on have no criminal record, but they say they are justified in storing their information because they may associate with individuals police deem to be extremists – or even, perhaps, one day become extremists themselves. 'Just because you have no criminal record does not mean that you are not of interest to the police,' explains Anton Setchell, the senior officer in charge of the domestic extremism machinery for six years until 2010. 'Everyone who has got a criminal record did not have one once.'

Only a small number of so-called 'domestic extremists' have succeeded in obtaining their files. They give an alarming glimpse into the types of people being spied upon by police – and the breadth of information being stored. The first to get his hands on his file was John Catt. He is an 88-year-old peace campaigner from Brighton with no criminal record, known among local activists for his tendency to arrive at protests with a sketch pad to draw the scene. His file revealed police were taking a surprising interest in his artwork. 'John Catt sat on a folding chair by the southernmost gate of EDO MBM and appeared to be sketching,' said one log, from a protest outside an arms factory. Another noted the pensioner was 'using his drawing pad to sketch a picture of the protest and police presence'. In total, Catt's attendance at 55 demonstrations between 2005 and 2009 was assiduously recorded by police. They did not just note his participation in these protests but recorded details such as the slogans on his T-shirt and whether or not he had shaved that morning. In 2013, Catt won a landmark ruling against the police, after the court of appeal ruled his details were being held without lawful justification.

Another 'domestic extremist' who managed to see his file was Guy Taylor, a 45-year-old campaigner in an anti-capitalist group, Globalise Resistance. Police logged his activities at 27 separate protests between 2006 and 2011, ranging from demonstrations against the Iraq War and racism. They even managed to monitor him at the Glastonbury music festival and report that between listening to music, he had worked on a stall selling 'political publications and merchandise of an extreme left-wing anti-capitalist nature'. Other activists discovered that police had been recording meetings they organised, people they were seen speaking to and even the precise brand of bike they were riding when cycling to demonstrations. Where does all of this information come from?

The answer is that the NPOIU has become adept at drawing in intelligence from dozens of different streams. Police chiefs insist that some of their information is sourced publicly, from internet websites, pamphlets and open email lists. Since the 1990s, police have also deployed overt surveillance teams equipped with cameras to float around demonstrations or stand outside meetings to openly record everything that happens. These small teams of officers, usually numbering two or three, are not used quite as frequently as they once used to be. But for around a decade these Forward Intelligence Teams were notorious for tracking activists wherever they went during a protest. These cops with cameras stick to their targets like flies. There have been occasions when FIT officers have pursued protesters, travelling with them on buses and trains to film their every move. A number of activists have even left their homes in the morning to find groups of FIT officers waiting for them on the pavement. One was once followed as he walked his children to school. Another recalls being tracked all the way to the supermarket.

Occasionally the police cameras have even turned on journalists covering protests. A surveillance video shot by police at a demonstration against a power station in Kent in 2008, and later obtained by protesters, reveals quite how interested police appeared in reporters.

'A lot of press officers aren't there,' an officer says as he zooms into a group of TV journalists. 'Just think they can bloody wander in and out of the field. It's wrong, I think. I trust them less than the protesters.'

Moments later, the camera pans to two photographers across the road.

'Inquisitive, ain't they – these two, by the pole,' the officer says. 'He don't like having his photograph taken – that one there with the bald head.'

Incidents like these have caused consternation among civil libertarians. But the truth is that FIT teams form only a small fraction of the intelligence picture collated on the domestic extremism database. For a long time, they were a useful distraction for police. It is covert surveillance – true spying – that is most intrusive, and most useful for the authorities.

One source of covert information has always come from paid informants. It is impossible to know how many activists have been persuaded to grass on their comrades, although lots say they have been offered money in exchange for information at least once by police, usually after arrest. Quite a few activists had been unable to live with the guilt and confessed to their friends that they have been speaking with police. Usually they have ended up expelled from the group or frozen out of important meetings. One informant who spied on climate activists says police threatened to prosecute him for possession of cannabis if he did not agree to the deal. He met plain-clothes police down a country lane once a day and was paid just £30 for each report.

It is a murky world, but one that was laid bare thanks to the cunning of an environmental activist. Tilly Gifford was a member of Plane Stupid, an anti-airport expansion collective that occupied runways. In 2009 she was approached by two plain-clothes detectives in Glasgow and asked to inform on her friends. At the time she was on bail for vandalism and breach of the peace. A few weeks earlier she and her friends had barricaded themselves onto the runway at Aberdeen airport dressed as the American tycoon Donald Trump.

Gifford had an idea. The 24-year-old decided to play the cops at their own game. She would pretend she was open to selling information about Plane Stupid, but secretly record the discussions with the handlers. She sewed a secret recording device into her tweed jacket. Gifford ended up recording three conversations with two plain-clothes cops from Strathclyde police, a detective constable and his assistant.

'There's no one on this earth, and there's no one certainly in this room, who is going to condemn you for your – if you want, your ideologies, for what Plane Stupid are trying to achieve,' the detective said during their first encounter. But he warned that involvement in protest could leave her with a criminal record and even a prison sentence.

His assistant – adopting the 'bad cop' role – warned Gifford there were 'hard, evil' people in Scotland's women's prison, Cornton Vale. 'And they would make your life a misery.'

'All we're here for today, Tilly, is simply to ask you: is there some way we can work together in this?' said the more concil-iatory detective. 'We have a responsibility to the people of the country to look at groups like Plane Stupid, like other groupings who appear out of nowhere.'

The men hinted at the kinds of questions they wanted answered.

'Who is the leader? Who is the head honcho?' the detective asked. 'In a nutshell, Tilly, look: we basically have a responsibil-ity to the people of Scotland – to their safety. How we go about that – there are ways and means. And as in any, shall we say, big groupings, there's always people within those groupings willing to speak to us.'

He explained more explicitly what these informants were doing. 'Feeding to us what's going on in the groupings – the actual dynamics of the groupings, who's saying what, who's doing what, who's running it, who's not running it.'

'Why would they do that?' she asked.

'People would sell their soul to the devil,' the assistant said.

The detective suggested other motives. 'Moralistic. Financial gain. Cos they've been in bother with the police...'

'They don't want to get in further bother with the police,' the assistant said.

'You're caught up in the whole wishy-washy ideology of it,' the detective said. 'You don't see the bigger picture. Look at the big picture – we work with hundreds of people, believe me, rang-ing from terrorist organisations right through to whatever ... We have people who give us information on environmentalism, left-wing extremism, right-wing – you name it, we have the whole spectrum of reporting. The point we're making is: they come to us with the concerns, because within the organisations for which they have strong ideologies and beliefs they are happy to go along with that, but what they will not get involved in is maybe where it's gonna impact someone else. That's when they come to us and say, "By the way, so and so – in my opinion – is maybe getting a wee bit too hotheaded."'

That was the opening gambit. By the second meeting the police officers were themselves growing a little suspicious. One asked if Gifford was covertly recording their conversations.

'Ha!' she laughed. 'Quite possibly!'

'We're just asking you to consider a proposal,' the detective said. 'It is effectively entering into a business contract. Let's not use the word "work" – you would assist us. But equally we would be assisting you – be it financially or whatever.'

He told her she could use the money for her university fees or donate it to charity. 'Cancer Research, Save the Whale, whatever.' She would become one of thousands of informants secretly working for police.

'They then go home to their families,' he added. 'They go home to husbands, wives, children. We are way, way down. That would be exactly the same with you. You would still have your life, Tilly.'

He added: 'You wouldn't pay any tax on it. So you could do with it what you want.'

Finally Gifford asked the important question. How much would she be paid?

'Oh, you'd be surprised, Tilly,' said the detective.

She said she would be unlikely to help them for a mere '20 quid'.

'UK plc can afford more than 20 quid,' the assistant said. 'Years gone by, people have been paid tens of thousands of pounds.'

For the NPOIU, paid informants are undoubtedly an essential source of intelligence. The same was always true of the Special Branch. The problem is they can never be fully trusted. The information supplied by activists is patchy and can be unreliable – and occasionally it is deliberately misleading. When Conrad Dixon came up with the idea of using SDS spies in 1968, he did so explicitly because the senior ranks in Scotland Yard felt that informants were not providing the calibre of intelligence that was required. And that central belief – that undercover operatives were needed to provide sufficiently reliable intelligence – was what led to the further proliferation of police spies since 2000.

By 2005, both the SDS and NPOIU had full fleets of spies planted in protest organisations. With two rival units, it was sometimes impossible to work out who exactly a police spy was working for.

One undercover officer for example was caught out when a conversation was accidentally recorded on an answerphone. It was 2005 and the spy, who used the fake identity Simon Wellings, was infiltrating the anti-capitalist group Global Resistance. He worked as the group's unofficial photographer, a useful excuse for documenting their activities.

One day he accidentally called an activist friend on his mobile phone and was diverted to answerphone. The two-minute recorded message was in large parts inaudible although the sound of bleeping police radios could be heard in the background. It captured the infiltrator in discussions with a police officer, presumably his handler. Wellings could be heard discussing photographs of protesters, and it seemed the pair had the images spread out in front of them as Wellings was asked to put names to faces – a key role fulfilled by all undercover cops.

'She's Hannah's girlfriend, they are very overtly lesbian,' Wellings told his colleague. 'Last time I saw her, her hair was about that long, it was bright blonde, week before it was black, so you get the picture. She's definitely her girlfriend, they have been together for a long time.'

'Thing is, we've got the CO11s. They're like, "Who are these people?"' said the other officer. He was referring to the Met's public order branch who regularly like to identify prominent activists at protests. 'Do you know who they are?' the officer asked. 'Have you just photographed them?'

Wellings seemed unsure. He identified one protester as 'in the Socialist Workers Party, I don't know his name'. He said another 'sort of flirts with the anarchist side'. He described a third as a 'central bloke'.

It was the tiniest snippet of dialogue. But the recording was sufficient for his friends in Global Resistance to realise he must be an infiltrator. Leaving the answerphone message was an amateur error to have made, and one that resulted in the immediate end of his deployment. By then Wellings had been in the group for four years and managed to get himself onto the main committee of around 20 activists who ran the group. He had originally turned up in 2001, claiming to have a job installing security systems. His friends described him as amenable, considerate and caring. Over the years he joined them on demonstrations in the United States, France, Switzerland and Spain. The fact he was based in London suggests he may have been one of the last spies to serve under the SDS.

A short, rotund man with a brown goatee, Wellings appears to have been satisfied lingering on the fringes of serious protest. He never immersed himself in activism. He was always at demonstrations, but never did much. In SDS speak, he paddled in shallow waters. He told friends he had been travelling for a long time and was separated from his wife and son, who were living in Australia. Looking back, there was never that much suspicion about Wellings. He stands apart from fellow undercover cops infiltrating protest groups for one reason alone: he is the only known spy who did not have sex with activists. That may not have been for want of trying; according to a friend, Wellings moaned that he 'wasn't getting any'.

When Wellings was confronted by his friends over the recorded answerphone message, he spent 10 minutes trying to deny he was an infiltrator and then disappeared. He has not been seen since.

CHAPTER 13

The Clown and the Truck Driver

Lynn Watson was one of the more professional undercover operatives to work for the National Public Order Intelligence Unit. She was also the only known police spy who was a woman and, by one measure at least, the unluckiest.

It was a warm day in Leeds in July 2004. Watson was deep undercover. She had large red dots painted on her cheeks and a green feather duster in her hand. Dressed in military trousers and jacket, she was festooned with bright strips of pink and orange cloth. The outfit was all in the name of duty. She was at the frontline of a covert police war on domestic extremism.

The Clandestine Insurgent Rebel Clown Army was one of the most harmless protest groups to campaign against the invasion of Iraq. They used street theatre and comedy as a tool of dissent. 'We are clowns because what else can one be in such a stupid world?' the group declared. 'Because inside everyone is a lawless clown trying to escape. Because nothing undermines authority like holding it up to ridicule.' Cringeworthy it may have been, but proponents of clowning argued it was a light, refreshing alternative to earnest banner waving.

This particular excursion in Leeds – supposedly a mock 'invasion and liberation' of the city – was recorded on a video camera. It began in a church hall, where around a dozen clown recruits stood in a circle and introduced themselves. Watson was one of the more awkward members of the group who, when it came to unveiling her clown character, was stuck.

'I am Lynn,' she said. 'And I don't have a clown name either.' She made a sad face.

'Let's play Tango!' said another clown. Watson and the others lifted their arms in the air and huddled together. Moments later, they were marching out of the hall, banging drums and blowing kazoos. Watson ran up to the person holding the video camera.

'We're checking for clowns,' she said, staring into the lens. 'We need more clowns in this country! More clowns! Bla!'

Their first destination was the constituency office of the pro-war Labour MP Hilary Benn. 'Can we go in and clean the office?' one clown asked an office employee.

'Please, please, please!' shouted the other clowns.

By the time uniformed police arrived, workers in the constituency office assured them it was a peaceful demonstration and nothing to be worried about. The constables laughed when the clowns ran outside, stood in a line and bent forward, wiggling their bums at the building. Of course, the police had no idea that one of the clowns was a fellow officer of the law.

Next, the clowns went to a recruitment centre for the armed forces. Watson took part in a game of cricket outside, using a feather duster as a bat, and then sat down in the street and sucked a lollipop. Later, the invasion of Leeds finished with the clowns sat beside a tree in a park.

One clown played guitar. 'Where is my mind?' he sang. 'Where is? My mind?'

Watson had climbed the tree and was wearing a steel colander on her head. She looked down at her friends and said in a squeaky voice: 'Tickle the tree! Tickle the tree!'

*

Life for undercover cops in the NPOIU could be quite different to the adventures of the Special Demonstration Squad. Veterans from the SDS might have winced at the idea of clowning around in the street, but the NPOIU's determination to monitor all kinds of protest activity meant this kind of surveillance was on the rise.

Watson was one of the first in a team of 15 spies who would be sent undercover in one six-year period. She initially appeared in May 2002, attending a local campaign to conserve a patch of woodland near Worthing on the south coast. Watson introduced herself as a care-home worker from Bournemouth, doing shifts at care homes for the elderly. She slipped one of the campaign organisers a piece of paper containing her email address, but was never seen there again.

It was a full year before Watson made her second appearance, this time at the Aldermaston women's peace camp, which had been running a sustained campaign against nuclear weaponry since the mid-1980s. She quickly befriended Kate Holcombe, who was another novice showing an interest in the monthly camping events outside the atomic weapons establishment.

'She sort of appeared from nowhere one day and said she had been very bothered about the war and nuclear stuff and she could not sit by and do nothing any more,' she says of Watson. 'She felt she had to get up and start protesting about it.'

Watson was an intelligent woman with an acerbic wit and she quickly made friends with the feminist protesters. She joined in some of the attempts to blockade the weapons site and showed she was up for causing a stir. 'There was a big giggle one day when a Ministry of Defence policeman ended up chasing her about three-quarters of a mile down the road,' Holcombe adds. 'She's very, very fit, and a runner, and everybody thought it was hilarious that she'd been chased by a policeman and she'd basically outrun him. He ended up pulling a muscle in his leg.'

In 2004, after a few appearances at other anti-war protests and peace events, Watson told friends that she needed to get away from an ex-boyfriend. The spy was never explicit about it, but some friends were given the impression she may have had an abusive partner. 'The story was the relationship had ended badly and she didn't want to talk about it,' says one friend. Watson said the agency she worked for had a number of promising placements in care homes up north. She was moving to Leeds, a city that would become her home for three years.

Despite its rich protest history, Leeds at the time lacked an epicentre for radical campaigning. There were some squats and meetings were occasionally held in community halls and school gyms, but no space dedicated to activism. Watson quickly became involved in a group planning to create a new hub for activism in the city. Action for Radical Change had received a £10,000 grant to rent a space that would be used to organise protests. When they decided to convert a former pork factory into a community centre called the Common Place, Watson offered to become its founding director and treasurer. Her name still adorns the company documents. An activist who helped set up the centre recalls the police spy sitting through boring meetings about whether stocking cow's milk would offend vegans. 'It was all of this tedious, dull stuff,' he says. 'There was a two-hour discussion about whether we wanted to call ourselves "The Common Place" or just "Common Place".'

From the outset, there were reservations among some Leeds activists about the newcomer. Watson said she was 35 and from an upmarket town in Hampshire, although her parents were Scottish and she often joked around in an authentic Glaswegian accent. She looked a little different to other activists; she sported big hoop earrings and a baseball cap and always wore a lot of make-up. For a little while, behind her back, some people in the

Common Place started calling her 'Lynn the cop', but it was not a nickname that stuck.

The Common Place was attracting a broad range of people interested in effecting social change. It hosted meals for homeless people and English classes for asylum seekers. At the weekends, there were free bicycle maintenance workshops. The premises had an entertainment licence from the council, and campaigners quickly discovered that hosting musical events could provide a much-needed source of revenue. Local police, however, started clamping down on the parties. During one of several raids on the premises, police burst in to find a handful of people listening to 1920s piano and watching a Czech surrealist cartoon being projected on the wall.

Despite the money these events brought in, Watson made it clear she disapproved of using the space for anything other than activism. 'She was arguing for keeping the focus far more political,' says a co-founder of the Common Place. 'She felt that music was side-tracking us into becoming more of a performance venue.'

Another activist wonders whether Watson had ulterior motives. 'We had a licence, and I imagine that would have been quite a problem for her professionally,' he says. 'She would need to be investigating something at least vaguely dodgy.'

The main purpose of the Common Place did however remain overtly political. It was used to mobilise support for a huge demonstration against the G8 summit in Scotland in 2005. The protests around Gleneagles, where Tony Blair, George Bush and other world leaders were holding their meeting, were among the largest of their kind in a decade. Watson attached herself to a group of first-aiders who volunteered to look after injured protesters. The Action Medics Collective was a fringe group and not the best of roles for an undercover police officer who wanted to be at the centre of action. Certainly, it was not the kind of position an SDS operative would have chosen. But it gave Watson the opportunity to meet a wider group of protesters in and around Leeds.

'We met over the *Guardian* crossword,' says Catriona, one of the city's most radical activists. 'I instantly liked her because she was cynical and sharp.' She and others who got to know Watson recall how dismissive she could be about the more farcical aspects of protesting. Disparaging the stereotype of activism would become something of a trait for NPOIU spies. Counter-intuitively, it often worked, with many activists finding the dose of realism refreshing. 'Those remarks can be lacking sometimes in the sort of dreary, hippy end of the activist scene,' Catriona explains.

John, a part-time bouncer who also became a close friend of the undercover police officer, says he was also attracted to her 'irreverence and sarcasm'. He often visited Watson in her two-bedroom terraced house in the Hyde Park area of the city. 'She kept quite a neat, tidy and well-ordered house,' he says. 'It was fairly plain, vaguely tasteful, cheaply done up.'

John, like almost everyone else who visited Watson at home, was struck by two things that were odd about her house. The first was the fact that she always kept one upstairs room locked, never allowing anyone to peek inside. The second was the artwork on her wall. Beside a photograph of Watson in clown costume there were two clip-framed 1980s posters from the anarchist collective, Class War. One glorified police being attacked on the street, and the other advocated the death of the Queen Mother, who was shown with a punk haircut.

The posters seemed incongruous. Watson was a straight, matter-of-fact person with a dry sense of humour. She would not hesitate to tell friends to 'fuck off' if they were getting on her nerves. She also liked to tell heartless jokes about the elderly patients she was supposedly looking after at care homes. The outdated protest art on the wall did not seem to fit her image. 'It felt a bit like something a teenager would put on the wall to represent who they are,' says Catriona. 'People did comment on the pictures quite a lot because it all felt a little naïve for Lynn. Everyone took the piss out of her about it. She was quite defensive.'

The focus of Watson's deployment was the infiltration of the first two protest gatherings called Climate Camp. This was around the time concern about global warming was gaining traction across the country. The Conservative party leader, David Cameron, travelled to Svalbard in Norway to be towed by huskies and witness first-hand the effects of glacial ice melt. Nicholas Stern, the economist, was in the process of writing his landmark report into the economic consequences of climate change. It was fast becoming a mainstream cause.

Climate Camp was an attempt by radical activists to exploit the shift in sentiment with a peaceful, open demonstration that might appeal to the wider public. Overnight, activists would occupy a patch of land near a major carbon emitter and construct a completely self-sustaining village with tents and marquees. There were five major Climate Camp protests in total; they defined an era in environmental protest and presented a new challenge for police. The first camp was held beside Drax power station, the UK's single biggest emitter of carbon dioxide. The second was based near Heathrow airport, in protest at plans to build a third runway. These were large gatherings, attracting hundreds and even thousands of people, many of them curious locals who came to attend workshops about sustainability and climate science. There was always at least one collective attempt of civil disobedience – such as entering the grounds of the power station – but they tended to be largely symbolic gestures.

Because the camps were at the peaceful end of the protest spectrum, organisers felt they could be open about their plans, although there was some need for security, particularly around the reconnaissance visits to select a suitable site and, on the eve of the protest, the carefully planned swoops on the land under the cover of darkness. Anyone could join the organisation but the more secretive tasks were restricted to cells of trusted activists. Watson managed to get onto these groups during both of the first camps, providing a fruitful source of intelligence for her NPOIU handlers.

During the first gathering, and when camping near the huge cooling towers of Drax power station, Watson had her first and only sexual encounter with an activist. It was a one-night stand and instigated, according to the man who slept with Watson, at the insistence of the undercover police officer. He says the pair had been flirting for some time but their dalliance in a tent was 'nothing meaningful'.

That night was also an aberration for Watson, who abstained from intimate relationships for the rest of her deployment. On the whole, her behaviour was less morally dubious than that of her male counterparts in both the NPOIU and SDS. Indeed, her infiltration in Leeds provides a useful example of exactly how undercover police can thrive without the need to sleep with the people they are spying on.

For her first 18 months in the city, Watson used the excuse of her recent break-up, saying she was not ready for any new relationships. One day at the start of 2007, she surprised her friends by announcing that she had a new man in her life. He was not a political campaigner. Instead she said she had met him randomly during the 40th birthday party of an old friend.

His name was Sean and he was supposedly a locksmith from Northampton. He immediately raised eyebrows. A dishevelled and socially awkward man, Sean seemed a strange match for Watson. He instantly acquired the nickname 'Frank Gallagher', after the fictional drunk on the British TV show *Shameless*. 'Lynn also called him Frank,' Catriona says. 'She was quite disparaging about him.'

Sean was almost certainly another undercover police officer seconded to the NPOIU. It is not unusual for undercover operatives to work in pairs and sometimes that means pretending to be sexual partners or spouses, although it was never a technique used by the SDS, which always preferred its spies to have intimate relationships with real people.

The fake boyfriend deception was actually a rather clever ploy. Watson could spend days or even weeks away and claim to have been staying with Sean. But for whatever reason, the NPOIU decided to terminate the relationship after less than a year.

Watson's second fictional boyfriend played a decisive role in her disappearance from Leeds. Toward the end of 2007, Watson had begun to tell some close friends she was depressed. They had known her as someone who was prone to mood swings, but she seemed to be deteriorating. She had always been a big drinker and now claimed she felt she had a problem with alcohol. She was also increasingly worried about a skin condition that, she said, resulted in blotchy markings on her face whenever she was exposed to sunlight. 'I was being there for her as a friend, listening to her cry,' says one close friend. 'Being someone's emotional support and then realising later it was all made up doesn't feel very nice.'

At the time Watson seemed to be drifting away. She pulled out of a six-week cycle trip around Spain, despite having already bought her ferry ticket. She also spent less time socialising, choosing instead to meet friends at their home.

It was around this time that Watson introduced her new boyfriend, a man who appeared to improve her outlook on life. His name was Paul and he claimed to be a former bouncer at nightclubs from Coventry who had now become a photographer. Watson said she met him during a hen party in another part of the country.

If Sean had seemed a strange partner, Paul left her friends totally dumbstruck. The general consensus was that her new lover was boring, uncouth and prone to bouts of misogyny.

'He looked absolutely like a cop, by which I mean a beefy white male, about six foot tall, with a shaved head and a slightly intimidatory attitude,' says one friend, Matilda. 'He clearly had not had too many feminists in his life. Lynn told me that she had tried to introduce her friends to Paul in Leeds and no one seemed to like him.'

Catriona is even more forthright in her judgment. 'He was a meathead and not attractive. Lynn could have done better, even for a pretend relationship. The first time I met him he managed to really fuck me off. He made a comment about my tits: "I like your eyes and I like your rack." At the time I thought, what a dickhead!'

The introduction of a controversial boyfriend into the equation may have been a deliberate strategy by the NPOIU, driving a wedge between Watson and her friends. But it is perhaps more likely that Paul was just not particularly suited to undercover work in protest circles. Despite the reservations of her friends, Watson gave every impression of being enamoured by the photographer from Coventry. It was a whirlwind romance. He bought her a Staffordshire bull terrier puppy. She named the dog Bridget. They had only been seeing each other for a few months when Watson told her friends that her new love was helping her overcome her depression. In January 2008, Watson announced she was moving to Coventry to live with Paul and start a bookkeeping course.

It all seemed rather sudden. Watson emailed friends the details of her leaving party: 'I am moving to Coventry for the beautiful scenery and its highly regarded ring road,' she wrote. 'It's not the back arse of nowhere (just strongly resembles it) and of course I will be back in Leeds lots and lots.'

The leaving party – a curry followed by a night in a rough pub – reinforced the opinion some friends had formed of Paul. Toward the end of the night when everyone was drunk, he started persuading Watson to kiss her female friends in front of him.

Watson and Catriona snogged a little, between giggles. But after a few seconds Catriona stopped. She felt uncomfortable about the 'creepy' way Paul was goading the situation. 'It seemed like a controlling man thing to do – kind of like he was extending her lead,' she says. 'It was not a respectful polyamorous thing.'

Two days later, Watson's friend John helped drive a removal van to her house in Leeds to pick up her things. The pair drove down to Coventry. When they were at Paul's apartment he cooked them a fry-up breakfast and suggested they head over to the nearest pub.

The couple visited Leeds a few times after that to meet Watson's old friends. Each visit left the impression that something was not quite right. The couple always insisted on staying in Travelodge hotels. It struck Watson's friends as an extremely odd thing for them to do. Why shell out money for a hotel in the city when any number of friends had spare rooms? Perhaps the two undercover police officers wanted to avoid a situation in which they were forced to sleep in the same bed. But by insisting on sleeping elsewhere they were raising suspicions. During one trip to Leeds, Watson and Paul were spotted drinking tea in a branch of McDonald's. 'Pretty much no one else I know in that scene would ever buy something from McDonald's,' John says. 'It is just alien.'

It was as though Paul was pulling Watson away from radical politics. That much was confirmed when, a few months later, she phoned friends to say Paul was taking her to Lithuania, where he had found work. She emailed a few times, claiming to be in eastern Europe. Not long after, the contact dried up.

Activists in Leeds were now suspicious. 'She seemed to have gone off the radar,' says John. He and two friends formed a committee to start investigating Watson and her background. They explored every possible trail, beginning with her family, who Watson had always said lived in Farnborough. They telephoned every Watson household in the area but there was no trace of any Lynn Watson. Then they began looking into her boyfriends. They called every locksmith in Northampton and asked if somebody called Sean worked there. They did the same for photography agencies in and around Coventry, where Paul said he worked. 'Basically, everything came back blank,' says John. 'My take on it was that something had to be wrong. People don't just disappear like that.'

The friends drew up a list of scenarios that could explain her disappearance. The possibilities included that she had suffered some kind of mental breakdown or been in an abusive relationship with Paul. They even speculated about whether he might have killed her. In the end, however, the more plausible explanation was that their friend of four years had been a mole.

Around that time, there were some anarchists 200 miles away having similar doubts about a member of their group. The Cardiff Anarchist Network (CAN, for short) was a small collective of campaigners at the forefront of radical activism in Wales. There were around a dozen of them: lecturers, musicians, a social worker and a trade unionist. They would meet weekly in pubs around the city, campaign on a range of issues, from the Iraq war to the inequities of capitalism, and build links with networks of anarchists elsewhere in the UK and Europe. A number of them had been arrested for criminal damage after travelling to London and forcing their way into a Coca-Cola factory. On Saturday afternoons they stood outside branches of Starbucks distributing coffee produced by revolutionary co-operatives in Mexico. Anyone could attend their meetings, receive their weekly email update or read the minutes of their meetings online. 'New people were coming all the time,' says Janine, one CAN member. 'We were not a closed activist group that treated everyone with suspicion.'

In the summer of 2005, one of the more eccentric people to join the group was a man in his 40s calling himself Marco Jacobs, who claimed to be a truck driver. He was in fact a police officer seconded to the NPOIU, working alongside Lynn Watson and Mark Kennedy. Extremely hairy and weighing around 15 stone, Jacobs had a notorious ability to drink huge quantities of alcohol without becoming drunk and liked to adopt the persona of a Northern comedian. 'Big, burly, brash and blokey,' says Janine.

Jacobs originally surfaced in Brighton a year earlier. It is not uncommon for undercover police officers to first appear hundreds of miles from the place they are being sent to. However, in this case, it appears that Brighton was Jacobs' first mission. It did not go to plan. Soon after he turned up at the Cowley Club – a social centre like the Common Place in Leeds – activists in Brighton say they became suspicious. Jacobs told people he worked as a landscape artist and also drove trucks. He bought lots of rounds of drinks and asked activists prying questions about where they lived.

'The word was, that man is a copper, everyone knows he is a copper,' recalls Terry, one of the spy's few friends in Brighton. 'It was something about his deportment that just screamed "pig" to some people.' A meat-eating truck driver who boasted about getting into pub brawls was perhaps not the best alias to have used in Brighton, which has reputation for a bohemian, cliquey activist scene. 'I was telling people that we cannot say, "Oh, he isn't a student with pink dreadlocks, therefore he must be dodgy,"' says Terry.

Despite the apparent reservations, Jacobs was allowed into some groups, and even convinced activists to hold meetings in his house, which he assured them would be free of surveillance. One weekend, he drove a group of Brightonians to Shepton Mallet in Somerset, the site of a dispute over proposals to build a Tesco store. In the end, though, he sensed that he was being frozen out. Less than a year into his deployment he turned to his friend Terry and said: 'Everyone thinks I'm a copper, don't they?'

A firm rule in the SDS was that undercover officers could never be given a second chance. If an SDS spy could not win the trust of the group of activists they were infiltrating after a short while, they were pulled out and their undercover tour terminated. The NPOIU, however, had a different view. It chose to send Jacobs to Cardiff.

Life in Cardiff seems to have been smoother for the undercover police officer. The South Wales anarchists were a more diverse, welcoming crowd. Now on his second attempted infiltration, Jacobs had the chance to learn from mistakes in Brighton. He became a vegan and changed his appearance, growing his hair to his shoulders and dying it purple. He also put more effort into explaining his back-story. He told friends that he had once been on remand in prison, but suddenly went cold whenever they asked what for. 'He was making out that he used to be a bit of a fighter and he had moved away to start a new life,' says a friend. 'I just thought he was a bit of a sad character, who had no family or had some sort of dodgy past.'

That past included a messy divorce. Jacobs told his friends that his ex-wife, a woman called Sam, used to beat him up. There must have been a real person called Sam in the police officer's life because he had the name tattooed on his lower back. His other tattoo was a Celtic knotwork on his shoulder that he claimed to have acquired when he was an 18-year-old member of a biker gang. When his friends joked that it was strange he still had the name of an ex-wife on his body, Jacobs visited a tattoo parlour to have it covered up with a black star. It meant the undercover police officer now had the traditional symbol of anarchism permanently etched above his backside.

Jacobs rented a first-floor apartment near Roath Park, on the fringe of the student area in Cardiff. Janine describes that flat as 'entirely without personality'. It was virtually empty except for a small amount of furniture and a heavy metal CD collection on the floor. 'There were no photographs or anything else that you would have by the time you were in your 40s,' she adds. But on the whole Jacobs appears to have gone to great lengths in his commitment to his undercover role.

He was always keen for example to talk in detail about his supposed work as a truck driver, hauling boxes of shopping catalogues around the country. He would spend hours explaining how he had executed complicated reversing manoeuvres, parking HGV trucks in parking bays 'designed for Tonka cars'. He had a permanently suntanned right forearm, which friends noticed was noticeably browner than the left, even during the winter. It was, he said, the result of having one arm constantly rested on the truck door by the window. Tom Fowler, a 26-year-old then at the centre of Cardiff activism, says Jacobs talked so much about truck driving he became annoying. 'I would be like, "I don't care, Marco!"' he says. 'He always had anecdotes from roadside cafés. We would be going down the motorway and pass somewhere and he would announce, "Worst cup of coffee on the M4, that place."'

When Fowler and some other Welsh activists were contacted by friends in Brighton, and told to be wary of Jacobs, they thought the suggestion he could be a mole was unfair. Cardiff activists did not want to fall victim to the paranoia they felt had hampered protest groups elsewhere. 'We used to be suspicious of people who used to only come to a couple of meetings then not be seen again,' says Fowler. 'We never really thought that someone living permanently among us, one of the core, if you like, would be a spy.'

.If there was one thing that really enamoured Jacobs to his friends in Cardiff it was his humour. 'He just had so many jokes, constantly,' says Fowler. 'His catchphrases were just endless.' One of his most frequently used catchphrases was: 'Strong European lager is my drug of choice.' It was like he was parodying the idea of a lonely middle-aged man and his tomfoolery could make people cringe. One day he put on some elbow pads and told Fowler he would use them in a ruck against the police. 'I laughed and said: "What the fuck, you idiot! That is ridiculous!" But that was Marco: an affable prat.' Another day, when deciding which takeaway to order, Jacobs opted for Chinese by saying he liked 'Chinky, chanky, chonk'. 'Everyone sort of went quiet,' says Fowler. 'He just said, "Oh, sorry, that wasn't funny." Apart from that incident his comedy was pretty right on.'

When people arrived late to meetings, Jacobs would take a look at his watch and say: 'We're on anarchist time, are we?' When discussions dragged on too long, he would quietly text message others in the room suggesting a delegation should head to the bar. He always took the minutes and his reports of meetings were works of satire. 'Hardened anarchists, sickened by the oppression offered by the states and governments, met in the quiet nice surroundings of The Oasis Club in Cwmbran,' the spy wrote in a typical dispatch.

After another get-together in a pub, Jacobs recorded that they had met in 'an atmosphere of revolution and soft lighting'. Part of the discussion turned to a forthcoming protest over the aviation industry. 'It is about planes, but a lot of the time the planes are involved in military-type scenarios. All at the meeting thought this was absolutely negative,' he wrote. 'Food for thought innit?' He finished that report: 'All agreed the meeting was successful. There were new people there. There were no fights. We had a pint afterwards. People had actually volunteered to do things. We are the future. The future is now.'

Most Cardiff activists could laugh at themselves and appreciated the light touch. But others detected a sinister tone in his mockery. They say the NPOIU spy sowed discord within the group, emphasising differences between people and making others feel self-conscious. One friend who joined him on protests recalls: 'He would always stand at the back and if I said I wanted to get more involved, he acted as though I was being really childish. He made it all seem stupid and pointless.' It was like Jacobs had been instructed to hold up a distorting mirror to anarchists in Cardiff, to dig away at their spirit. 'He basically trivialised what we were doing to the point that I started to question why we were even bothering,' says another friend.

The NPOIU was aware that there was a lot going on in south Wales at the time. Jacobs joined protests against an oil pipeline and the proposed construction of a nearby military academy. He took part in campaigns against immigration and asylum policy and showed an interest in animal rights. His gateway into many of these worlds was the dreadlocked Fowler, one of the best-connected anarchists in the country. There was almost a twenty-year age difference between the two men but they became close friends. They went to gigs together and watched rugby in Newport.

'For a while, Marco was privy to all of my decision-making around activism and personal relationships to a really deep level,' says Fowler. 'He was like my best mate. He was the most reliable person in my life.'

It was in 2008, three years into his Cardiff deployment, that the undercover policeman began secretly courting Fowler's girlfriend behind his back. Deborah was 29 and a social worker from Cardiff. At the time her father was in hospital, terminally ill with cancer. Fowler was dealing with his own personal tragedy, having lost his beloved grandmother. 'Neither of us were able to cope very well or treat each other as we perhaps should have,' Fowler says of his relationship with Deborah around that time. 'Marco very much put himself in the middle of that. He acted as a father-like figure to her. My relationship was breaking down and I confided in him about that. Perhaps I should have been more aware of his intentions. But I wasn't.'

When Deborah's father died, Jacobs attended his funeral and offered her a shoulder to cry on. Later, he tried to seduce her. Initially Deborah resisted the sexual advances. She only gave in when the undercover police officer said he loved her. The relationship was a brief but traumatising affair. The pair slept with each other a few times, before Jacobs suddenly lost interest. By then it was too late. Deborah had already broken up with Fowler, believing she was about to begin a serious relationship with the truck driver.

She was the second woman Jacobs slept with while undercover. The first was Sarah, a 26-year-old. 'He always said he could not tell his family or friends about us because of the age difference,' she said. 'If it had been anyone else I would have thought that was strange, but because he had been such a good friend for so long it really did not enter my mind that he was anything but a stand-up honest man.'

At the time the NPIOU was keen for its spies to travel to the anti-G8 summit protests in Heiligendamm in Germany. Exchanges of covert operatives between European countries was becoming far more common than in the days of the SDS, but it was important that they travelled with the right people. Sarah was friends with some particularly well-connected activists who were forming their own delegation.

Two months before the summit took place, Jacobs told Sarah that he wanted to take their relationship further. She agreed and they travelled together to Germany. A week after their return to the UK, the relationship became sexual. They continued to see each other for a few weeks, before Sarah decided she did not want to continue. Years later, when Jacobs' role as an undercover policeman was revealed by the *Guardian* newspaper, Sarah was aghast. 'I was doing nothing wrong, I was not breaking the law at all,' she said. 'For him to come along and lie to us and get that deep into our lives was a colossal, colossal betrayal.'

Another Cardiff resident used by Jacobs – but in a very different way – was a 50-year-old vegan cake baker called Fran Ryan. She met the undercover police officer through Fowler, although she was not herself politically active. Her energies mostly went into Eat Out Vegan Wales, a group that promoted alternatives to animal food products. On the weekends, she ran a vegan stall in the Cardiff, giving out free homemade cakes and leaflets about where to buy vegan food.

She quickly formed a rapport with the undercover police officer. 'I like *The Archers* on Radio 4, and I can't talk to anyone about it because they don't know about it,' she says. 'But he knew about it and was quite knowledgeable about a lot of things.' One day, Jacobs approached Ryan to see if she wanted to accompany him to a meeting of European animal rights activists in Vienna.

Ryan was shocked by the proposal: 'I said, "What would I want to be going there for?" I won't even go to a protest gathering in this country, never mind Vienna.' Jacobs suggested an alternative: a similar gathering of animal rights campaigners in the south of England. 'I wasn't into animal rights activism, I was more just promoting veganism,' she says. 'But he made it sound quite exciting, and he was always good company, so I agreed to go.'

When they approached the field in Essex where the gathering was being held, something happened to make Ryan suspicious about her companion. His car was stopped by police for a routine check-up. When it emerged that his insurance was out of date, she says Jacobs appeared nervous. 'He explained that he had changed his insurance recently and he did not remember which one it was. The police were checking this out and Marco was getting more and more upset.'

There was a tense standoff over the next few minutes. A frustrated Jacobs repeatedly walked away from his car to make telephone calls, ostensibly to his insurers. Eventually, the traffic police officer lost his patience and said he would need to seize the vehicle. 'Then I heard Marco tell the officer: "Do you mind if we just walk away from the car please?"' Ryan says. 'I just thought: why would he do that?' When Jacobs finally returned to the car he said the situation had been resolved and they drove off.

In turning to someone like Ryan, who was not particularly interested in activism, Jacobs was behaving like an operative who was running out of options. By now, the NPOIU would have wanted him to have infiltrated some national protest groups, to have done more to befriend prominent campaigners outside of Cardiff. As it was, there was not much going on in Cardiff for police to spy on.

Fowler, for so long a linchpin in the city, had lost his enthusiasm following his break-up with Deborah. Like many in Cardiff, he was losing his passion for activism. Some would end up blaming Jacobs for driving apart what would otherwise have been a cohesive group. The last CAN meeting Jacobs took minutes for was in June 2009. It was one of his typical reports, full of remarks that trivialised the meeting. He concluded with a description of how the meeting ended, which read like he was saying goodbye. 'Some went home for an early minibus to catch, some went for a takeaway, and I did my usual trick of continuing to support brewers and distillers around the world. We then all went our separate ways.' A few months later, anarchist meetings in Cardiff stopped happening altogether.

Jacobs' leaving party at the Mango House curry restaurant in August that year was a sedate affair. He had told friends he was going to Corfu where he had been offered a job maintaining holiday villas. Fowler still had no idea that Jacobs had slept with his girlfriend, and the men remained close. The 26-year-old recalls joking to his older friend: 'If you disappear in a few months, you do realise that means you're a cop, don't you?'

Jacobs kept in touch with his friends for just a few months. The very last communication was a text message, sent to a friend toward the end of the year from a Greek mobile number.

'Never, ever, ever, get in contact again!' it said. 'Never, ever, ever, text me!'

It is unsurprising that Jacobs ended his deployment with a difficult to understand joke. 'It sounds ridiculous, but it was the kind of message he would text us all the time,' Fowler says. 'He always texted things like, "Ignore me! I don't mean shit to you!" You know, he was just taking the piss. That one was his last text message. After that, his Greek phone number was dead.'

There is one fear that keeps undercover cops awake at night. It can happen to any spy, anywhere, from the moment their deployment ends. There is not a whole lot former covert operatives can do to prevent it from happening. Some will just be unlucky.

It was an unseasonably cool day in July 2010, but the sun was shining on the Dorset coast. The SDS had ceased to exist two years earlier. The NPOIU however was still going strong. It had a new array of spies in the field and had overseen the departure of officers who had done their time. Marco Jacobs had been missing for a year. Lynn Watson had been gone for two.

Matilda, one of the undercover policewoman's friends from Leeds, was walking a coastal route with her family when they decided to stop for a pint at the Square and Compass, a Dorset pub overlooking the sea. She was squeezed by the bar waiting to be served when she glanced to her left and saw a ghost from the past.

"Lynn! How the fuck are you?!' she said. 'We've all been really worried about you!'

Matilda can still remember Watson's facial expression. 'Her face dropped. She just looked really shocked, horrified almost, to see me. Then she just switched and said, "I need to go to the loo."'

One can only imagine the thoughts that were racing through Watson's mind. In an instant, she had to resume her alter ego, an identity she had tried to put behind her. She too was on a coastal walk with friends and family who could now easily give away her real identity. Her decision to head to the bathroom was quick thinking. It should have given her time to think up an excuse for why she was in England and not Lithuania, the place where she had ceased contact with her friends.

Back in the pub, Watson briefly introduced Matilda to her walking companions and took her outside. The two women sat on a bench outside the pub, the sound of seagulls overhead. Matilda still remembers how the conversation unfolded.

'To be honest, Lynn, we had just assumed you were an under-cover cop,' she said. 'We hadn't heard from you. It was like you dropped off the radar.'

'No, it isn't that, I've just been really depressed.'

'So have you got a phone on you now?'

'No. I haven't been in the country long enough to get one.'

Moments later, there was a ringing sound. Watson pulled two phones out of her pockets and hung up the call. 'She just looked and me and said, "These are not my phones, they belong to my family,"' Matilda says.

Watson started to explain what she was doing in England without her boyfriend Paul. She said her father had recently died and she had returned for the funeral. Paul was in Iowa in the United States, where the couple had been living for some time.

'Iowa?' Matilda said. 'My God. Why there?'

The reply was a little convoluted. Watson said their initial move to Lithuania had been an attempt to escape some 'dodgy' individuals Paul had been in business with. 'The implication was that it had something to do with a criminal gang or perhaps drugs,' says Matilda. 'Paul owed someone a lot of money and he was in trouble.'

Watson said the couple were tracked down to eastern Europe and then had to move suddenly again. They had hoped Iowa, a remote midwestern state, would make a more suitable hiding place, but they were still on the move. In three days, Watson said she was flying to New York, where the couple were now relocating.

The story did not seem to add up. If Watson was in serious trouble, then why had she not told her friends? If the trip to Lith-uania had all been some desperate escape from a drug gang, then why were they so open about where they were going? And how would the British couple now live in New York without visas?

Mid-conversation, a man from Watson's walking party emerged from the pub. He introduced himself as Chris.

'He was coming to check on her,' says Matilda. 'He said, "Lynn, are you OK?" She said, "Don't worry. Just go back inside."'

That was just one of several incidents during the hour-long conversation that left Matilda feeling suspicious. She began asking more questions, pushing her friend to explain why she had not confided in her, and insisting she should not disappear again. Matilda asked for a postal address for Watson's family, so there would always be a way of keeping in touch. Watson refused.

'Lynn, I'm not being funny, but where do your family live?' Matilda said.

'In Hampshire.'

'Where in Hampshire?'

'Farnborough.'

'Where in Farnborough? Can you tell me?'

'No.'

That was the point at which Matilda says she decided her friend must be lying. 'I must have asked her more than five times to give me her family's address. She just refused flat out. I was like, "Look, to be honest, we thought you were an undercover cop and now you can't even tell me where your family live." Lynn just said, "I'm sorry. I'm really upset. I don't want contact with anyone and I feel a bit weird about all of this."'

Before they said goodbye, Watson assured her friend that she would call her before she left for New York. She never did. Instead, exactly a week after their chance encounter in the pub, Watson sent Matilda an email.

'Sweetie! It was really lovely to see you on Sunday, I'm only sorry about the circumstances and that we didn't have much time,' she said. 'It was difficult to talk because I was with Chris who is supposed to be looking out for me on this visit and is very protective.'

Watson gave another feeble attempt to explain her absence. 'I can't go into it all but I haven't been able to keep in touch because of some business difficulties Paul has been having. We thought things would've been sorted out whilst we were in Lithuania but that wasn't the case (so six months spent in a shit hole for no good reason!). We've had to drop out for a while and I promised Paul after the problems followed us to Lithuania that I wouldn't get in touch with anyone but family back home. I've not checked my email in months and I won't be using this one again. I shouldn't be sending this one but felt I owed you an explanation.'

Watson finished the email saying she was now in New York and did not plan to return to the UK soon. She said that Paul 'has some contacts out here' who could arrange visas for them. 'Anyway, I should go. Can you let people I care about (don't have to tell you who) that I'm fine and just be a bit discreet about it? Probably best not to do it by email if you can. Take care of yourself lovely girl.'

CHAPTER 14

Birth of the Hound Dog

The man called Mark walked into the toilets of the Green Man pub shortly before 8.25pm. An audio tape was wired into his sleeves and he had £80 cash in his pocket. He was wearing the paint-flecked overalls of a painter and decorator. Mark found the man he was looking for relieving himself at one of the urinals. His target had short hair and was wearing white trainers and a blue Adidas jacket. Mark walked casually over to the urinals, unzipped his flies and began to pee.

'Did you want anything tonight?' the man in the Adidas jacket said. 'You asked me last week, didn't you?'

'Is there anything about?' Mark replied.

'Yeah, what do you want?'

'A little bit of white, say?'

'What? Charlie?'

Mark confirmed he wanted to buy cocaine. The drug dealer offered him half a gram of the class A drug for £25, warning him that the powder was not the best quality. It was about the going price for half a gram of cocaine picked up in a north London pub in 2001. Mark said he would buy it. Just before handing over the drugs, the dealer paused and scrutinised the talkative customer. He had a wide nose and a wonky left eye.

'Obviously, you're not Old Bill?' the dealer asked.

Mark zipped up his trousers and laughed. 'Fuck off, mate.'

*

Mark Kennedy was, indeed, Old Bill. He was a police officer with a quite extraordinary future ahead of him. He would go deeper undercover, and take far more risks than either Marco Jacobs or Lynn Watson, or indeed any other spy known to have worked for the National Public Order Intelligence Unit. But his success would lead to his downfall. In just over a decade, his life would unravel with remarkable speed, making him, for a period of time, the most talked-about undercover police officer in the world. 'He was as deep a swimmer as there ever was,' says fellow police spy, Pete Black. 'He was absolutely professional. He was just like Bob Lambert – he lived and breathed the role.'

Given the man he was to become, Kennedy had an inauspicious start to life. He was raised in the commuter-belt town of Orpington, in Kent, the son of a policeman, John. Kennedy and his brother Ian seem to have had a contented upbringing as they grew up in the 1970s, with one notable exception. As a two-year-old, Kennedy stumbled across an empty cardboard box and started playing around with it. A staple came loose and became lodged in his left eye, causing instant and irreparable damage to a muscle. The injury left Kennedy permanently suffering from a strangely appropriate disfigurement for someone who made a living from duplicity: he always looked as though he was glancing in two directions at once.

It was a tough start in life for Kennedy, who soon developed a stammer. He tried to overcome his impediment by speaking in a slow, deliberate way that would later in life lead people to assume he lacked intelligence.

At 16, he left school with few qualifications to his name and took a lowly job as a court usher, before deciding to follow in the footsteps of his father. Years later his father John Kennedy would say he encouraged his son to become a police officer. 'Being a policeman was a way of life for the family. You'll never be rich. But you will be proud of what you have done.'

A photograph from 1990 shows a young-looking Mark Kennedy, squinting at the camera from beneath a helmet embossed with his constable number. He had joined the City of London police, a small force that only has jurisdiction over the financial district of London. He settled into the suburbs, moving into a house with his parents and then marrying an Irish retail manager, Edel. The couple had two children, a boy and girl. It was the foundations of the kind of quiet, sedentary life that Kennedy showed every sign of disliking.

He bought himself a motorbike and took up long-distance running. He was an enthusiastic rock climber and started travelling further afield in search of the adrenaline of dangerous climbs, including one expedition to Pakistan. By 1998, Kennedy had transferred to London's Metropolitan police and begun going undercover briefly to purchase drugs from dealers.

And so it was that in October 2001, a few years before he turned his attentions to spying on protesters, Kennedy found himself walking into the Green Man pub in Barnet in search of cocaine. He was working on Operation Smoothflow, a sting to bring down one of the most notorious places to score drugs in the area. The man in the Adidas jacket who sold Kennedy a wrap of cocaine in the toilets had no idea he was an undercover cop. Kennedy and three other police officers had been drinking in the pub for weeks, posing as manual labourers with wires sewn into their outfits.

When police eventually got round to raiding the pub with sniffer dogs, they arrested a couple of dozen customers and hauled them off to the station. Prosecutors charged 13 people, mostly for supplying small quantities of drugs or for possession. Only one decided to plead not guilty and risk a higher sentence: the man accused of being the drug dealer who gave Kennedy cocaine in the toilets.

From the start, detectives had a problem trying to identify the dealer in the Adidas jacket. When he sold Kennedy drugs, he refused to give him his name or telephone number. There was no DNA or fingerprint evidence on the wraps of cocaine. The audio recordings were so muffled that it was not possible to identify the culprit's voice. Eventually police decided the guilty man was the pub's 18-year-old barman, Gary Pedder.

The teenager denied ever having sold drugs to anyone and pointed out there were several other people in the premises wearing Adidas clothes. His mother, Josephine, insisted her son would never deal drugs and said police had the wrong man. Police searched their home but found no evidence of drug paraphernalia or suspicious stashes of cash.

Several months later, Pedder found himself in the dock at Hendon magistrates court. 'All the way through I said I never did it. It wasn't me. You've got the wrong person,' he says. It was his word against that of Kennedy, who testified under oath that Pedder was the man who sold him drugs. Pedder says none of the other undercover police officers felt confident enough to finger him as the suspect.

As he was leaving, Kennedy bumped into Pedder outside the courthouse. 'He walked past me and my mum and my girlfriend,' Pedder says. 'He said "sorry" and then just got on his motorbike and drove off. My mum was there and said, "Did he really just say that? Did he just say 'sorry'?" Everyone was in shock.'

A few hours later, the jury returned its verdict. Pedder was found guilty of five counts of supplying a class A drug. He was sentenced to five years in prison.

Kennedy declined to comment on the Pedder case. However, reflecting on his years purchasing drugs for the police, he once told a journalist: 'I was a natural at undercover work and I loved it. Drug work was black and white. You identify the bad guys, record and film the evidence, present it in court and take them down. I did that for four years and loved it.'

Kennedy's enthusiasm for undercover work did not go unnoticed. By the time Pedder began his prison sentence in 2002, the constable who put him behind bars had made an important career move. Kennedy twice asked to transfer to the NPOIU, but initially, for some reason, was considered an unsuitable candidate. On his second application he was accepted and told he would work on Operation Pegasus, the same mission to target left-wing environmental campaigners as Lynn Watson.

He would have to relocate and start a new life in Nottingham, on a salary of £50,000. This new deployment was quite unlike his brief forays into pubs purchasing drugs. His targets were a close-knit group of eco-activists in Nottingham and Kennedy was told he was expected to spend years living among them. They socialised around the Sumac Centre, which contained a vegan fast-food business in the basement. Upstairs, there was a library and space for parties, film screenings and workshops. There was also a bar with a small sound system and a garden out the front growing organic food. It was not unlike the Common Place in Leeds, which Watson helped set up, or Brighton's Cowley club, where Marco Jacobs made his first, faltering introductions.

Like the other NPOIU spies, Kennedy invented a fictional identity that might make him useful to activists. In some respects he stuck to the usual formula. He too, for example, would tell friends that he was recovering from a messy break-up with his girlfriend and had moved cities to get away from her. He decided he would be a 'rope access technician', or professional climber, a job that would allow for a van, and long absences from Nottingham when he could claim to be in distant parts of the country painting cranes or cleaning skyscraper windows. He would also tell friends he did part-time work as a driver, for an uncle named Phil.

But if Kennedy was going to justify his generous expense account, his alias would need another source of funds. He decided to make his fake persona a former criminal who had earned a small fortune smuggling cocaine into Europe from Pakistan. This was not something he would ever announce. Instead it was a secret that would unfurl slowly, providing a second layer to his identity. He could be a risk taker thirsting for excitement, and someone wanting also to seek redemption for past failures.

There were of course threads of truth to this deception. He had travelled to Pakistan, so if he was ever pressed he knew he was familiar enough with the country. His previous undercover work also gave him some grasp of the cocaine trade. All told, it made for a clever ruse. Kennedy could have plenty of cash, and an excuse for not wanting to speak about his past.

Once an undercover police officer has established their legend, the rest was no more than ritual. Kennedy selected a name, settling for two clean syllables: Mark Stone. His surname was 'just an easy name to remember. It is a popular name. It is not difficult to forget in stressful circumstances.' He says he spent 'about a year' researching neighbourhoods and schools in London, joining Friends Reunited so that he could talk convincingly about his fake background. He was given the codename UCO 133 and introduced to his NPOIU handler, a sergeant called David Hutcheson. Finally he was issued with credit cards, bank accounts and a fake passport and driving licence. Both identity documents had photographs of a podgy-looking Kennedy with cropped hair.

By then, however, Kennedy was morphing into his new identity. He purchased a new wardrobe of mostly black clothes, pierced his ears and let his hair grow. When he looked in the mirror, the glance would have been returned by a stranger. He had the same damaged left eye, but Mark Stone looked completely different to his former self. He now had a gingery beard and shiny long hair.

No one at the Sumac Centre can say exactly when Mark Stone turned up. He just appeared. One day, he was sitting in the Sumac's vegan café taking part in a letter-writing campaign to call for changes to the prison system. He enquired about a poster hanging on the wall advertising transport to Earth First, an annual gathering of environmentalists. The NPOIU knew this to be a must-attend event in the calendar of many radical green campaigners.

In 2003 it was held on Lime Tree Farm, near the village of Grewelthorpe in North Yorkshire. This was what activists liked to call a 'safe space'; rescued from its previous life as a dairy farm, the fields had been transformed into a spiritual sanctuary and nature reserve. The organisers of Earth First tried to create a campsite without hierarchy, in harmony with its surroundings, to meet, socialise, debate and plan for the year ahead. There was a communal kitchen, bicycle-powered generator, compost toilets and, for those so inclined, a nude hot tub. 'It was like a very straight festival,' says a key Earth First activist. 'Workshops all day, everyone eats the same vegan food for their meal, cooked by the Anarchist Teapot collective, and a bit of drinking and socialising in the evening, but not an all-night party.'

Central to the workings of the camp was that decisions should be reached by consensus, rather than vote, and the activists used a strange-looking ritual known as 'jazz hands', in which they wiggled their fingers in the air to express support for speakers.

One decision reached that year was to target the German biotech company, Bayer, which was entering the global market in genetically modified crops. A few weeks later, Kennedy was taking part in his first direct action protest, driving a people-carrier filled with activists to a small subsidiary of the company in Huddersfield.

It was 5am and the road was empty. Two activists were wearing cartoon stuffed animals on their heads. Another had brought a Chinese jaw harp to play. Activists blocked the road with a large metal tripod, locked themselves to the entrance of the building and handed out leaflets to office workers. Kennedy was getting his first taste of domestic extremism.

If Kennedy was going to burrow deeper, he needed to make friends. The Nottingham Crew, as one group of activists from the city were called, were an older crowd, and many of them had ties stretching back decades. Friendships had been forged in the anti-roads movement in 1990s, made famous by the battles against plans to build a bypass near Newbury. Others had been involved in Reclaim the Streets, and had been around long enough to encounter other police spies, such as Jim Boyling. It was never going to be easy for Kennedy to persuade these strangers to trust him. They were serious activists, and could be suspicious of outsiders.

Kennedy would have been provided with a detailed briefing about the group he was infiltrating. Much of this information is likely to have come from other undercover police. His suspected predecessor in Nottingham was an infiltrator who posed as an activist called Rod Richardson. Named in parliament as a suspected police officer, Richardson turned up in 2000 and disappeared shortly before Kennedy was deployed, claiming to be migrating to Australia. He drove a dark blue Peugeot 505 and claimed to be earning money working as a fitness instructor. He was extremely camera-shy; on one occasion, at the G8 summit in Genoa in 2001, he scratched out his face from a photograph of British activists. In other images from the summit, Richardson's face is concealed behind a gas mask, as he poses next to a burning car that has been turned upside down. In all other photographs, he appears to be hiding his face. Richardson rented a room in another activist house and painted the walls with bright red sperm he called his 'worms of doom'.

Kennedy, who was presumably briefed by Richardson about the best way to gain access to activism in Nottingham, chose a similar strategy: renting a spare room at a house near to the Sumac. It was rented by five politically engaged campaigners. Kennedy took a room on the top floor and built himself a four-poster bed from discarded scaffolding. He tried to be the model housemate, washing, cleaning, doing odd jobs around the house. He also made a point of giving his room-mates gifts.

One housemate, the recipient of a T-shirt, says Kennedy was 'a breath of fresh air'. 'He was very creative – good with his hands – and he drove around a lot,' says Loukas Christodolou, then aged 26. 'It was like he was there to enrich our lives.' But there was something about Kennedy that made him a little too keen. 'He was like an Afghan hound with his long hair and puppy eyes. He had this air of extreme vulnerability while also wanting to get stuck in,' Christodoulou adds. 'People in the early days called him "dodgy Mark". He just didn't seem right.'

It was as though Kennedy's housemates could see through the mask. 'Mark Stone looked like a copper,' says Christodoulou. 'He was heavy-built, a kind of lower-middle-class man. He had a certain physical readiness about him. I remember people saying: he can't be a copper, he has a funny eye – he wouldn't get into the police with dodgy eyesight like that.' Others around at the time agree that Kennedy initially struggled to fit in. As one friend puts it: 'Mark needed to prove himself.'

One strategy he used was an NPOIU favourite. One day, Kennedy told his housemates that he had some childhood friends visiting and asked if they could sleep on the sofa. 'They were both heavily dreadlocked and bearded,' says Christodoulou. 'One of them was strawberry blond and had huge amounts of hair – he called himself Ed and he was really jocular. He was just relaxed and joking.' He says the second man was 'dark, with a bit of a beaky nose' and much taller. 'He was totally silent and seemed scared out of his wits. I just assumed he had taken bad drugs back in the day.'

Both of these friends were almost certainly fellow undercover police officers. Lynn Watson used a similar strategy when she introduced two operatives as her boyfriends. So too did Rod Richardson, who occasionally introduced his friends to a woman called 'Jo' who they now believe must have been a fellow spy. Kennedy of course had no reason to introduce his friends to female undercover police, to pretend they were his girlfriends. Doing so would have been counterproductive.

His alter ego was more in keeping with the template used by the SDS for decades: Mark Stone, as activists knew him, was a bachelor looking for a long-term girlfriend.

Within just four months of his Nottingham deployment, Kennedy had chosen his first woman. Lily was a bright and popular 23-year-old whom he met at a political event in Nottingham. 'We started hanging out after that meeting,' she says. 'He was very charismatic, exciting, good fun. He claimed to like country music, caravans. He claimed to be interested in climbing, in travelling, in all kinds of political projects. He seemed like a really nice guy. He was quite a lot older than me – nearly 10 years older. He was very romantic and set the tone for our relationship.'

Kennedy appears to have had no qualms about getting deep into the life of the young activist. On the frequent occasions they passed through London they stayed at her parents' flat in Putney. 'They both had long hair so they would sit down and watch TV, combing each other's hair after it was washed,' says her mum, Pauline. 'He used to eat with us and slob around watching TV with us. All the stuff you do in a relaxed way with people in the family.' The spy worked hard to gain the affections of his girl-friend's family. He bonded with her brother over Chelsea football club and when her mother's choir group sang outside East Putney Tube, Kennedy stood beside them rattling a can for donations. He also accompanied Lily and her mum Pauline on a trip to the theatre, telling them it was the first time he had ever worn a suit.

So close did he become that within just a few weeks of going out with Lily, he found himself at her grandmother's 90th birth-day. There is a photograph of him there, wearing a roll-neck sweater beneath a quilted waistcoat. Pauline said she found her daughter's new boyfriend 'quite funny, good company' but thought he was different to her previous companions. 'Mark was laddish, compared to some of Lily's more cerebral friends,' she says. 'He was not particularly bright or articulate and didn't have a hugely broad vocabulary. He talked about politics in a much more naïve, down to earth kind of way.'

Kennedy's relationship with Lily was profoundly different to the one he had with his Catholic wife in his real life. Lily believed in open relationships, more formally known as polyamory. Propo-nents of open relationships say that this unconventional approach is no less meaningful than traditional, monogamous partnerships, which can leave people feeling shackled. Open relationships are different with each couple, but often the arrangement allows both people to have more than one sexual partner, which advocates say encourages honesty.

This of course allowed Kennedy to have more than one girl-friend at a time. 'He was a bit different from all of us. He ate meat, had a pickup truck and was just not very hippy in a way,' says Anna, a 21-year-old Kennedy slept with around 20 times.

'I knew he was seeing other people at the same time and it was never, you know, any type of romance involved.' It is not possible to know exactly how many women Kennedy slept with during his six years undercover. He claims it was only two. His friends in Nottingham can name more than 10 women he slept with while living in the city and expect there were more. 'It just seemed he was up for sexual liaisons anytime, anyplace, anywhere,' Christodoulou says. 'He had just come on board and he was at it right away. One person I know who had a romantic relationship with him challenged him and said: 'I'm not going any further because I think you're a copper.' Then Mark said something to her which apparently calmed her down.'

Not long after Lily's grandmother's 90th birthday, the effort Kennedy was putting into his second life was paying off. He was attending various political meetings with her up and down the country. He travelled to a May Day protest in Dublin with an anarchist collective called the 'White Overalls Movement Building Libertarian Effective Struggles', or WOMBLES for short. They were famed for their tactic of covering their bodies with white overalls, padding and helmets to protect themselves from riot police, a tactic they anointed 'self-protection from the depredations of the constabulary'. It was the same group that Richardson had infiltrated just a few years earlier.

Kennedy returned from Ireland boasting that he had been drenched in water cannon and nursing his first protest injury, a damaged knee. It was his first bruising encounter with his colleagues in the riot squad, and Kennedy seemed to have relished it. He cut out a newspaper photograph of himself stood in a line of masked anarchists and hung it framed on his living-room wall. After that, Kennedy delved into a panoply of activist events. 'It was really a smorgasbord of grievances,' says a friend. 'It could have been saving the animals one day, stopping the BNP the next day, protesting against a war in some far-flung corner of the world the next day, and then trying to stop an asylum seeker getting deported or a post office closed. I just assumed he was a bit of a lost soul looking for something he could believe in.'

By the following year, Kennedy had inveigled himself into the core of the group mobilising ahead of the G8 summit in Gleneagles. There was no greater NPOIU priority at the time than gleaning intelligence about how protesters planned to disrupt the meeting of world leaders in July 2005. Kennedy would come to view his surveillance operation at the G8 summit as one of the high watermarks of his entire deployment, and claim his reports were reaching the desk of the then prime minister, Tony Blair.

The anti-summit protests were months in the planning. Blair had suggested the G8 would deliver agreement among leaders on two totemic issues: climate change and economic development in the world's poorest nations. Protesters were loosely split into two camps. On one side, there was a large and moderate coalition of trade unions, charities and campaign groups that coalesced under the Make Poverty History banner. They planned a huge demonstration through Edinburgh, capitalising on the spirit of the protests against the Iraq war. On the other were the more radical contingent of anti-capitalist protesters, of whom Kennedy was part, mobilising under the name Dissent. Their objective was to stop the G8 summit meeting from taking place by blockading roads to the fortified hotel and other forms of 'resistance' to the state.

If they were going to be organised, the protesters needed a base, and they chose to construct an Earth First-style campsite 12 miles from the Gleneagles Hotel. It would be another sustainable camp, host to thousands of protesters from across Europe. Kennedy volunteered – and was considered sufficiently trustworthy – to co-ordinate the immense logistical challenge of ferrying equipment to the camp.

He hired a convoy of vans and began touring the country to pick up ropes, portable toilets, tent poles, canvas and other supplies. He was accompanied by a 22-year-old student from Holland named Wietse van der Werf. 'Mark was willing to take stuff on,' he recalls. 'He seemed keen and took the initiative. People just let him get on with it. If you have someone that has a credit card ready to hire any vehicle, and a political movement that doesn't have a lot of funds, then that person becomes very valuable, very quickly.'

The Dutchman remembers a laptop placed on the back seat of Kennedy's pickup truck which was connected remotely to the internet. 'This was 2005 – that was quite uncommon back then,' he says. Kennedy often encouraged activists to borrow his laptop to send emails, presumably to spy on their electronic communications. He was also a fast driver, and had some curious routines. It was only years later, and with the benefit of hindsight, that it dawned on Van der Werf that his friend's driving habits were those of a police officer. 'He took tea breaks all the time and bought food whenever we stopped,' he says. 'He also made a point of keeping all of his receipts.'

In the end, the G8 protests, like the summit they intended to disrupt, did not quite live up to expectations. There were some roads blocked, although never for that long, and an attempt to break through the perimeter fence of the hotel ended when riot police emerged out of Chinook helicopters.

But for Kennedy, the G8 was an impressive milestone. The NPOIU had a whole network of spies at the protests, including both Watson and Jacobs. So too did the SDS, and foreign police spies were invited to attend too. Germany alone sent five undercover police officers. But no infiltrator is believed to have come close to securing the kind of access Kennedy achieved.

He now had a reputation among activists as a reliable and trusted campaigner who could get things done. Just two years after first showing his face in Nottingham's Sumac Centre, Kennedy had wormed himself into the close-knit group of radical activists and, with the help of Lily, landed himself a key role by taking care of logistics, and a new nickname: Transport Mark. He was no longer being viewed through the prism of suspicion. He was just Mark Stone. And he was on a roll.

CHAPTER 15

International Playboy

The commotion started in the semi-darkness, just as the sun began to rise over the peaks of Mount Kárahnjúkur. Kennedy looked on as masked protesters locked themselves to an enormous yellow dump truck. They were in a remote corner of the Icelandic wilderness, battling to stop the construction of a 690-ft dam. And for Kennedy, watching from the sidelines in a flat cap, undercover work was about to get personal.

Among those clambering all over the huge truck was his new girlfriend, Megan, to whom Kennedy had grown very close. The pair had been together for a few months, and it was a whirlwind romance. Now Kennedy watched as Megan used a bicycle D-lock to attach her neck to the vehicle, a tactic often used by activists as a form of civil disobedience. Usually, police will have to spend hours using special cutting equipment to break the lock. Megan and the others hoped that by locking themselves to the truck, they would halt its progress, blockading a major construction route to the dam. Suddenly, there were terrified screams. The protest was not going to plan. Chinese construction workers commanding the truck had turned on the engine and started to inch it forward, protesters still draped to the side. Bones were about to be snapped. Kennedy and some other activists leaped onto the front of the truck, pleading with the driver to stop. Kennedy yanked open the bonnet and started to rip at cables and levers in the dark until the engine fell silent, before pulling the keys out of the ignition and throwing them into a ditch.

Kennedy was furious, believing that Megan had come within an inch of being killed. He scuffled with police guards and was dragged away with his arms held behind his back. 'He possibly saved her life – and he certainly likes to point it out as if he was some kind of hero,' says Olafur Pall Sigurdsson, who led the Saving Iceland campaign. Sigurdsson was not present when Megan chained herself to the yellow truck, but the incident was relayed to him afterwards in detail by Kennedy and others. It even appeared in the newspapers. The Icelandic press were briefed by the police that the incident on the yellow truck was an act of sabotage, and evidence of the violent intent of foreigners flocking to the island. They reported it as such, unaware that the man who immobilised the truck was in fact a British spy.

The battle to save a pristine region from destruction was becoming a priority for European conservationists. The enormous Kárahnjúkur dam was rising out of the bleak volcanic terrain of the eastern highlands like an alien structure. Situated near Europe's largest glacier, it would become the largest of several hydroelectric plants the Icelandic government wanted to build in the area, supplying energy to a huge aluminium smelter plant, 75km to the east.

Kennedy's role in Saving Iceland has been vastly overstated. He was not, Sigurdsson says, involved in any of the direction or control of the campaign. Instead, he was one of the many British activists who joined the campaign, heading to Iceland immediately after the 2005 G8 summit. But Kennedy did show a real interest in the battle against the dam project, and tried to get close to Sigurdsson.

The following year he and Megan joined the Icelandic campaigner on a road trip through Spain, to raise awareness about Saving Iceland. The activists were living a hand-to-mouth existence, camping under the stars or staying in squats. A number were 'freegans', scavenging unused foods from supermarket bins. Kennedy chose a more comfortable existence, a decision that raised eyebrows. 'People were getting a bit pissed off with Mark because he was treating it like a holiday,' Sigurdsson says. 'He was eating in really nice restaurants when everyone else was eating some horrible vegan grub.'

During the trip, an editor of an environmental journal asked Sigurdsson if he could pen an article about the campaign in Iceland. Kennedy offered to write the piece for him. But rather than use his activist identity Mark Stone, Kennedy wrote the article under a pseudonym, 'Lumsk'. It is not uncommon for activists to use aliases when writing online, and Kennedy told his friend that Lumsk was the name of a Norwegian folk-metal band he liked.

Sigurdsson, however, was aware the word had another, somewhat suspicious, meaning in his native tongue. One day, he confronted Kennedy about his choice of pseudonym, telling him that the Icelandic translation was 'duplicitous'. 'He was jolted,' Sigurdsson recalls. 'It was like I had given him a small electric shock – he became aggressive for a few seconds. I thought that was a bit odd.'

As the trip through Spain continued, Kennedy managed to annoy Sigurdsson even more. The Icelandic campaigner was heading a peaceful campaign against the dam project and was finding himself labelled as a dangerous radical on the island. But he says Kennedy began to cajole him to go even further. 'He kept coming to me to say: what you're doing is not really working, is it?' he says. 'All these lock-ons and protest tactics you are using are not effective.'

Sigurdsson believes the undercover police officer was trying to plant ideas in his head. 'The way he said it was: "I know some extremely heavy people. I can get hold of them and they can do some real damage. I can get these people to come over to Iceland." He was talking about seriously damaging the infrastructure of the dam – sabotage.' Sigurdsson says he told Kennedy he wanted nothing to do with violence. 'He kept coming back to me, like some sort of parrot. I was just like, "It is very nice you know these people, Mark, but don't come to me – as far as the Icelandic police are concerned I am already like a Bin Laden."'

Back in Nottingham, Kennedy was settling into his new life with Megan. He had moved out of the shared home and started renting a terraced house near the Sumac, occasionally letting out his spare room to a lodger. It was neatly furnished, with framed pictures from various protests he had been involved in. There was not a huge amount for Kennedy to do during the day. When he wasn't away, telling friends he had found climbing work, he would often wake up early, go for a run, and then disappear for a few hours, saying he had odd jobs to do. It was a domestic life, often revolving around Megan.

They had been together by then for two years and the relationship was serious – equivalent, friends say, to that of a married couple. A warm-hearted and principled woman from Wales, Megan was in her 30s. She has never spoken publicly or been interviewed about her relationship with the undercover police officer, but her friends say she loved him deeply. They would end up being with each other for six years.

They spent time living together, travelled on holiday abroad and spoke to each other every day. He got to know her family in much the same way as he did with Lily, who had split up with him the previous year. It is impossible to know how much, if any, of Kennedy's affection for Megan was genuine, but those who know the couple believe it must have been. Without irony,

Kennedy would one day declare: 'The love I shared with her and the companionship we shared was the realest thing I ever did ... Yeah, there were no lies about that at all.'

Megan was an obvious choice for an undercover police officer to target. She was connected with activists across the country and 'trusted and respected by everyone', according to one friend, who adds: 'She was one of the most universally loved people you could find.' Like Lily, she was also an advocate of polyamory. When she first met Kennedy she had another boyfriend, a thickset man with purple hair called Logan. When Kennedy arrived on the scene, the dynamic obviously shifted. 'We were seven years in by that point and she had not had a relationship with anyone on the scale of what we had,' Logan says.

Logan was keen to accept Kennedy; he says he was pleased that his girlfriend had found a second meaningful relationship. It was an unconventional set-up. In simple terms, Megan had two boyfriends – Kennedy and Logan – and they became good friends. 'He was a really gregarious guy, and for all his kind of blokey, cockney-geezer bluster, there was a real sensitivity and generosity there,' Logan says. 'I used to call him detective inspector Mark. I didn't for a second really think he might be a cop. It was just a comment made in jest, because it was funny how he fit the mould of an infiltrator: turns up out of nowhere, works away all the time, has loads of money, starts seeing somebody who is really central in the protest movement.'

Although, for a few years, Megan had intimate experiences with both men, she eventually chose Kennedy. She had been seeing Logan since 1997, and they remained close. When her father died, both men attended the funeral. Although, according to friends, Megan never agreed to Kennedy's requests for a monogamous relationship, he did become the most important man in her life. 'Both of the women Mark had close, intimate relationships with were very trusted women in the movement,' notes one friend. 'That cannot have been a coincidence.'

Lily, Megan and the other women gave Kennedy access to the heart of radical protest, a place few of his colleagues in the NPOIU are believed to have reached. Routinely, Kennedy found himself at the centre of all the action. One day, he scaled a tree outside the BP oil company's headquarters in Grosvenor Square, in London. On another, he joined a small group of activists who climbed a tower at Didcot power station to hang a 'Climate Crime' banner. Later he locked himself to the gates of a nuclear power station in Hartlepool, wearing a black cap, sunglasses and scarf covering his face.

His friends were noticing a change in the man they knew as Mark Stone. When he first turned up in Nottingham, they had been amused to find his iPod full of 'edgeless rock'. By the middle of 2006 he had started listening to drum and bass dance music, buying himself mixing decks so he could DJ at all-night raves and squat parties. He rarely if ever took drugs but, like his colleagues Lynn Watson and Marco Jacobs, enjoyed a drink. 'Mark drank, certainly most nights,' says Logan. 'And drinking to that really, really, gone state – that memory void thing for him was not uncommon.'

Kennedy was immersed in another world, far away from the staid Tory suburbs where he left his wife and children. He and Megan would go on tree-planting weekends or on long camping expeditions in the Scottish Highlands. One ritual among the group involved savouring a bottle of expensive Port Ellen whisky and talking late into the night. On one such weekend Kennedy arrived with six whisky glasses, each engraved with the name of a friend in the group.

Years later Kennedy would reflect on his life undercover and remark: 'I began to live the life and enjoy it. People have this image of hairy tree huggers and, yes, there is an element of that. But there are also a lot of educated, passionate people with degrees who really believe in what they are doing. There were people who, if they had only a couple of quid left, would buy you a pint. So many people I knew, or Mark Stone knew, became really good friends. It wasn't just about being an activist all the time.'

But the lifestyle came with a cost. For much of the time he was undercover, irrespective of what he was doing, Kennedy was earning overtime. 'Every day I was on the job, even if I was at "home" in bed watching telly and doing the laundry, I got five hours' overtime. My handler got the same,' he said. 'I was taking home more money than an inspector who was two ranks higher than me.' Kennedy was also blowing several thousand pounds a month on rent, petrol, rope equipment, parties, a fleet of new vehicles and flights abroad. He bought himself two bicycles, a top-of-the-range sound system and a Mitsubishi Warrior pick-up truck. His life of adventure, parties and domesticity with Megan was costing the British taxpayer close to £250,000 a year.

Some friends felt his spending habits were incongruous with the lifestyle of an anti-capitalist. But Kennedy was unapologetic, telling friends he was earning 'Hollywood wages' doing climbing work and revelling in his new nickname: Flash. He set up an email account beginning 'flashwheels@' and introduced himself to new people as 'Flash Mark'. By then, some of Kennedy's closer friends were under the impression that he was living off the proceeds of a criminal fortune. 'The story was Mark had been a cocaine courier, and he had made a lot of money doing that,' Logan says. 'But people in that drug world had done his head in. It was just a lot of coked-up, superficial gabbling twats, so he wanted to do something meaningful with his life. It seemed plausible for somebody who was not educated, not especially intelligent, not very old, and yet he had got a wad of money.'

It was not just his persona that was evolving. As he spent more and more time living as Mark Stone, the police spy's appearance changed too. As time passed, he seemed to look like an exaggerated caricature of himself. He started wearing bigger earrings and tight black vests that exposed his torso and an ever-growing collection of tattoos. He was becoming obsessed with a genre known as biomechanical body art. Etched into his forearm was a tattoo that depicted his skin being peeled back to reveal mechanical levers beneath the flesh. It suggested Mark Stone was a shell, and beneath the surface were the mechanics of a robot.

That summer, Kennedy had an altercation that tested his loyalties and left his managers asking who exactly was in control.

The brawl that took place in the shadow of a power station was not a fair fight. On one side was Kennedy, red-faced and with his hair loose and ruffled in the wind. His assailants had helmets and metal batons. It was him versus a handful of armed men, who had no idea that the protester they were beating was a fellow constable, receiving a painful introduction to police brutality.

It was August 2006 and the climax of the Climate Camp gathering in North Yorkshire. There had already been one march, in which protesters donned white paper boiler suits and walked toward the power station carrying a puppet ostrich, to symbolise people with their heads in the sand. Now a splinter group of protesters was trying to break into the grounds of Drax power station to force a temporary closure. The previous night, protesters had crawled through some woodland to bury cutting equipment near the perimeter fence. Kennedy was among a dozen activists, including his girlfriend Megan and his fellow spy Lynn Watson, who were hidden in some bushes, waiting for the right moment to cut open the fence and run inside. With two officers involved in the plan, the NPOIU knew what was about to happen. Unbeknown to the protesters, police were themselves hiding nearby, preparing an ambush.

Kennedy watched as a handful of excited activists scurried out of the shrubbery, snipped the wire fence and started wriggling through the hole like rabbits. One by one, they squeezed into the grounds of the power station. Watson got through. So did Megan. But another woman had only crawled halfway through when riot officers pounced and started beating her legs. Kennedy snapped and lashed out at the officers to distract their attention.

The riot police later described how they were assaulted by a bearded protester without justification. Kennedy told a very different story, claiming that he was dragged to the ground and subjected to a senseless beating. One officer stamped on his back, causing a prolapsed disc. As he was dragged away he was heard shouting: 'This is the face of peaceful protest.'

Back at the camp, he removed his top to allow his friends to photograph his injuries: a badly bruised back, broken finger and a cut forehead. 'He looked like he was in serious pain,' one recalls. 'He said his back was seriously fucked. I remember he said: "They kicked me in, but I beat up some of the coppers so it was worth it."' Kennedy told another friend how the officers pinned him on his back and took turns to punch him in his face. He claimed to have shouted back: 'Your mum punches harder than that.'

The police spy was fuming. He felt he was the victim of an unprovoked attack and believed his assailants should be disciplined. His supervisors at the NPOIU saw the situation rather differently. Operatives were not supposed to engage in hand-to-hand combat with their uniformed colleagues. When Kennedy's handler asked to meet with him, he refused. Instead he emailed his superiors pictures of his injuries and took to the activist website Indymedia to decry the 'deluge of police brutality' meted out at the power station. When the NPOIU ordered Kennedy to leave his activist friends and return to his wife and children, he replied with an astonishing text message. 'I'm going to stay here for the time being, where people are actually going to take care of me,' it said. 'You've completely fucked it up.'

Police chiefs now had a rogue officer on their hands. Kennedy was openly disobeying orders. He was out of control, a loose cannon. If he had been an officer in the SDS, Kennedy would almost certainly have been pulled from the job with immediate effect. Managers like Bob Lambert were conscious of the risks of long-term spies showing split loyalties, and would terminate deployments at the slightest whiff of disloyalty. Senior officers in the NPOIU, however, were reluctant to lose their top operative. Kennedy had undergone a number of assessments with psychologists, none of which returned any concerns. He was delivering superb intelligence, both in the UK and abroad.

Toward the end of the year, after a stern warning about who was paying his wages, Kennedy was allowed to return to Megan. The couple headed straight to Germany, where Kennedy had been developing some promising friendships. It was the start of a sustained period of foreign travel for the undercover police officer, who made Berlin a base for his activities on the continent. 'He knew quite a few people already,' says Jason Kirkpatrick, an activist Kennedy stayed with in the city. 'We went out pretty much every night. And we drank a lot. It is no secret that Mark loved Berlin. He told me it was his favourite city.'

Some people who knew Kennedy in Germany say he adopted a more brooding, dark persona over there. He spent some of his time infiltrating black bloc anarchists, famed for hiding their faces behind ski masks and military balaclavas. The spy himself claims to have met some 'fairly serious people' in Berlin, and obtained a manual about how to construct incendiary devices and derail trains which, he says, was accidentally shredded by the NPOIU.

Kirkpatrick says he was unaware the police officer was meeting violent campaigners, although he seemed to want to. The Berlin resident recalls one awkward conversation with Kennedy after a night of heavy drinking. 'He said to me: "Jason, I've been meaning to ask you, do you know any serious neo-Nazis? Because if you know anyone that needs to be taken out, I've got the crew in England who can sort them out."' Kirkpatrick says he was 'shocked to hear him talk of violence like that'.

While working in Germany, Kennedy was listed as an 'informant' by police authorities in the country. The status should have explicitly barred him from having intimate relationships with women he was spying on, which is prohibited under German law. He is known to have had sex with at least two women in Germany, but there could have been more. But Kennedy's trips to the country did not appear particularly impeded by rules or regulations. He was only formally authorised on two operations, first to gather intelligence about plans to disrupt the G8 summit and second to infiltrate protests against a NATO meeting near Strasbourg. However, Kennedy came and went from Germany as he pleased, once after no more than a phone call informing German authorities that a British spy was on his way.

He was twice arrested in Germany, the second time after a mysterious incident involving an arson attack in the street. It was unclear whether he had received clearance to even be in Berlin at that time, let alone to commit crime. He was becoming something of a lone agent. At least once, Kennedy travelled abroad despite being instructed by the NPOIU not to go. These foreign missions occasionally appear to have taken his colleagues by surprise.

On one occasion, he was spotted in Berlin by Watson, who appears to have been stunned to see him there. She was in the city for the annual May Day protest with her friend Matilda, when they saw Kennedy appear suddenly out of a bustling crowd, the lower part of his face covered with a bandanna. 'Lynn just looked so shocked,' says Matilda. 'I was saying to Mark: "What are you doing here?" He was like, "Oh, I just came over, I've kind of got to go." Then he rushed off.'

Whatever Kennedy was getting up to in Germany, it was not the only place his services were required. In the space of just a few years he travelled to Denmark, Greece, Italy, Spain, Iceland, France, Poland and America as well as Germany. In France, he claimed to have witnessed activists practising bomb-making near a small village, a claim that was later cast in doubt. In the bureaucratic-speak of European intelligence sharing, Kennedy was monitoring 'Euro-anarchism', and was one of a fleet of British spies travelling all over Europe. So many resources were going into these trips that, during one European protest meeting in Poland, two out of the three Britons present were police spies. The British delegation, who travelled to Poland together, consisted of Kennedy, Jacobs, and just one genuine protester.

In total, Kennedy worked in 11 countries. One of his more curious foreign deployments was to New York in 2008, a visit that resulted in a special commendation from the Federal Bureau of Intelligence. It is not exactly clear what Kennedy did to earn the approval of the FBI, other than attend a meeting in Manhattan, amid the first stirrings of what would become the Occupy Movement, and tip them off about a supposed French revolutionary who had visited the country.

Back in Nottingham, Kennedy was gaining a reputation as a committed activist with a thousand connections abroad. He was fast becoming one of the people activists turned to when planning an ambitious protest, particularly if they needed help with transport. When friends concocted a plan to take over a train delivering coal to Drax power station in 2009, Kennedy agreed to ferry them to the location in a transit van. Posing as railway workers, the activists used red flags to wave the train to a halt on a bridge over the river Aire. They then clambered on board and politely informed the driver they were taking over his cargo. The campaigners were commended by a judge for making an 'eloquent, sincere, moving and engaging' case for why they stopped the train, but he found them guilty of obstructing a railway engine under the Malicious Damages Act of 1861.

Kennedy was also known as the master of logistics. He helped build more Climate Camps, first near Heathrow airport, and later at Kingsnorth power station in Kent. It was always a huge upheaval, and could take months to prepare. Like his colleagues Watson and Jacobs, the police spy was often unable to conceal his frustration with his activist friends. Kennedy often complained that activists could be disorganised and moaned about the effort that was required to pick up protest camp equipment – the generators, marquees and tools that activists call their 'tat'.

It was partly for this reason that Kennedy pushed for the creation of a group called the Activist Tat Collective. They found a warehouse in which to store protest equipment, and conducted a proper audit of the materials they owned. The idea was that the ATC provided a more centralised, efficient system, and that anyone organising a major protest could loan out equipment on request. In practical terms, that meant asking for a key for the storage depot from the director of the group – Kennedy.

It was a remarkable achievement. The go-to man for anyone wanting to organise a big protest camp was an undercover spy from the NPOIU. Kennedy even wrote the manual, or 'recipe book', as the collective called their guide to building protest sites. The document detailed the quantities of food needed for a vegan kitchen (5kg of bulgar wheat will feed 60–80 people) and contained diagrams for constructing toilets from straw bales. The chapter about transport was written by 'Lumsk'. He opened with a wry complaint about the 'endless meetings focusing upon going round in circles' that he had endured over the years.

Kennedy's chapter, which detailed the kinds of trucks, vans and quad bikes required to construct a large campsite overnight, was his opportunity to impart advice that had been gleaned, as he put it, 'from the experiences, adventures, trials and tribulations of a few who have burnt some rubber'. He cautioned that drivers in the world of activism were in short supply and warned that arguments could often degenerate into 'sarcasm, tears or a few terse and sharp words between gritted teeth ... You must remember that you will be collecting generously donated yurts and tepees from people who have a different understanding of time management to the efficiently clockwork-like and synchronised transport collective,' he added. 'An element of frustration at this point is inevitable.'

The tone was classic Kennedy: jokey, laddish, perhaps a little self-important. It was a persona that had served him well over the years. By the end of 2008, Kennedy was reaching the zenith of his undercover deployment. He projected the image of a veteran activist who could be confided in with the most sensitive of plans. That reputation would enable one last major act in Kennedy's undercover mission. And it would end in a catastrophe.

CHAPTER 16
Rock and Roll Star

It began at 11.07pm one Sunday night, when a police chief with a pot belly stood in a warehouse in the city and began addressing his men; there were around 200 of them, stood in rows and dressed in the black protective clothing of the riot squad.

'Right, ladies and gentleman,' he shouted. 'First of all, can everybody hear me? I don't intend to use a microphone if I can help it. Right. Welcome to Operation Aeroscope. Many of you, I guess, will be wondering what we are doing here and what all of this is about. I am not going to go into all of the information that surrounds this, only to say that there is information that a group of individuals intent on ... erm.'

The senior officer was lost for words. 'How can I put it? Disrupting a major ... erm.' He scratched his bald head and folded his arms: 'Erm...'

The crowd of riot officers started laughing.

'Power station!' their boss barked. 'Within the east Midlands area!'

Regaining his composure, the police chief gave a brief rundown of the operation to intercept activists who were planning to disrupt the Ratcliffe-on-Soar power station. 'There is information that these individuals are at this moment at a location called Iona school, which is off Sneinton Dale. We're expecting up to 100 individuals at the premises. They are in possession of

items that would allow them to disrupt a generating establishment for up to seven days, which is probably unprecedented in
this country. They are in possession of lock-on equipment. They
are in possession of food which will keep them going for seven
days and vehicles to assist them in that.'

He paused and looked out at the crowd of officers. They had
been drafted in from across the region, some of them taken off
leave during the long Easter weekend in April 2009. It was dawning on the men that they were going to see some action and the
excitement showed on their faces.

'The intention of this operation is to enter their premises, by
force, under warrant, and arrest all 100 of them,' the commanding officer said. 'Again, pretty unprecedented in this force and
you can imagine the planning that has gone into it.' Both sides –
police and activists – had been preparing for this moment for seven
months. They were less than an hour away from the crescendo.

The plan to break into the power station was hatched by five
eco-activists. Two were undergraduate students, Tom and
Penny. Childhood friends, they typified the new crop of articulate, young campaigners pouring into the movement against
climate change. By their own admission, they were also a little
naïve. Tom, who was 21, was initially surprised that the veteran
campaigners wanted to collaborate with two students. 'You do
know we don't know anything about direct action at all?' he
remembers telling them. 'Are you sure you want us involved?'
Penny, a 20-year-old, was also taken aback. 'We were rookies,
basically. I was amazed they wanted to work with us. We were
in our early 20s and working with seasoned activists and they
respected us. We were so excited.'

The other three activists involved in the plot were older and
more experienced, and two already had experience of breaking

into power stations. But none of the group had ever taken part in a demonstration on the scale of what was now planned. The idea was to quietly recruit more than 100 activists from across the country for a showpiece act of civil disobedience: breaking into the Nottinghamshire station, turning off the generator and occupying the plant for a week. If they pulled it off, this was likely to be the most high-profile direct action against global warming in British history.

Discretion had to be absolute, and the security precautions were a baptism of fire for Tom and Penny, who were quickly exposed to the rigours of 'activist security' and counter-espionage. None of the five could confide in anyone outside the group, discuss their plans on the telephone or behave in a way that might raise suspicions among family or friends.

During one of the first meetings, Penny and Tom were told to sit on a bench outside Angel Tube station in north London. They waited there until a man cycled past and gave them an address scribbled on a piece of paper. It was for a terraced house in nearby Finsbury Park. When they arrived, the man on the bike and two other activists were waiting for them. At each meeting, they were given the address of the next rendezvous, and instructed to write down the details on pieces of paper in code. Meetings took place in London, Oxford, Nottingham and Leeds and they chose locations they were confident would not be bugged; church halls, crowded pubs or student houses.

'We were never meeting in activist-related places,' says Tom. Fearing their phones might be tracked, they left them switched on in their homes each time they met. If police were monitoring their movements through their phones, they would assume they had been at home. And they always paid for bus and train tickets with cash. For the university students, life was overtaken with some elaborate routines.

Penny, whose job, among other things, was to take notes at meetings, was told to periodically destroy the evidence. One night every few weeks she would wait until the early hours of the morning before stepping outside her Oxford college dorm. When she was sure no one was watching, she hurried along a cobbled path, past a lake, to what she thought was a suitable hiding place. Wrapped in a red overcoat and carrying matches, lighter fluid and a tin pot filled with the incriminating pieces of paper, she kneeled down and started a fire. 'I never felt so safe as when I had burned everything,' she says.

Tom had his own curious ritual. In order to make sure his friends did not know he was missing from university in Swansea, he made a point of going out drinking with them the night before he had a planning meeting. They would often end up in a nightclub. The only thing that made Tom stand out was his backpack. At 3am, when his friends were drunk, he would slink off into the darkness and head straight for the train station to catch the night train into London. 'No one would know I was gone,' he says.

Two months into the planning, Tom, Penny and the three other activists had reached a crucial stage. They had drawn up detailed plans and studied maps of the power plant. Now it was time to undertake a reconnaissance visit. After weeks of silence and caution, the time had also come to allow a sixth person into their plot. They needed a driver to take them to the power station. It had to be somebody who was totally trusted and experienced, a driver who was familiar with the local area.

'We were told we were going to get driven up to the power station by this guy called Flash,' says Tom. His friend Penny says the decision made sense at the time. 'Mark Kennedy was just known as the man when it came to activist skills,' she says. 'He was always up for it and at the centre of everything and just completely trusted and sound.'

At 6am on January 10, after a night at the Sumac Centre in Nottingham, the activists were woken by tapping on the window. They came out of their sleeping bags and opened the curtains to see Kennedy standing outside in the semi-darkness. He looked worried. Despite his efforts, he claimed to have been unable to hire a car. They were going to have to drive to the power station in his personal vehicle. 'We just thought: we cannot possibly go in Mark Stone's own car because he is such a prominent activist – he must be known to police,' says Tom. 'But we had no choice.'

An hour later, Kennedy's Octavia estate was parked up in a layby in the village of Thrumpton, 12 miles outside Nottingham. Kennedy, as ever, was in the driving seat. He and another activist were going to drive around the power station to assess the access routes. Meanwhile, Tom, Penny and a third campaigner were tasked with getting as near to the power plant as possible to take photographs with a long-lens camera. They got out of the car and walked south, the silhouettes of cooling towers appearing in the dawn light. They found their way through a muddy field and a small wood before they reached the footpath that circles the reinforced steel fence defending Ratcliffe-on-Soar power station.

'It was absolutely terrifying because we were just thinking about all the ludicrous security precautions we had taken to not get found out,' says Penny. 'And here we are, at the perimeter of the massive power station with the biggest long-lens camera I have ever seen in my life, taking photographs of all of the mechanisms. We were photographing how the site was laid out, the infrastructure, the access routes.'

It did not go to plan. Out of nowhere, two security guards stopped them in their tracks. The guards demanded to know what they were doing. 'We had a cover story,' says Penny. 'We were arts students at Nottingham Trent university and we were doing a project on the intersection of nature and industry. We wanted to get some images of this crazy futuristic architecture and the beauty of the nature around it. We were absolutely terrified so I was just babbling telling this story. Eventually we were basically sent on our way.'

They returned to Thrumpton and waited for Kennedy and the activist in a village hall. When the car arrived, they nervously bundled into the back and headed back to Nottingham. They had been driving for a few minutes when someone in the rear of the vehicle shouted: 'Shit! Where is the camera?' The large camera, containing dozens of incriminating images of the power station, was missing. 'Mark just reversed and turned around the car and said: "OK, stay calm people,"' says Tom. 'He said we should retrace our steps and we went back to the village hall and found the camera in the toilets.'

It was a close shave and, for Tom and Penny, perhaps a little embarrassing. They were the youngest in the group of five core organisers, and the least experienced. Mostly, they were treated as equals. However, both of them got the feeling that Kennedy was looking down at them. 'I was torn between thinking he was really cool – a super-experienced activist – and a bit of a cock,' says Penny. 'He was just quite arrogant and definitely clearly enjoyed the company of young women. I felt Mark just had this attitude towards us that we were kids who had bitten off more than we could chew.'

As it turns out, that is more or less what Kennedy did think about the two students. His verdict is contained in the reports he was sending back to his handlers at the NPOIU. The restricted documents, marked 'secret', reveal another side to Kennedy: his work as an intelligence source. He made a parting reference to Tom and Penny, describing them merely as 'youths believed to be based in London'. One NPOIU document, based on Kennedy's intelligence, states: 'Youngsters are getting more and more involved with climate change issues on the back of this year's Climate Camp.' It adds that they are less of a threat than other activists and 'just want to save the world from climate change'.

Kennedy's communications to his bosses provide a revealing insight into the inner workings of the NPOIU. The reconnaissance trip to the power station, for example, is covered in remarkable detail, even recording the incident involving the lost camera. 'The two girls realised that they had left the telephoto stills camera somewhere,' Kennedy reports. 'It apparently contained photographs of strategic points of Ratcliffe power station. They were very worried. I got them to retrace their steps verbally. It transpired that one of the girls had taken it into the toilet in the village hall. We returned to the hall and the camera was retrieved.'

The police operative's secret reports to his managers reveal the depth of access he had. Remarkably, given all the precautions taken by the five activists, Kennedy knew about the plan to break into the power station before he was even asked to drive them to the plant. Two months before Kennedy was approached by the activists, his superiors had authorised a surveillance operation, stating in internal NPOIU documents that they were aware there was a protest that could 'damage' a power station and could cause a 'severe economic loss to the United Kingdom and have an adverse effect on the public's feeling of safety and security'. Kennedy was the undercover officer tasked with finding out as much as he could.

A few weeks after he drove the activists to the power station, Kennedy filed another report, this time detailing the precise time and date the protesters planned to occupy the plant. By now he had also established the scale of what they were attempting, telling his bosses that protesters were 'hoping to recruit 150 people to take part'. This was intelligence gold dust. It enabled the NPOIU to liaise with the Nottinghamshire police force and devise a plan to scupper the protest, exploiting the fact they had Kennedy in a prime position.

The question was: how far should the undercover officer go? Kennedy was asked by the activists to perform his familiar role as driver, carrying a truckload of equipment to the power station on the night of the occupation. But the campaigners also wondered whether he might use his rope expertise to help them with another critical part of their plan: climbing. Getting into the power station was not going to be the hard part. The challenge would be forcing the plant to turn off its generators and prevent it from operating for a week.

The activists had figured out that if they immobilised key parts of the infrastructure, the energy giant E.ON would have no choice but to turn off the coal-burning furnaces for health and safety reasons. They would switch to an emergency supply of gas-produced energy, thereby leading to a huge reduction in carbon emissions for the period during which the plant was occupied. If they could keep the furnaces turned off for seven days, they calculated that they would be preventing the emission of 150,000 tonnes of carbon dioxide into the atmosphere.

That was where the climbers came in. The plan was for a team of climbers to scale one of four chimneys and force the furnaces to be turned off. One activist would abseil down inside the shaft and hang a 'bat tent'; an expensive, cradle-like contraption used by professionals to suspend themselves beneath vertical cliffs. There was no way E.ON could turn on its furnaces with an environmental campaigner hanging inside one of the chimneys. If things went to plan, and they had sufficient food and water, the climber would be able to stay suspended inside the chimney for a week.

Kennedy was in a Wetherspoon's pub at Leeds railway station when the elaborate plan involving the climber and the chimney was relayed to him for the first time. It was just two weeks before the Easter protest was due to commence. He was sat drinking a beer with a veteran campaigner, one of the five, including Tom and Penny, who had been organising the direct action from the start. The two men scrutinised aerial images of the chimney stacks and talked about what was required. Kennedy recounted his conversation in one of his NPOIU reports.

'He started to explain the Ratcliffe action,' Kennedy wrote of the conversation. 'He asked if I was prepared to be the main climber on the action.' The activist who met with Kennedy that day denies he proposed the undercover police officer should take the star role of abseiling into the chimney stack. However, according to Kennedy's account to his bosses, this was exactly what he was asked to do. He told his superiors that, if he agreed to the role, he would have a mobile internet device so they could broadcast updates from inside the chimney. 'I would then be able to take pictures of the event and myself wearing a gas mask and send them around the world,' Kennedy reported. 'He said I would be broadcast around the world and jokingly said I would be a hero. He said if we pulled it off it will be amazing.'

Kennedy may have wanted to take the lead climbing role in the protest, but he was informed by his supervisor that this was out of the question. Detective inspector David Hutcheson had been Kennedy's cover officer for the last six years. He had been his shadow, tracking his movements, reading his emails and text messages, staying in nearby hotels in case of an emergency and sanctioning his every move. In theory, it was Hutcheson's job to make sure Kennedy never crossed the line. On April 9, the eve of the planned Easter weekend protest, Hutcheson met with Kennedy. The two police officers went through a familiar ritual that takes place before covert operations: the senior officer reads aloud a set of guidelines called 'instructions to undercover officers', recapping what they have been tasked to do and the limits of their powers.

Technically, like all the other SDS and NPOIU officers, Kennedy was supposed to only ever be an observer, taking part in criminal activity as a last resort. His instructions for the next 48 hours were explicit: his job was to obtain 'pre-emptive intelligence' and explore 'possible opportunities to disrupt' the protest at the power station. He only had permission to hire a van and drive activists to the gates of the power station. He was prohibited from entering the site and barred from taking part in the demonstration.

That much was standard practice. But this particular operation would differ from the others in one crucial way. Rather than just monitoring the activists, Kennedy's supervisors wanted him to gather evidence against them, using a specially modified covert watch.

The following morning he went to the Nottingham offices of All Truck Vehicle rentals and hired a 7.5-tonne lorry. He gave the manager of the company Mark Stone's fake passport and driving licence, which contained a recent speeding fine. He used Mark Stone's Maestro debit card to pay £278.48 for the rental and left a £500 cash deposit. The manager of the hire company later provided this description of the customer: 'I would describe Mark Stone as a white male, 5ft 10in to 6ft tall, mid- to late 30s in age, of a medium build, with long brown hair tied in a ponytail. He had distinctive boss eyes, in that his eyes looked in different directions.'

Kennedy drove the van to the Iona primary school in the suburbs of Nottingham, where activists from across the country were scheduled to meet the following day. One campaigner had keys to a disused wing of the school and it was empty over the Easter break. If anyone asked, the activists planned to say that they were hosting a weekend of workshops, teaching sustainability through street theatre. To add credibility to this cover story, they had even advertised the Ecological Showstoppers weekend and printed hundreds of flyers for the fake event. All of the protesters who were heading to Nottingham knew, of course, that they would be involved in something more exciting than amateur dramatics. But they had no idea exactly what kind of protest was planned. Details of the protest had only been shared on a need-to-know basis – the core group of five had expanded now to around a dozen. Only they knew the magnitude of what was being planned.

Over the next 24 hours, scores of minivans would depart towns and cities across the UK and bring activists to Nottingham. Each minibus driver had a set of instructions, maps and a mobile phone with an unregistered SIM card. They were told to stay in touch with base at the Iona school for further directions. There was always the chance the protest would be pulled at the last minute, so the drivers were told not to set off on their journey until the phone beeped with a text message confirming the all-clear. If organisers had counted correctly, more than 100 activists would start arriving at the school the following morning.

Once everyone was at the school, they would be split into groups and given a detailed briefing about what the direct action involved and the specific role each individual would have if they decided to take part. It was inevitable that some people would drop out. This was a radical direct action protest, and anyone inside the power station was likely to face arrest for trespass. It was a risk some would take out of conviction to the cause, but not everyone. Those activists who agreed to the plan would be ferried to the power station in the middle of the night in three 7.5-tonne trucks, two people carriers and a Ford transit. The vehicles had already been packed with bolt cutters, angle-grinders, ropes, metal fences, food, concrete blocks and bicycle D-locks. They had prepared for every eventuality, except perhaps the possibility that they had already been rumbled.

The activists first began to grow concerned that police knew about their plan that evening. There were still only around a dozen activists at the school and some of them decided to take a quick drive around the power station to go over the route they planned to take the following night. They returned to the school with some bad news: parked around the power station, in what looked like strategic spots, were three police cars. 'We just thought: Oh, no! Oh fuck! They know about it!' says Tom. 'It was just completely gutting. All of the work we had put in over the months and now it seemed there were police there guarding the station.'

It would have been foolish to attempt to break into the plant when the entrance was being protected by police. For a brief period, they considered changing the target of the protests, heading instead to Kingsnorth power station in Kent. After lengthy discussions, they decided it was impractical to switch power stations at the last minute. If the police cars remained outside the Nottinghamshire power plant, there was no choice – they would have to abandon the protest altogether. The organisers phoned the minibus drivers and told them not to set off in the morning; the protest would have to be put on hold until further notice. Tom remembers the look on the face of a stalwart of the protest scene, someone who, like him, had spent months preparing for this moment. 'He looked absolutely broken. We all did, I suppose.'

There was a sombre mood at the Iona school the next morning. Activists had intermittently driven past the power station through the night and each time the three police cars were still there. It looked like they were on the verge of having to pull their plans. It was 8.30am on that Sunday morning when Kennedy told activists he would make one last visit to the power station to see whether police were still guarding the facility. He left the school in a taxi. Away from the activists, he would have been expected to call his superiors at the NPOIU, and explain that the protest was about to be called off because activists had seen police guarding the station. At that point, police could have chosen to arrest the dozen depressed-looking activists sat around the school. They could be sure they were arresting some of the key organisers, before all the other protesters had even started travelling to Nottingham. Instead, they chose a different course of action.

When Kennedy returned to the school 90 minutes later he was smiling. 'They've gone,' he told the other activists. 'There are no police there. No cars. No nothing.'

The other campaigners were ecstatic. With police apparently no longer outside the power station, there was still a chance they could get inside. They sent messages to the minivan drivers: the protest was on again, and they should bring the activists to Nottingham as soon as possible. Tom recalls the irony of that decision: 'We did not know we were phoning up activists across the country and telling them to come to Nottingham for what was essentially a police trap.'

Kennedy walked away to find a quiet corner of the room where he could not be heard. He rolled back his sleeve and lifted his watch to his mouth. 'I am an authorised undercover police officer engaged on Operation Pegasus,' he whispered. 'This weekend, Easter weekend, I am together with a group of activists that are planning to disrupt Ratcliffe-on-Soar power station.' He paused. 'Shortly gonna go, to record briefings that subsequently take place throughout the day ... The time on the watch is 10.06am.'

Kennedy's reports to the NPOIU record what happened next. 'People arrived at the school throughout the day. I recognised many people and knew them from various parts of the UK, including London, Bristol, Manchester, Sheffield, Leeds,

Nottingham and Scotland.' What Kennedy omitted from this report was that these people were by now his friends; some were pals from the Sumac Centre, including Logan.

The school was transformed into a buzz of activity by the arrival of the activists. Small parties arrived throughout the afternoon, unloading sleeping bags and carrying stocks of food into the school, while others slipped out of the back, to burn bundles of incriminating paper at a nearby allotment.

By the evening, all 114 activists were gathered in one room in the Iona school to hear a briefing about the planned protest. It was around that time that the pot-bellied police chief was briefing the riot squad in a warehouse a few miles away, preparing them for the impending mass arrests. In just a few hours, these two worlds would collide.

Kennedy was sat with his fellow activists in the school and, for the second time, activated his watch to work as a recording device. It picked up the excited murmur of more than a hundred campaigners against global warming packed into a single room. It was now dark outside and everyone who needed to be at the school had arrived. Above the chatter, the watch strapped to Kennedy's wrist captured snippets of his brief discussion with a man sat next to him.

'Gonna get a bit hot in here as well, ain't it?' Kennedy said.

'Yeah, in about an hour's time,' the man replied.

'Yeah.'

'There's no air flow and there's lots of people.'

The conversation was interrupted by the sound of applause. Someone at the front of the room had stood up and was beginning to talk in a deep voice. It was one of the five organisers.

'Everyone bear with us a bit. It has been a long night and this is amazing,' he said. 'The basic plan – there is a big power station over there, it emits 10 million tonnes of CO_2 every year. That's more than the 41 lowest-emitting countries in the world. We're gonna go and shut them down for seven days.' The man's voice was drowned out by the sound of cheering and clapping.

Taking turns, the five activists explained various aspects of the plan. They stressed that even though people had travelled for miles to reach Nottingham, they should not feel obliged to participate in the protest. Each person had to decide if they wanted to be involved and agree to abide with strict safety procedures, avoiding interference with the water flow system and the potentially toxic cooling towers.

The direct action was laid out with clockwork precision. At precisely 3am, they would climb into their allotted vehicle and head to the power station in teams. The convoy of vehicles would first drive to a 24-hour café for truck drivers that was perhaps a mile from the power station. They would wait a few minutes and then drive off in a pre-planned order. Activists were divided into colour-coded groups, each assigned a different role. At the front of the convoy would be the people carrier and transit van containing the orange team. Their job was to force their way through the gate and ensure the other vehicles could get in. Once everyone was safely inside the grounds, they would use arm locks made out of fire-extinguisher shells to form a human barricade across the entrance, preventing police from accessing the site and buying time for everyone else.

The bronze team, dressed in suits, would make a beeline for the power station control room and calmly inform managers that a peaceful protest was underway, demanding they turn off the furnaces for the safety of those involved. Meanwhile, the blue team would head toward the nearby river – used to channel water into the cooling towers – and lock themselves to the pump facility. They were instructed not to tamper with the water pump mechanism – their role was simply to distract police and security guards by causing a nuisance. The silver team was also a decoy. Tasked with creating the 'illusion of chaos' inside the power station, they would splinter into small groups and lock themselves to any components they could find. When police arrived they would be baffled by the mayhem and forced to attend to activists locked on to various parts of the plant.

All of which was the perfect distraction, allowing the two most important teams in the protest to get on with their work. One was the black team, which would be driven to the power station in the back of Kennedy's truck. Its role was crucial: immobilising the enormous conveyor belt that delivers coal into the four furnaces. It was a tricky climbing task. When Kennedy parked his truck inside the grounds of the power station, the back doors would be flung open and activists would come streaming out wearing harnesses and helmets and carrying rope equipment. Halting the conveyor system by pressing an emergency button, they would clamber on top and wrap their ropes around the huge, car-sized teeth used to scoop up the coal. Once secure, they planned to suspend themselves underneath the conveyor belt, preventing the power station managers from turning it on. Police would arrive to find a handful of protesters dangling 20ft off the ground and the furnaces would be starved of fuel and turned off.

If the protest went to plan, the ground would be prepared for the most important group of all: the green team of specialist climbers who by then would have scaled one of the four towering chimney stacks. High above the rest of the power station, they would be able to see the glow of Nottingham beyond distant hills, and a snake of cars making its way along the nearby M1 motorway. These activists would harness themselves to the stack to avoid being blown over in the wind and then begin the delicate procedure of entering the chimney, abseiling down and suspend-ing their bat tent. By the time the sun appeared over the hills, they would spot the first TV satellite vans parked down below, as news spread of the occupation. Whoever was inside the tent would turn on a small laptop and begin broadcasting live around the world.

The bubble was popped shortly after midnight, when most activists were inside their sleeping bags in the school, trying to get to sleep. 'Bang,' recalls Tom. 'Something gets smashed. Then we just see police storming in from every direction.' A police video camera captured the scene inside one room in the school minutes after the raid: two dozen sullen-looking activists, staring at the floor in silence. The camera panned round at the sound of banging and glass breaking elsewhere in the building.

'Sir, there is a locked door here,' an officer shouted.

'We're going to enter here by force, OK,' said another. 'We haven't got a key.'

Inside, some activists were hurriedly trying to eat scraps of paper containing their notes. Moments later, a senior police officer stood in the middle of the room and said: 'You are all under arrest on suspicion of being involved in a conspiracy to commit aggravated trespass and/or criminal damage at a power industry facility.' One activist began singing Vera Lynn's 'We'll Meet Again' and, slowly, everyone joined in. Then they began a chorus of Dolly Parton's '9 to 5 (What a Way to Make a Living)', to mock the banality of police work. 'It was a surreal moment,' one activist remembers. 'But it lifted everyone's spirits.'

The police raid was unprecedented. Throughout the history of the SDS and NPOIU, police always waited for a protest to happen before arresting the suspects. Sometimes there would be clever ploys to disrupt a planned demonstration. But never before had riot police stormed in to arrest this number of activists before they had even begun. This was the birth of a new strategy: wait for activists to gather in one place and then pre-emptively arrest them on charges of 'conspiracy'. Kennedy had just facilitated the largest pre-emptive arrest – for any type of crime – in modern policing history.

Over the next few hours, activists were frogmarched, one by one, into the school gym where they were searched and made to pose for a police camera. Among the less co-operative was Kennedy, dressed head to toe in black and still wearing his watch. The arresting officers had no idea he was a police spy.

'You're being mass-arrested mate, just face here,' a policeman told him. 'You've been arrested and now you will be individually arrested by this officer.'

Kennedy turned to one side and stared into the middle distance. He looked drained. He was handcuffed and taken with the others to the waiting police vans parked outside the school to be transferred to a police cell. Among the last to be escorted out was Penny. 'I remember walking out the school and there were so many flashing police vans,' she says. 'I couldn't see anything but blue.'

The barn in Herefordshire was packed to the rafters with a drunken crowd. A bunch of veteran activists were turning 40 and this was their joint party: a weekend celebration in honour of eight old-timers who had been born in a year synonymous with protest: 1969. They had formed a rock band for the occasion called 'The 69ers', and the amateur musicians were about to take to the stage. They were all wearing black T-shirts printed with an image of a couple going down on each other in the so-called '69' position. It was five months after the raid on the school, and many of the people in the barn were on bail over the planned occupation of the power station. Now, though, they were in a mood for partying. Logan looked the part on drums, his purple hair draped over his shoulders. So too did Kennedy, who was wearing a black trilby hat and posing with an electric guitar.

Kennedy had been waiting for this moment for months. It was the peak of his six-year deployment, a final moment in the spotlight for Mark Stone, his alter ego. Kennedy was the person who first suggested the joint 40th birthday bash for him and his friends. A trail of email correspondence reveals quite how much the party meant to the undercover police officer. One of the first emails came from Logan: 'Following a suggestion from the venerable Flash Mark, over the last year or so we've made noises about having a joint party in 2009 for all those of us turning 40,' he wrote. He summarised the idea of the weekend party, a kind of Earth First without the politics. To prevent 'a ruck with the cops' they would hire a venue instead of squatting in a field. It would be a family affair, with space for camping and activities for guests with children. Logan wanted to incorporate just a bit of political activity as 'a great affirmation of our common politics'.

Kennedy could not conceal his excitement. He promised to DJ a 'flash drum and bass set' and even offered to pay for a Croatian band called Analena to fly over to perform a set. 'Eastern Europe anarchist punk,' Kennedy told his friends. 'It keeps you young, a must-have for any 40th.' He didn't like Logan's suggestion of adding politics to the mix, but told the others they could 'crack on if you feel the need to wave banners in front of something'. Transport Mark promised to 'rustle up' a marquee from his Activist Tat Collective and said he would take care of logistics for the weekend. 'Whatever we want,' he told his friends. 'It's all possible.'

The police spy promised to write some poems for the occasion and said he would buy everyone themed printed T-shirts, joking he could get them from an ethical supplier who would guarantee 'water, food, a bike and education for a family of 16 in Mozambique'. The celebrators calculated they could fit around 350 of their closest friends on the farm. Kennedy's list of potential guests was testament to the friendships he had forged during his years undercover; it was filled with the names of hundreds of activists, including some from Germany. A flyer produced for the party was composed of pictures of John Lennon and Yoko Ono and a hippy confronting police with a flower.

In the dozens of emails Kennedy sent to his friends in the lead-up to the party, there was one topic he mentioned more than any other: the 69ers band. When his friends agreed to form the rock group 'for one night only', Kennedy replied: 'Excellent, excellent. I have a lead guitar and an amp, I'm sure we can borrow drums from the bands that play. I also have a banjo and a large bongo. Or so I am told!' He added: 'I have lyrics already forming in my head for a bit of a song about all of us and 69 and crazy times.' A few months later he told his friends he had been practising guitar 'until my fingers bleed' and learned 'a bunch of tunes I can thrash out in an angsty punk style'. He seemed obsessed.

Of course, thoughts of his imminent debut on stage as a rock artist distracted Kennedy from darker thoughts. Dozens of his closest friends were on bail over the planned occupation of Ratcliffe-on-Soar power station. As a result of his betrayal, they were facing the prospect of jail. 'I just felt so bad, I felt fucking awful,' Kennedy reflected months later. 'I did my job very well but I had got to a point in my deployment where it was becoming very hard to do those things against people who really meant a lot to me on a personal level.' At the back of Kennedy's mind, he knew that he may have to help prosecute his comrades. If that were to happen, it would be a significant departure for the NPOIU which, like the SDS, always avoided its officers appearing in court. 'I'd be facing people I'd known for seven years – and who were really good friends – across a witness box,' he said.

Even if the case against the activists never reached court, Kennedy was increasingly paranoid that activists would work out he was the mole in the Ratcliffe protest. Out of all the 114 activists who were arrested that night, Kennedy was the only one who was not represented by the same firm of London-based lawyers, Bindmans. Kennedy was furious with the NPOIU, who did not want to risk one of their operatives being represented by the human rights firm. 'I said: look, everybody else has got a solicitor, Mark Stone hasn't – it looks really odd,' he said.

If Kennedy was compromised by being the only activist without a lawyer, the situation was made even worse when prosecutors began deciding who out of the 114 should be charged. A decision was taken to let most of the activists walk free, to concentrate on bringing charges against a smaller group for conspiracy to commit trespass. In a terrible error, Kennedy was placed in the smaller group who potentially had to go to court. When police realised the mistake, the case against Kennedy was suddenly dropped. He believed that made him stand out even more. Kennedy felt suspicious eyes were turning toward him. It was a concern that may have been shared by his supervisors at the NPOIU, who seem to have believed their prized agent was running out of time.

The truth is that Kennedy was not quite as exposed as he feared. Everyone knew Mark Stone as an eccentric character with a dodgy past, and he had a good excuse not to want to share the same lawyer as everyone else. Other people were suspected as possible infiltrators, but not him. When the birthday festivities got underway on the farm in Herefordshire on a warm September Friday, Kennedy must have felt reassured that his friends still trusted him. It was an impressive turnout for a 40th celebration.

Although Kennedy had not wanted a political festival, it was impossible to escape the fact this was a party for veterans of the radical protest movement. The menu consisted of black-eyed bean, nut and parsley stew with rice and green salad, and food was supplied by Veggies and the Anarchist Teapot, two collectives which had been feeding protest camps for years.

During the day, friends lounged on bales of hay and drank organic local cider in the sunshine. There were egg and spoon races, football matches, a mud-wrestling contest, a traditional Gaelic céilidh dance, cabaret and a barbecue. Inside one of the barns, Logan had pinned up photographs of all of the 40-year-olds, showing how much they had changed over the years. It was the first time that most of Kennedy's friends had seen images of his previous life. One showed Kennedy as a young boy in the 1970s, stood next to his brother. Another, from the 1990s, captured a dazed-looking Kennedy at the end of a long-distance running race, caked in mud and wrapped in a blanket. His hair was bleached blond, separated by a centre parting and held back with a headband. Finally, there was a photograph of Kennedy a few years older, around 2002. It was the old Kennedy, the man as he was just before he went undercover in Nottingham. He was wearing the same dark sunglasses that helped to conceal his injured eye, but his hair was shaved short and his arms looked naked without the tattoos.

Another barn was converted into a music venue for the highlight of the weekend: the live Saturday-night performance by Kennedy and the 69ers. This was the part of the weekend that Kennedy had been looking forward to most. 'He had been saying how it was his dream since he was a kid to be in a band and he had never had the chance,' one friend says. 'It seemed really genuine.' Kennedy's emails confirm his emotional investment in the band. He told friends he had purchased a DVD with 'rare amazing event footage' from 1969, to be projected on the wall behind them when they played. He hired a sound studio in Leeds so the band could rehearse more than a dozen times. And he helped plan a detailed set-list.

Everyone turning 40 had the chance to sing at least one song. The opening track would be the Stooges' cover, '1969', followed by 'Anarchy in the UK' by the Sex Pistols and T. Rex's '20th Century Boy'. Logan would sing 'White Riot', the classic punk anthem by the Clash. Megan would also have a chance to come on stage to sing a song. Kennedy was determined that he should sing Johnny Cash's 'Folsom Prison Blues', in honour of all the comrades who had gone to prison for the cause.

Kennedy emailed each of his friends in the band, giving them specific instructions. Clearly, he had given a lot of thought to the performance. Before each song, band members should take to the microphone and engage in 'a little banter' with the crowd. 'Let's not ramble on,' he said. 'I like to think it's more about the punk rock.' Before anyone walked on stage, they would play a pre-recorded tape, mixing a drum roll by American rock band MC5 and Jimi Hendrix's 'Star Spangled Banner' medley from Woodstock in 1969. Via email, Kennedy told his friends that, after individualised introductions from the master of ceremonies, each band member would take it in turn to jump up onto the stage 'to raucous applause, wolf whistling and screaming groupies'.

That was pretty much what happened on the night. The room was packed full of friends. The mix tape was played, building up to a crescendo before the band jumped on stage, smiling and waving. Megan did a turn on the microphone as a guest vocalist. Then the master of ceremonies, who was dressed in a tailcoat peppered with glittery sequins, took to the microphone and introduced Kennedy. 'On guitar, direct from the bar!' he shouted, as the crowd began to cheer. 'Diamond geezer, he's a rock and roll star! It's Flash!'

The crowd went wild, but Kennedy was not feeling the love. He looked dejected for a reason. Moments before he was called onstage, he had received a text message from the NPOIU. 'The operation is over,' it said. 'At least you had a great party and now it's over.' He had three weeks to 'get out' of Nottingham.

Friends recall a forlorn-looking Kennedy walking onto the stage in a daze and singing his Johnny Cash song. The band played the chorus again and again, accelerating the rhythm each time, as the crowd stomped and cheered. When the performance was over, Kennedy removed his guitar and walked through the barn, friends patting him on the back. Later, when the live music was over, he took to the decks to play one of his favourite records: KRS-One's rap anthem: 'Sound of da Police'.

Kennedy did not appear to want to talk to anyone. Friends presumed he must have been overwhelmed with the love and attention he was given. He told Logan: 'I've never had so many people do something that is about me.' It seemed the occasion had got to Kennedy and he was feeling melancholy. 'Having a couple of hundred people love you and sing happy birthday to you – maybe that does unsettle you,' Logan says. 'But there was something not right in the way that he said it.' Kennedy went to bed early, and the party carried on in his absence until dawn. 'It was absolutely the best party I've ever been to, or expect to go to,' says Logan. 'Except now it has all been spoiled.'

The next morning, when hungover revellers awoke for Sunday brunch, Kennedy was missing. His friends found him lying in bed in the campervan he was sharing with Megan. He refused to come out. Word spread that he looked terrified and was hyperventilating. 'He was freaking the fuck out,' says Logan. 'Panic attacks had never happened like that to Mark before. And after that, he was a very different person. He appeared jumpy, very paranoid.'

The next three weeks seemed to pass in a blur. Kennedy became frosty and cold toward his friends. He told them he was worried police were on to him and they might find the secret stash of money he earned as a drug courier. Once or twice, he phoned friends telling them in a paranoid, hurried voice that he thought he was being followed by plain-clothes detectives. He told his closest friends he wanted to start a new life and talked about moving to the United States to live with his brother, Ian. Just as generations of SDS and NPOIU officers had done before him, Kennedy was feigning some kind of breakdown, preparing the ground for his exit. However, in his case, the symptoms may have been genuine.

'It seemed a bit fucking weird,' admits Logan. 'But the jumpiness and the paranoia was quite intense. He moved out of his house in Nottingham not long after. Well, he didn't actually move out, he just didn't come back. He sent a bunch of us in to clear the house for him. He said he was going put some stuff in storage, but basically we should get rid of the rest – the crockery, the furniture – just throw them out.'

Kennedy disappeared from Nottingham in October 2009 as abruptly as he had arrived six years earlier. His friends cleaned his house in his absence. He had stopped calling or answering emails, although he continued to speak with Megan on an almost daily basis.

That month, Kennedy was summoned by his managers to a meeting at an anonymous truck stop. It would have made a strange sight: a ragged-looking man with long hair stood by the roadside in sombre conversation with men in suits. Mark Stone was being dismantled. As traffic rushed past, the police spy formerly known as UCO 133 handed over his fake credit cards, car keys, passport and driving licence.

'As of then,' Kennedy says. 'I'd vanished.'

CHAPTER 17

The Phantom Returns

The resurrection of Mark Stone began two months after he was supposed to have vanished forever. Just a few weeks after his 40th birthday party in Herefordshire and the roadside meeting at which he relinquished his fake ID documents, Kennedy was missing his previous life. The prospect of a return to his friends in Nottingham was supposed to have been out of the question. His deployment had been terminated by the NPOIU. He was out of the field now, his spying days over, and expected to shave, cut off his hair and return to some kind of desk job at the Metropolitan police.

It was not a prospect that appealed to Kennedy and he knew that there was another option that would allow him to continue living the life of a political activist with Megan and the others. Not long after being pulled from his undercover job, Kennedy was approached by a former Special Branch officer, a man well known to old-timers in the SDS. Rod Leeming had built his career monitoring animal rights activists in the 1990s, in a separate unit that worked alongside the likes of Boyling and Lambert in the SDS. He retired early and moved into the private sector, setting up a company called Global Open in 2001. The detective agency was the corporate equivalent of the NPOIU; it promised to keep a 'discreet watch' on campaigners on behalf of business clients such as the energy giant E.ON and arms manufacturer BAE and used many of the same techniques.

Global Open was one of many detective agencies making money out of spying on protesters. Others firms that go by the names Inkerman Group, Vericola and C2i International ply a similar trade. Senior police say that 'without question' there are more corporate spies posing as protesters other than those run by police, and the private sector is 'completely uncontrolled and unrestrained'. It provided an enticing proposition for Kennedy, involving a smooth transition from the public sector to corporate espionage. Kennedy already had the contacts and the undercover identity. He had invested six years of his life, and the taxpayer more than £1.75m of public money, into creating Mark Stone. Why let him go?

Two months after his official deployment ended, Kennedy resigned from the Met and began working as a 'consultant' for Global Open. Now he set about planning the reappearance of Mark Stone in Nottingham. In one sense, it would be far easier turning up the second time round, when everyone already knew and trusted his alter ego. But the private sector involved some new challenges. Kennedy was now alone, without the generous expense account given to him by the NPOIU or supervision from commanding officers. He no longer had a passport, driving licence or bank accounts in the name of Mark Stone. He was a lone operator.

This time around, Kennedy had to spend his own money to reconstruct his life as an activist. He purchased a white Ford transit van and travelled to Lincolnshire with his brother to buy a canal boat. The 55ft-long vessel, named *Tamarisk*, was his new home. He moored the vessel in Nottingham and wandered down to the Sumac Centre to catch up with people he had not seen in three months.

His friends were pleased that he had come back but still concerned about his unexplained disappearance. And they were concerned over his welfare. The man they knew as Mark Stone appeared to be a different person since his absence; he was quiet, reflective and prone to mood swings. Friends say he was behaving strangely toward Megan and, presumably in the knowledge that he needed to rekindle his access to protesters, began an intimate relationship with another well-connected female activist. 'He would be subdued and unreliable in a different way from usual,' Logan recalls. 'It was that no confidence, sunken thing of depressed people.'

Kennedy had reason to be worried, not least because he was running out of money. He set up his own company, registering the address at the offices of a solicitor who worked for Global Open. He called it Tokra Ltd, a name apparently derived from the science fiction television series *Stargate*. It was another example – like his tattoos – of Kennedy's tendency toward fantasy: in the TV show the 'Tok'ra' are an alien race symbiotically inhabiting their human hosts. He also founded a second business, ostensibly to work as a freelance rope access technician. Yet the name of the second company – Black Star Access Ltd – suggested it was another front; living again as Mark Stone, he could provide corporates with rare 'access' to radical anarchists, known by their 'black star' symbol.

Whatever hopes Kennedy had of making money, he was struggling. He told friends the downturn in the construction industry meant there was scant work for professional climbers. He also let a few people know that the stash of money he had supposedly earned as a drug trafficker was running dry. On one occasion, Flash Mark even took a loan from a friend. 'That was weird,' says Logan. 'But then again it is not uncommon for people to suddenly run out of cash, especially when they say, they have been living off a single pot for years which has now run out.'

If Kennedy was going to make money from corporate espionage, he needed to revive some old contacts. He resumed his role as Transport Mark and became involved again in the leasing of equipment through the Activist Tat Collective. He attended meetings and returned briefly to Germany. His interests, however, appeared to be shifting, as he tried to gain access to the kinds of activism his paymasters were interested in. Suddenly, Kennedy, who had always been a meat eater, said he was anti-vivisection and opposed to industrial farming. For the first time in his life, Kennedy took part in animal rights meetings, first in England and later in Milan, where campaigners were staying in a squat. Some of his friends were confused that Kennedy was now showing an interest in animal rights campaigning.

It all added to the sense that Kennedy was not quite behaving like himself. 'He clearly had some sort of crisis thing and was figuring himself out,' says Logan. 'He just seemed very lost.' On a camping holiday in Scotland, Kennedy admitted to friends that he was feeling depressed and suffering from paranoia.

The spy was right to fear that his former employers were on his trail. Senior officials at the NPOIU would have viewed the reappearance of Mark Stone with total disbelief. Kennedy had always been a loose cannon, but the NPOIU could always clamp down on his excesses. Now he was a free agent, breaking every rule in the book. As soon as the NPOIU was aware that Kennedy was back, they began monitoring him. One suggestion – denied by senior police – is that Kennedy was pursued by a four-man police surveillance unit who installed covert cameras aboard his canal boat. The hidden CCTV was said to have captured Kennedy having sex with another activist.

True or not, police were certainly scrutinising Kennedy's every move, trying to work out what would happen next. But they were not the only people on his trail. Within a few weeks,

Kennedy's friends, the people who had trusted him for over seven years, and welcomed him on his return, would be meeting behind his back, trying to unearth his real identity.

The chance discovery occurred in rural Italy. Kennedy and Megan were on a road trip and sleeping on a makeshift bed in the back of his van. The trip through Europe was intended to mark a fresh start for the couple. They had experienced a turbulent few months, but Kennedy had told Megan that he loved her and he wanted to reaffirm their relationship. It was early July 2010, and baking hot. Megan was looking for her sunglasses in the glove compartment when her hand pressed against the leather cover of a British passport. She opened it. The photograph was of her boyfriend, the man she knew as Mark Stone. But the name was not.

It appeared to be a stranger's passport in the name of someone called Mark John Kennedy. Under a section listing dependents, it said: 'one child'.

Logan recounts what happened next: 'Obviously this freaks her the fuck out. And she goes looking around the van for anything else that might provide some clues. Finds an iPhone – turns it on, there's hardly any battery left. Quickly, she scrolls through emails. She finds some messages from two children, one of them called Jack, calling him 'Dad'. And some emails from someone called Edel. Then the battery goes.'

Megan has never spoken about the discovery of the passport, or the train of events that followed, to anyone other than her closest friends. They say she felt sick, questioning everything she knew about Kennedy. The passport suggested he had some kind of double life, while the emails indicated he had secretly fathered children. Megan mulled over the implications of what she had found for two days. Eventually, while still in Italy, she decided to confront him. Friends of Megan say that she told him: 'I need to talk to you. I saw your passport and it is in a different name. What's going on?'

That was the point at which Kennedy's undercover training kicked in. Just like Lynn Watson, who had a ready-made story for her chance encounter with an activist friend in the pub on the Dorset coast, Kennedy had a back-up. Suddenly, he broke down in tears and told Megan that his mother's maiden name was 'Stone'. He said he had chosen voluntarily to adopt it as his own because of his hatred for his father, an accountant whose surname was Kennedy. He described his father as an oppressive man who had abandoned the family. By relinquishing the surname Kennedy, he hoped to vanquish his father's presence from his life. It seemed a strange explanation, but a plausible one; it fitted with how Kennedy had described his father in the past. He said he only realised the value of the two separate identities when he started working as a drug courier. He could use one passport when entering a country, and another when leaving, making it harder for border authorities to track his whereabouts.

When asked to explain the emails on his iPhone from a boy called Jack, Kennedy broke down and began to sob again. He was behaving as though he was revisiting some dark, painful memory. He told Megan that he had kept an important secret from her. It dated back to his former life as a drug courier. Rather than work alone, he had a partner – a childhood friend. The two men had been like brothers, travelling the world with drugs stashed in suitcases. However, one day their luck ran out when a deal went wrong and they were taken hostage by armed men. According to Megan's friends, Kennedy told his girlfriend the incident was the 'scariest moment of my fucking life'; he had a gun put to his head, but was spared. His friend was less fortunate. He was killed right in front of him.

When his friend perished, Kennedy said he felt an obligation to his next of kin, including his friend's wife and son. Jack was not his own son, but the child of his now dead friend, and a boy he had vowed to treat as his own. The boy's mother was called Edel, and when she gave birth to a second child, a girl, after falling pregnant with another man, Kennedy resolved to take responsibility for the entire family. He felt he owed it to his dead partner in crime. He had therefore become something of a surrogate father to the two children, visiting them occasionally and paying maintenance.

Kennedy had conjured up a vivid fabrication. Friends of Megan say that however implausible the story might sound in retrospect, she was convinced by his acting skills. By the end of the story, Kennedy looked totally devastated. He told Megan that the abiding regret of his life was that he had not done more to look after Edel and her children. He wished he could have been a better father. He was weeping inconsolably.

It is hard to imagine the thoughts that must have been racing through Megan's mind. Friends say the suffering she endured in the weeks and months after that moment left a deep psychological scar. Kennedy was the man she had wanted to share her future with. During their six years together she had got to know him like no one else. They had spoken of a life together. Now she felt she did not quite know him as before. Every time she questioned his account of the passports or the children, she was wracked with guilt for doubting his story.

Part of Megan wanted to believe her boyfriend. He had always been a complex character and finally it seemed she had discovered his true secret. But she was still torn. Kennedy's explanation was so far-fetched it was almost unbelievable. How could he have lived a double life for so long? Why had he never introduced her to these two children that he claimed he loved? Who was he, really?

Back in Nottingham, Megan spent three months trying to work out whether or not she believed Kennedy. Another woman might have sided with the man she loved, buried any doubts and got on with her life. If she had done that, the truth about Mark Kennedy, and all of the other undercover police officers, may never have surfaced. One incident that tipped her into doubting her boyfriend occurred at a music festival. She met some old activists from Reclaim the Streets who were talking about Jim Boyling. They had recently had contact from his ex-wife, Laura, who confirmed he was a police spy. Megan listened as the group talked animatedly about how Boyling had seemed like an ordinary activist. They were stunned that an undercover police officer would live a double life for years, cultivating close friendships and even long-term sexual relationships with campaigners. Hearing those stories was a turning point for Megan.

When she got home, she logged onto a computer and searched the electoral roll for any records of a Mark Stone born in 1969. There were none. Unlike the Special Demonstration Squad, the NPOIU was no longer using the identities of dead children. It was as though the man she had known for the best part of a decade did not exist. There were, however, records for Mark John Kennedy – and they told a different story. The records indicated Kennedy was not just a friend to Edel, but her husband. The couple had lived on Dowlerville Road, a suburban street in Kent, between 1997 and 2002. That was immediately before Mark Stone appeared out of nowhere in Nottingham. In the days of the SDS, inquiries into records of an ex-spy would have immediately triggered an alert at Scotland Yard, informing senior officers that one of their former operatives was coming under suspicion. For whatever reason, the NPOIU does not appear to have had similar powers. No one, it seems, knew how close Megan was getting to the truth.

It was by now September 2010, a few months after Megan discovered the passport and emails in Italy, and just a couple of days after she heard the news about Boyling. She decided to share her discovery with Logan, her ex-boyfriend. She relayed the story about the dual identities, the drug deal that went wrong and the family that Kennedy claimed to have adopted. 'In all this time he's not mentioned that he had a best friend who died?' Logan said. 'Why has he not told you before that he had responsibility for these two kids? It doesn't ring true to me.'

Logan was a good person for Megan to confide in. He had been knocking around the protest scene for almost two decades and she felt she could trust him. He was something of an expert in genealogical research and knew how to navigate the bureaucracy of public records. He searched an ancestry website and found a Mark John Kennedy who had a wife, Edel, and two children, one of whom was called Jack. The same Mark Kennedy had a brother called Ian. 'We can't jump to conclusions,' Logan said. 'It is somebody called Mark Kennedy but this might not be our man. But frankly, whoever this is, these are his wife and kids.'

Logan could see that Megan was distraught and desperate for some firm answers. He felt that he needed to prepare her for the worst. 'You do realise,' he said, 'that if Mark was a cop this is exactly what it would look like?' It was a daunting thought and not one either of them wanted to believe without evidence. They felt that it was important to give Kennedy the benefit of the doubt. 'Mark always had his dark side and there was a sense that if he had a wife and kids, that was probably something we could handle,' Logan adds. 'He has always been a bit unreliable – he has always been a fucking liar. He was just so charming that we cut him slack. There might be reasons for the secret family; there might be an excuse. We kind of thought: anything but cop is all right.'

Part of the reason they held back from jumping to conclusions was that there were gaps in the story. Although Mark and Edel Kennedy appeared to have married, there was no evidence of their marriage certificate. In fact, it was harder to find any documents relating to Edel than her husband. One night, Logan ordered copies of all the relevant birth certificates from the public records. Rather than wait for hard copies to arrive by post, he paid extra to have scanned versions of the birth certificates sent to his email account. The first attachment he opened was the birth certificate of Kennedy's son Jack, born in 1998. It was registered in Kent. That much, Logan had presumed. It was only when he scrolled down that he read two words that left him stunned.

Section five of the document required the child's father to provide his occupation. Beneath the name Mark Kennedy it stated: 'Police Officer'. Logan's heart began to race. He was too shocked to know what to do. He inspected the document again to make sure he was not confused. Even with the words 'police officer' staring out from the screen, Logan wanted desperately to believe it was not true.

He still felt there were scenarios that might exonerate his friend. What if this was all just a coincidence, and there was another Mark Kennedy, born around the same time, with a wife called Edel and a son named Jack? The other possibility, which Logan described as his 'second most plausible explanation', was that Kennedy had written 'police officer' on the birth certificate of his son for a joke. 'If Mark was an international cocaine courier, then he was not going to write "international cocaine courier" as his occupation, was he? What was he going to put then? It would be quite funny to put "police officer". To be honest, if I had a child and I was doing something illegal for a living, my sense of humour would probably lead me to write something like that.'

Logan quickly opened the second attachment: a scan of Mark Kennedy's birth certificate. It stated he was born in Dulwich in south London on July 7 1969. Just as with the first document, Logan scrolled down before reading that Kennedy's father, John, was not an accountant, as he had always said. The handwritten note from the registrar listed his job as 'Metropolitan Police Constable'. Logan recalls thinking: 'So his dad is a cop – it's a family thing. God, this is looking worse. That is the point at which the scales have tipped. It looks like Mark was a cop.'

Logan met with Megan to show her the documents. They were still minded to give Kennedy the benefit of the doubt for two reasons. First, despite the documentary evidence, they felt the story remained incomplete. The birth of Kennedy's second child, in which he said he was a police officer, was dated 2000 – three years before Kennedy became involved in activism. It was therefore possible that Kennedy was a police officer, but had seen the light and abandoned his uniform to dedicate his life to activism. 'He could hardly walk into activist circles and say, "Hi, I used to be a police officer until a couple of years ago,"' explains Logan. 'No one would ever talk to him. We'll have a former cocaine dealer, we'll have an ex-soldier who has murdered people and done war crimes, but we are not going to have a copper. Never trust a copper – it's the one thing.'

The second reason for suspending judgment was the remote possibility that they were dealing with a case of mistaken identity. Their search had turned up seven births of men called Mark John Kennedy in England between 1959 and 1979. What if they had the wrong details and their Mark Kennedy was another man? They needed to be able to connect Kennedy with Edel, the woman he had apparently married. They searched hard for their wedding certificate, but despite weeks of trying, that was the one document they were unable to locate. It was the final piece of the jigsaw, but it was missing.

Then the answer suddenly dawned on them: Edel Kennedy, maiden name Cashman, was born in Ireland. What if the couple had chosen to marry in Ireland?

Logan picked up the phone and called a friend in Dublin. He said: 'I know this is weird, but you are not allowed to tell anyone about this phone call. I need you to do me a favour. Can you quickly go down to the general records office and look at the archives? You're looking for a marriage certificate – it is probably going to be somewhere between the mid-1980s to the mid-1990s. You need to look for a Mark John Kennedy who married an Edel Elizabeth Cashman.' He added: 'I hope one day I can tell you why you're doing this. But right now, I can't. You're not allowed to tell anyone – is that OK?'

A few days later, Megan and Logan met with three other trusted friends in a house in Nottingham. They were still one document – the marriage certificate – short of the truth. But they felt they had amassed sufficient evidence to share with three other friends to seek another opinion. They needed help and advice from close friends. It was October; the cold air outside marked the arrival of autumn. Kennedy was out of the country; he had told Megan he was going to visit Ian in America. He had no idea that his best friends were at that very moment mulling over a pile of documents pointing to his real identity.

Everyone agreed it did not look good for Kennedy. The friend in Dublin had still not called with news of the marriage certificate. But Kennedy's friends had another lead: a telephone number for a woman in Ireland called Edel Kennedy. It would be too obvious to ask outright if she was married to Mark Kennedy, so the friends decided to call the number and ask to speak to Jack. One of the five volunteered to make the call.

'Is Jack there, please?' he asked.

The reply was a male voice. 'Excuse me?'

'Jack, who is aged 12 or 13.'

'There is no Jack that lives here.'

The phone was hung up.

The friend who made the call was shocked. He recognised the voice on the other end of the line. It was Kennedy. He was not visiting his brother in the United States, as he claimed, but in Ireland, with his wife and children. The friends were still digesting the implications when Logan's phone rang. It was his friend in Dublin, fresh from a visit to the public records archives. He had a copy of the marriage certificate in his hand.

'What does it say?' Logan asked.

'Edel Elizabeth Cashman, she was born in 1967 in some tiny little hamlet,' his friend replied. 'She married Mark Kennedy in a Catholic church in 1994.'

'What does it say Mark Kennedy's profession was?'

'It says his profession was "policeman".'

Kennedy's friends decided they had to meet him face to face. There was talk about travelling to Ireland and visiting him at his family home. In the end they decided that Megan should call and ask him to come to Nottingham. Logan recalls the conversation.

'I've found out stuff about you,' Megan said. 'You have not been telling me the truth. I don't like it and I want you to come and explain yourself.'

'What do you think you know?' Kennedy asked.

'I'm not talking on the phone. You're going to come home and you're going to tell me what the truth is.'

Kennedy told Megan that he was looking after his children and could not just leave Ireland at the drop of a hat. A few hours later he seemed to have changed his mind. He called back. 'I'm coming,' he said. 'My flight gets in at 11.30pm. I'll be with you at 1am.'

*

The doorbell rang shortly after 1am. One of Kennedy's friends met him at the front door. She smiled and asked him to come into the living room. Kennedy walked in, looking nervous. He kept his jacket on.

Megan broke the silence. She told Kennedy that he had lied to her repeatedly and that she had foolishly believed him. She did not feel she could trust her own judgment and wanted their friends to be in the room with her. There were six people present: as well as Kennedy and Megan, there was Logan and three other close friends.

'We made sure the room was warm,' says Logan. 'We set up the seating in the round so that it wasn't like an intimidating tribunal. We had it arranged so that Kennedy would sit on the sofa, so that again was going to be less isolating for him.' Kennedy's friends knew that if the situation became hostile, he might storm out of the room and never be seen again. But there was another reason for their caution.

Despite all of the evidence pointing to Kennedy being an infiltrator, they still believed their friend deserved a chance to explain himself. However implausible it might seem, there may still be some eleventh-hour explanation, a reason for his deception that they had not anticipated. Before Kennedy had even arrived at the house, his friends had reached a decision: in the unlikely event that he managed to convince them that he was not a police officer, they would never tell any other activists about the documents, the telephone call or the visit to Nottingham in the middle of the night. But his friends were fearing the worst.

Kennedy had told them his flight landed at 11.30pm, but when had they checked the schedules, there were no flights from Ireland to any London or Midlands airports around that time. Kennedy must have arrived earlier in the day and his friends were worried about what he may have been doing. They presumed he must have met with police beforehand, and had come wearing a wire. They thought it was possible that a team of riot police was in vans outside, waiting to come storming in if Kennedy uttered a code word.

That was not the only reason the friends were determined to keep the atmosphere calm. Their aim was to get Kennedy to confess. By then, Kennedy knew that his friends were aware he had a secret family in Ireland. But he could not have known they had found documentary evidence he was a police officer. 'There was no way we were going to ambush him like some kind of kangaroo court and say, "You're a cop, you're a cop,"' says Logan. The plan was to feign some degree of ignorance, and entice Kennedy into admitting he worked for police.

Kennedy took his seat on the sofa, looking uncomfortable. His friends said they had found information that did not match up with what he had told them. They knew he was not the person he claimed to be. They asked Kennedy to be honest, to stop the trail of lies and tell them who he really was.

'He 'fessed up immediately to the wife and kids,' says Logan. 'I suspect he thought that was what he had been found out for. He gave a ridiculous story about how he had been a van driver in Battersea and then got this woman pregnant, with his first child, but he realised parenthood wasn't for him and so then he left her when she was pregnant with their second child. He claimed to have hardly ever seen his children. He said he was worried that his neglect of his family was turning him into his evil dad. Supposedly, it was a great curse on Mark's life that he had done this to his family and he had always wanted to tell us but was unable to.'

It was a bold start by Kennedy, but it did not wash. His friends continued, gently. 'There are a number of things you've just told us that are not true,' one friend said. 'Would you like to try again? Because we stress this is not looking good and this is your one chance to make it right. Tell us who you are. Tell us what has happened.'

Kennedy floundered. He refused to tell his friends the real name of his father, which they knew to be John. The conversation was becoming strained and Kennedy stumbled over the most basic questions. Then one of the friends just asked outright: 'And when did you join the police?'

Kennedy exhaled loudly. He looked at his hands. Then he stared up at the ceiling.

'You can't ask me these kinds of questions,' he said. 'I don't want to talk about this.'

After seven years of lies, deceit and betrayal, Kennedy could no longer conceal the truth. He confirmed he was an undercover police officer. He told his friends how he had joined the police two decades earlier, and gone undercover purchasing drugs before being recruited to the National Public Order Intelligence Unit, a secretive squad dedicated to monitoring protesters.

'The relief of that was colossal,' says Logan. 'Oh God, he's admitted it – thank fuck.'

Kennedy's friends cannot recall precisely what was said in the emotional hours that followed. The man they once knew as Mark Stone began telling them about Special Branch, the Special Demonstration Squad and the surveillance of domestic extremists. There were so many acronyms, they cannot recall them all. He told his friends that there were many other police spies who, like him, were living a double life among political campaigners. 'I am not the only one, by a long way,' he told them. 'There are lots of us.'

One friend asked Kennedy directly if Lynn Watson was also an undercover police officer. Kennedy nodded. 'Yes,' he said. 'But you knew that already.'

While there were parts of Kennedy's confession that were true, his friends were sceptical about other elements of his story. He told them he was sorry for the harm he had caused and said he regretted taking part in the spy operation. He claimed that life as an activist had changed him, that he had been converted into a true believer in the environmental cause. None of his friends believed him but, remarkably, the room stayed calm. Kennedy's friends just sat there, still stunned by his confession, watching him sob.

Some in the room even felt empathy for the man who, just hours earlier, had been their friend. 'It was [witnessing] the absolute wrenching bottom-of-his-guts crying that he was doing,' says Logan. 'You know, there are prisons up and down the country that are full of people being visited by the relatives who still love them, even though they know the dreadful things they have done.'

That feeling has long since disappeared. 'Now he is just that fucking undercover police officer and I don't feel anything like that for him any more,' says Logan. 'But at that time, when we had just found out, as well as being a traitor, he was still the man that I had loved like a brother for seven years. The man that I went through loads of stuff with and did amazing things with. He was still sat in front of me.'

CHAPTER 18

Business as Usual

'Oh, hello Mark,' the lecturer said. 'How are you? Are you in America?'

'I am,' Kennedy replied.

The telephone call took place three weeks after Kennedy admitted to his friends that he was an undercover police officer. The lecturer on the other end of the line, a friend Kennedy had known for some years, was sitting in his university office.

'I was trying to think where you were in the world, to be five hours behind. I thought it must be America,' he said. Kennedy sighed.

'I'm not doing so good, to be honest.'

'Yes, well. It is all pretty bad really.'

'Hurting Megan is just the hardest thing. I love her so much. What has happened is just devastating for everybody. If I can help, in whatever way I can, then I would like to.'

Less than a month earlier, in the early hours of a Wednesday night, Kennedy had been in Nottingham, sat on the sofa, surrounded by friends, making his confession. Now he was reflecting on events from thousands of miles away, staying with his brother in Ohio. Kennedy told the lecturer he was grateful to their activist friends for the courtesy they showed him on the night of the confrontation.

'They were so good, you know? That Wednesday could have been as bad as it could ever be. But you know, people were good. They were decent about it.' Kennedy paused before adding: 'They were always going to be.'

Kennedy's voiced wobbled repeatedly during the telephone call. He would later describe this period – the lonely weeks abroad after he was outed – as the lowest point of his life. He was unsure who he really was. Part of him, of course, was still Mark Stone, the activist, seeking atonement for his sins.

It was this that the university academic had in mind when he arranged the call. He wanted to persuade Kennedy to take a remarkable leap. The trial of 26 activists accused of conspiring to break into Ratcliffe-on-Soar power station was due to start in a few weeks. The lecturer was among those facing conviction and a possible jail term if found guilty. He was trying to convince Kennedy to switch sides, abandoning his loyalties to the NPOIU altogether so he could give evidence on behalf of his friends in the green movement. He made sure to record the call.

'In terms of the wider points, about police infiltration, who they go after and the methods that they use,' the lecturer said. 'It is quite an extreme thing that they are doing. This is not al-Qaida. It's fucking Climate Camp, you know what I mean?'

Kennedy agreed the surveillance was overkill. 'When you start addressing the cost and the finance of it all,' he said, 'I am not the only one, you know? Not by a long shot.'

'It seems patently obvious that Lynn was [a police officer],' the lecturer said. 'It just totally fits.'

Kennedy had already admitted to his friends in Nottingham that Lynn Watson was a colleague of his. This time he simply laughed and said: 'I can't really comment. But I am not the only one.' He added: 'You know, when you start looking at the way the law is used and it is manipulated, it's like, what the fuck?'

The lecturer explained the legal situation. The 26 who had been charged with conspiring to break into the power station were split into two groups. Twenty of them accepted that they planned to break into the power station, but were planning to run a 'necessity' defence. They would call on evidence from the world's leading climate scientists in a bid to persuade the jury that the attempted break-in was justified because, by temporarily halting emissions at the plant, they were saving lives that would be lost to global warming. Similar legal strategies had been successfully used by climate activists in the past. This group of defendants called themselves 'the justifiers'.

The second group of defendants had a different defence. None of them were involved in any planning of the protest against the E.ON plant. They were just part of the large crowd of campaigners who had descended on the school in Nottingham with a vague sense that there would be a protest.

When police stormed into the building shortly before midnight and arrested 114 people, these six activists had still not decided whether they wanted to take part in the occupation of the power station. Hence, they were called 'the deniers'; their strategy was to persuade the court that – contrary to the charge – they were never part of any 'conspiracy'. Some people had obviously planned the Ratcliffe-on-Soar protest. It just wasn't them.

Over the phone, Kennedy agreed this was the truth. The case being brought against the activists was unjust and flawed. It risked a miscarriage of justice. He expressed an interest in saying as much in court. He said he would spend some more time thinking about giving evidence on behalf of his activist friends and agreed to start liaising with their lawyers.

'I owe it to a lot of good people to do something right for a change,' Kennedy said. 'Most of all Megan.'

The lecturer also encouraged Kennedy to speak to two *Guardian* journalists – the authors of this book. Kennedy sounded interested in the idea of giving them his story and turning his back altogether on his former employers at the NPOIU. He was considering doing the right thing, but he was nervous.

'The potential to blow the lid on stuff is absolutely huge,' he said. 'I am out on a limb here. I am totally on my own.'

On the morning of January 10 2011 – two months after that call – there was a rare moment of theatre in Nottingham Crown Court. It happened around 10.25am. The six deniers were sitting in the dock, awaiting what should have been the start of their trial. As it turned out, Kennedy went back on his offer to help the activists. Despite telling their lawyer, Mike Schwarz, he would help their case, he pulled out. It seemed he did not have the courage to stand up in court against the police, in a bid to save his old friends from a possible jail term, or 'blow the lid' on police spy operations by speaking to journalists at the *Guardian*.

However, Kennedy's admission that he was a police officer, to his friends in Nottingham and, later, in the call to the university lecturer, had been sufficient to undermine the entire case. Shortly before Judge John Milmo entered the room, a woman clerk walked nervously over to the dock. She whispered a few words to the six men then ushered them out of the dock and across the courtroom, where they took their seats in the space usually reserved for the jury. It was a weird sight.

The public gallery was packed with reporters from national newspapers and TV stations. At the back of the court, behind the journalists, were a handful of detectives, including some from the NPOIU. They looked furious. By the time Judge Milmo walked into the room in his red robe, everyone in court understood the significance of the six deniers being removed from the dock.

That morning the *Guardian* had published the details of a special investigation into Kennedy's seven years undercover, without his co-operation. It included the revelation that the Crown Prosecution Service was abandoning the trial against the deniers. There had been a game-changer, and it was linked to Kennedy.

It all happened remarkably quickly. Prosecutors told the court they would no longer pursue the case and the judge agreed to enter not guilty verdicts for all six activists. They walked free and, moments later, stood on the steps outside the court as Schwarz gave a brief statement to the waiting media.

'On Easter Monday 2009, over 400 police officers were involved in a raid at Iona school in Nottingham, which led to 114 arrests. I represented 113 of those arrested,' he said. 'The 114th we now know was PC Kennedy, an undercover police officer. This is a serious attack on a peaceful, accountable protest on issues of public and pressing importance like climate change. One expects there to be undercover police on serious operations to investigate serious crime. This was quite the opposite. This was civil disobedience, which has a long history in this country and should be protected.'

For the first time since 1968, when Conrad Dixon began deploying spies in protest groups, a lawyer could prove that his clients had been infiltrated by police. Even though Kennedy pulled out from helping, Schwarz could request disclosure of all the evidence the undercover police officer must have gathered during the deployment. It was the equivalent of placing dynamite and a ticking clock beneath the case of the prosecution, which had little choice but to abandon the trial.

By then, the other 20 activists, 'the justifiers', had already been prosecuted separately. Their trial had taken place three weeks earlier. All of them were found guilty, but spared jail after the judge in the case declared they had acted with 'the highest possible motives'.

It was a bitter pill for Kennedy's handlers at the NPOIU. They had spent millions of pounds spying on environmental groups, justifying the operation to ministers as a drive against dangerous domestic extremists. Now they had to listen to the judge describe these PhD students, teachers, social workers and former civil servants as upstanding and even admirable citizens. These domestic extremists were, in the words of Judge Jonathan Teare, 'decent men and women with a genuine concern for others and in particular for the survival of planet Earth. And if I select some of the adjectives that recur throughout, they are these: honest, sincere, conscientious, intelligent, committed, dedicated, caring.'

The NPOIU might have felt relieved that, despite the judge's proclamation, the twenty 'justifiers' were still found guilty, their trial taking place before the Kennedy revelations were made public. But five months later, their convictions were quashed, after the court of appeal ruled that evidence obtained by Kennedy, and withheld from the activists' lawyers, would have exonerated them.

At the centre of the ruling was the Casio watch Kennedy used to record conversations at the school in Nottingham. The contents of Kennedy's surveillance tapes would have supported the activists' argument that they had planned to occupy the power station in a safe way to stop carbon emissions, rather than, as the prosecution alleged, a publicity stunt.

The three senior judges said 'elementary principles' of fair justice had been ignored. 'Something went seriously wrong with the trial,' they said. 'The jury were ignorant of evidence helpful to the defence, which was in the possession of the prosecution but which was never revealed. As a result, justice miscarried.'

The ruling personally criticised Kennedy, concluding his deployment among the campaigners could have been construed as 'entrapment'. They observed that the police spy 'was involved in activities which went much further than the authorisation he was given, and appeared to show him as an enthusiastic supporter of the proposed occupation of the power station and, arguably, an agent provocateur'.

For senior managers in the NPOIU, it was a catastrophe. The behaviour of one of their undercover police officers was now public knowledge. The activists he had spent years spying on had been praised in court for their high moral principles and found to be not guilty. Now, police were in the dock.

The story of Kennedy's undercover mission was making headlines across the world. There was astonishment that police would ever contemplate such an intrusive surveillance operation against peaceful activists. Most people never imagined undercover police would spend years posing as protesters, let alone form long-term sexual relationships as part of their cover. And the remarkable story of Kennedy's undercover life was only the start.

Kennedy, it turned out, was just the first in a line of falling dominoes of SDS and NPOIU spies. The second police spy to be unmasked in the *Guardian* was Lynn Watson. She was followed a few days later by Marco Jacobs. With their identities compromised, Jacobs and Watson were told they could never work as undercover officers again. The country was realising that Kennedy was not a lone wolf, but part of a team of undercover police targeting political campaigners. Senior officers contemplated the possibility that more officers would be exposed. They put in place a contingency plan to pull out as many as 15 undercover officers and tried to discourage editors from identifying any more operatives. In the top ranks of Scotland Yard, panic was beginning to set in.

But the dominoes did not stop falling. In the months that followed, there was a cascade of further revelations, first about Jim Boyling. The revelations included the claims made by his ex-wife Laura, that he had made her change her name by deed poll and disclosed classified information about the undercover operation. The day after Laura's story was revealed in the *Guardian*, Scotland Yard initiated a disciplinary inquiry into Boyling which, more than two years later, has still not beeen concluded. Still working for the Met police, Boyling denies that he 'committed any criminal or misconduct offence whilst carrying out my duties' for the covert unit. 'My actions whilst deployed on SDS duties were with the approval of the Metropolitan police,' he said. 'I have never opposed the work of the SDS and I have never compromised my work colleagues.'

One of his former colleagues, Pete Black, started to give the inside story about the SDS, revealing the truth about the operations, including the use of dead children's identities. Meanwhile, one by one, as activists began piecing together long-forgotten jigsaw pieces, more police were unmasked: Simon Wellings, Bob Lambert, John Dines and Mark Jenner suddenly found themselves splashed across the pages of newspapers and the subject of heated debates in parliament.

Apart from Black, none spoke openly about their undercover work. They have all tried to keep a low profile. Kennedy, on the other hand, was quick to cash in on his notoriety. He decided against speaking to any investigative journalists and did not co-operate with this book. Instead, he solicited the services of the celebrity publicist Max Clifford, who sold his exclusive story to the *Mail on Sunday* tabloid and arranged for a series of carefully managed interviews, allowing Kennedy to paint a one-sided and often misleading picture of his time undercover.

For many of his old friends in the activist movement, Kennedy's media tour was the ultimate betrayal.

At the time of his first interview, less than three months after he made his confession to friends in Nottingham, Kennedy pretended to be in hiding, claiming he feared he might be killed by violent political activists seeking vengeance. Posing for photographs in a neat shirt and sweater, he looked totally different to Mark Stone; he was clean-shaven, with short hair and a neat side parting. 'I can't sleep,' he said. 'I barricade the door with chairs at night. I am in genuine fear for my life. I have been told that my former bosses from the force are out here in America looking for me. I have been told by activists to watch my back as people are out to get me.'

Just a few weeks earlier, Kennedy had been on the phone to his friend, the lecturer, apologising for what he had done and thanking his friends for the kindness they showed him on the night he was confronted in Nottingham. Kennedy had been treated humanely, and he knew it, telling the lecturer during the call: 'I've frankly got nothing but gratitude for that.'

In his tabloid newspaper interview, Kennedy gave a wildly different account. For a start, he claimed that he only travelled to Nottingham to meet Megan and the other activists because he thought they might harm his family. 'I was extremely fearful for my children because I know what the people I had been involved with were capable of,' he said. 'I had been infiltrating a lot of very serious people for a number of years. I needed to find out what they knew to assess the threat level. So I went.'

If that seemed far-fetched, so too was his depiction of his arrival in Nottingham, when his friends calmly gave him a chance to explain himself. In Kennedy's account to the newspaper, it was more like a hostile interrogation. 'I was asked to sit down, which I did,' he said. 'Then three or four other people came in. They shut the door in a menacing way. They sat in a semi-circle around me. It was hugely menacing. I cried a lot. It was the end of my tether. They broke me.' He also denied telling friends that night that Watson was also a spy. 'I didn't give anyone up,' he said.

Worst still for Megan and his friends was his portrayal of life in Nottingham. 'What I found difficult was the dirt,' he said. 'They should have known I was a cop as I was the only one who ever cleaned anything. People didn't buy food; they either stole it or took it out of bins. Often vegetables in the kitchen had mould on them. You couldn't tell if they'd been there for a while or been salvaged. It would annoy me when I gave someone a lift and they put their filthy feet on the dashboard.'

On the whole, Kennedy gave every impression of a man wallowing in self-pity. It was not the people who he was spying on who were the victims of any injustice, but him. 'I am physically and mentally exhausted,' he said. 'I have had some dark thoughts. I thought I could end this very quickly. I don't have any confidence. My world has been destroyed. I don't have any friends; they were all in the activist movement.'

There is little doubt Kennedy was suffering from the same kind of psychological confusion that plagued Mike Chitty 20 years earlier. The parallels between the two men are obvious. Both formed intimate relationships while undercover, and both, after finishing their deployments, returned to their former lives, unable to let go of their disguise.

Kennedy was soon giving radio interviews in which he spoke about his dual identities in the third person. 'What Mark Stone believed in and his values are probably very similar to Mark Kennedy,' he said. 'It's a part of my life which has come to an abrupt end. It's very much like falling off a cliff. I'm trying to establish who I am now, but I think I have to put Mark Stone in the background and try and think about who I am.'

He was clearly confused, but perhaps Kennedy's most blatant deception related not to the hygiene of his friends in Nottingham, or the nature of his confession, but the vexed question of his sexual activities. Kennedy claimed to have been the victim of a 'smear campaign' by women, and claims he was celibate for the first year of his deployment.

'I avoided sexual contact, despite the fact that free love is part of that lifestyle,' he said. He admitted to only two intimate relationships – Lily and Megan – a claim he later repeated in testimony to parliament, in effect denying his sexual relationships with all the other women.

Lily, the woman who shared two years of her life with Kennedy, with whom he spent long weekends getting to know her family and even attended her grandmother's birthday, was reduced to a fling. 'She came on to me at a party. She seduced me. I know it was wrong,' Kennedy said. 'I didn't consider her a proper girlfriend.'

He was only a little more honest about his six-year relationship with Megan, who he described as a Welsh redhead. 'I was in a relationship with a really amazing person,' he said. 'I felt really trapped as to how I was going to extricate myself from such a position without hurting that person and without hurting everybody else that was connected to me. At the same time I was being tasked to continually provide intelligence and I didn't have time to think.'

He said his bosses knew about his relationships, and allowed them to occur because they were necessary for his cover. 'It was a very promiscuous scene. Girls on protest sites would sleep with guys in order to entice them to stay in these horrible places: cold, wet, with bad food and non-existent bathroom facilities.' He added: 'I lived undercover for eight years and if I hadn't had sex, I would have blown my cover. But I never used these women to gain information. The love we had was real.'

Of all the misdemeanours committed by undercover police, the most controversial question relates to long-term relationships. Senior police and ministers have contradicted each other over whether sex is permitted in undercover policing, although most have claimed it is discouraged. Kennedy claimed that he was told during his training not to have sex with his targets. On the other hand, he said his bosses must have known about his relationships. In that much, he is certainly correct.

It would have been impossible for Kennedy's supervisors not to have known about his relationships. Watson, Jacobs and other undercover police officers all saw Kennedy with women – indeed, one fellow NPOIU spy warned him he 'should be careful'. His movements were carefully monitored, and he had a tracking device fitted into his BlackBerry. He claims he 'could not sneeze' without the NPOIU knowing about it. 'My superiors knew who I was sleeping with, but chose to turn a blind eye because I was getting such valuable information,' Kennedy said. 'The police had access to all my phone calls, texts and emails, many of which were of a sexual and intimate nature. They knew where I was spending the night and with whom.'

Of course, Kennedy was not the only NPOIU officer who slept with activists. Jacobs had two serious relationships with women activists, and Watson is accused of having sex with a male protester in a tent. Top commanders, including those who had spent years working with the SDS, in which sex was routine and systematic, can hardly have been surprised that covert agents were having intimate encounters. It has been the modus operandi for undercover police infiltrating protest groups over the last four decades.

Of the 10 undercover operatives identified so far, nine had sex with their targets, and most of them developed meaningful relationships with the opposite sex. It may not have been officially sanctioned, but the tactic appears to have been standard practice, born from the culture of the SDS and its motto 'By Any Means Necessary'.

As more information about the undercover cops has surfaced, a growing number of women have realised that the men they shared their lives with were in fact police spies. Eleven women have begun a legal action against the Met, suing the force for the psychological trauma caused by their relationships with undercover police working for the NPOIU and SDS.

They include three of Kennedy's girlfriends: Megan, Lily and a third woman. Tom Fowler, who became best friends with Marco Jacobs, is the only man who is suing; his girlfriend, and another woman who slept with Jacobs, are part of the same legal action. So too are women who had relationships with John Dines, Mark Jenner, Jim Boyling and, of course, Bob Lambert.

The lawyers bringing the case – Harriet Wistrich and Jules Carey – say their clients have all suffered an unjustifiable emotional toll as a result of the spy operations, which reveal a form of institutional sexism in the police. In one of the first rulings in the high court, presiding judge Mr Justice Tugendhat said the events in the case were unprecedented. 'No action against the police alleging sexual abuse of the kind in question in these actions has been brought before the courts in the past, so far as I have been made aware,' he said.

His ruling found that damages to the women under common law, including misconduct in public office, deceit, assault and negligence, constituted allegations of 'the gravest interference' with their fundamental rights, and should be heard by the court. However, in a blow to the women, he approved the police's application to have the women's additional claims under the Human Rights Act heard first by the Investigatory Powers Tribunal, a secretive body ordinarily used to dealing with complaints about MI5, MI6 and GCHQ. Lawyers are anticipating a protracted court process that could take years before reaching its conclusion.

*

By the spring of 2013, the situation was getting worse for police. Revelations that SDS officers adopted the identities of dead children caused a public outcry. Parliament's influential home affairs select committee branded the practice 'gruesome' and ordered the Met to contact the families of the dead children to apologise. Summoned to parliament to explain what was going on, a deputy assistant commissioner at the Met, Patricia Gallan, refused to apologise.

However, she admitted that the NPOIU had been resurrecting the identities of dead children too, although it appears the practice may have stopped around 2001, before Kennedy, Jacobs and Watson joined the unit. Gallan would not be drawn on how many identities the two units had stolen over the years. However, it seems probable that the identities of more than 100 dead children were used over a 40-year stretch.

Shocked by what had been going on, the committee called for the law governing undercover policing to be overhauled. 'The impact of the conduct of undercover officers on the women with whom they had relationships has been devastating, and it represents a wholly improper degree of intrusion by the state into the lives of individuals,' said Keith Vaz MP, who chaired the committee. 'Equally shocking has been the revelation of the ghoulish and disrespectful practice of undercover officers looking to develop cover stories plundering the identities of dead infants.'

The MPs were persuaded, in part, after holding a private hearing, where women who had relationships with John Dines, Mark Cassidy and Bob Lambert gave evidence. They were joined by Megan, who plucked up the courage to speak for the first time about her relationship with Kennedy. It was an admirable step for Megan, who friends say had struggled, at times, to talk even privately about what had gone on. She was determined to prevent a repeat of the undercover operations in future.

'You imagine that [a spy] may be in public meetings that environmental groups have,' Megan told the MPs. 'You imagine there might be somebody listening in there. You could even imagine that your phone might be tapped or that somebody might look at your emails, but to know that there was somebody in your bed for six years, that somebody was involved in your family life to such a degree, that was an absolute shock. It felt like the ground had shifted beneath me and my sense of what was reality and what wasn't was completely turned on its head.' She added: 'The only reason that this has happened to us is because we were members of political groups. The only reason was because I was involved in environmental groups and I was campaigning for social justice.'

Megan said she still had many unanswered questions about the six years she spent with Kennedy. 'I cared deeply for somebody whose life was intermingled with mine, and that person's life story is a fiction,' she said. 'Who else was participating in the relationship that I believed was just me and one other person? Who else was seeing every text message that I ever sent him? Who was listening in to our most intimate phone calls? Who saw our holiday photos? Was there anybody following us when we were on holiday? Who made the decisions about what happened to my life, where I was allowed to go, who I was allowed to see, which I thought was my free will but actually was being manipulated by this person who was being controlled by other people?'

There are still many unresolved questions. But the secret is now out.

An experiment that began in 1968, when Conrad Dixon resolved to get to grips with protests against the Vietnam War, and decided undercover policing was the way to do it, became an enduring and permanent programme of state espionage, directed at political activists.

It is remarkable it took so long for the truth to surface. The torch ignited by Dixon all those years ago was carried by successive undercover police working first for the SDS and, later, the NPOIU. It was passed, like a baton in a relay, through generations of spies who transformed themselves into new people, living real lives, with jobs and friends and lovers and even children, before vanishing like ghosts.

It took more than 40 years for that to become public knowledge. Now that it has, what has changed?

Not much. It is business as usual for the NPOIU, which continues the practice of planting undercover police in protest groups. After the uncomfortable glare of public scrutiny, it seems likely that supervisors will be far more careful to ensure that its agents do not cross the line in the future. During her parliamentary appearance, Patricia Gallan assured MPs that undercover officers no longer use the identities of dead children and are prohibited from developing intimate relationships. 'I am absolutely clear that such activities should not be authorised or sanctioned,' she said. 'It is morally wrong.' Privately, senior officers say they no longer believe such long-lasting operations are healthy. One recent deployment of an NPOIU spy, suspected to have been directed against animal rights activists in Wales, lasted less than two years and did not, it seems, involve sexual activity.

There have been some other changes. After a number of years based at the Association of Chief Police Officers, where police admit it was not subject to proper scrutiny, the unit was returned to its original home. The NPOIU is now back at New Scotland Yard, under the command of counter-terrorist officers, the very place the whole spy programme was developed by Dixon back in 1968.

Next to nothing has been done to reform the system, or prevent further cases of abuse taking place again, despite a raft of proposals. Sir Denis O'Connor, the chief inspector of the police brought in to clean up the system after Kennedy was outed, recommended ditching the flawed concept of 'domestic extremism' and said police should separate out their investigation into serious criminals, which might justify undercover methods, and the routine policing of protest. He also proposed forcing police to obtain advance authorisation from independent surveillance commissioners before deploying undercover officers. As the police's chief watchdog, O'Connor was a hugely influential bureaucrat. Being a former chief constable, O'Connor rarely liked to rock the boat. When he did, it was for a reason.

Yet more than 12 months after he published his damning report, and despite support from senior officers for many of his key proposals, not a single one of the recommendations has been implemented.

His inquiry was just one of 15 separate official inquiries launched into various aspects of undercover policing since Kennedy was exposed. All have been held behind closed doors. None have come close to providing a full and open account of how police have used spies to monitor activists over the last four decades.

The largest inquiry – Operation Herne – is being conducted by the police themselves, with a team of Met officers conducting an investigation into their colleagues. Their inquiry into the SDS is supposedly a definitive review that, one day, will atone for past mistakes.

Under the command of a chief constable from Derbyshire police, a staff of 31 investigators are combing through 50,000 classified documents, tracking down former spies, and trying to speak with activists who were spied on. Just over a year into its deliberations, the inquiry has already cost the taxpayer £1.25m. It has not yet made a single disclosure about any undercover operation. The Met estimates Herne will not be completed until 2016.

But will the public run out of patience? 'Things have gone badly wrong,' says Ken MacDonald, a former director of public prosecutions. 'It seems only a public inquiry, taking stock of the picture both nationally and locally, receiving evidence and advice, and setting standards and mechanisms of control, is capable of rescuing us, and necessary undercover policing, from a steady drip of exposure and seediness.'

That constant flow of revelations will not stop. The 10 undercover police officers identified so far will not be the last to be exposed. There are around a dozen cases of suspected undercover police who are not mentioned in this book, but are known to be guilty of similar misdemeanours, who might be unmasked any moment.

There is no precise number for the total number of police spies who worked for the SDS or NPOIU. However, evidence in documents and testimony from police suggests there have been at least 100 covert officers, and possibly as many as 150. That means fewer than a tenth of the total number of spies have been unmasked so far. The scandal has a long way to go before it runs out of steam.

How many more undercover police who slept with women, used dead children's identities or lied in court will be exposed in years to come? How many will argue they were not properly looked after by police, deployed for years undercover without consideration for their psychological health? Will any of them follow the example set by Black, find the courage to come forward, and tell their story on their own terms?

Needless to say, there are tens of thousands of political activists who had police spies as friends, comrades or lovers. Many may now want to go public about the impact on their lives. These campaigners have video footage and photographs, postcards and letters of people they now suspect were infiltrators who lived in their midst. And, for the first time in almost half a century, they feel emboldened by the knowledge that their suspicions may well be true.

If there is one irony to this story, it is that political activists who had no faith in the state, who were labelled conspiracy theorists for claiming they were being watched by secret police, were not nearly paranoid enough. If they were culpable of anything, it was underestimating quite how far police were willing to go in the pursuit of information about their lives. They are unlikely to make that mistake again.

For any police spies currently deployed in protest groups, that must be a chilling thought. Undercover policing is never easy – one misplaced step, one slipped word, and the officer can be found out. Operatives deployed in protest groups today are working in an environment in which all activists are on the lookout for the next spy cop, in the knowledge that they do, after all, exist, and they could be anywhere.

The consequences for those spies who are exposed in the future are laid bare by the mixed fortunes of the officers in this book. Black continues to speak out about his days in the SDS, and believes he has found some closure in coming clean about the excesses of his deployment. He is campaigning for a public inquiry into the undercover policing of protest. If such an inquiry is ordered, he is committed to giving evidence to it without any disguise.

Those who have met Kennedy since his exposure say he seems profoundly unhappy. He has struggled to rebuild his life since he was outed and recently announced his intention to sue the Met police for £100,000 in compensation, claiming that, like Black and Chitty, he suffered post-traumatic stress disorder. He works for the Densus Group, an American security firm that specialises in spying on activists, and also provided some assistance to the

Los Angeles Sheriff's Department. He recently took on a role at a leisure company. He has confided in some friends that he would like to work for the FBI. Recently, after around a year adopting the clean-cut look of his days in uniform, he grew back his stubble and long hair.

But of all the police spies, it is Bob Lambert who faces the most uncertain future. He still faces questions over his role in the arson attacks on Debenhams in the 1980s, his role in the writing of the infamous McLibel leaflet, which gave rise to the court case with McDonald's, and his relationships with women, including the one which resulted in the birth of his son, an episode he says he kept secret from his bosses and his family for more than 20 years.

For some time, Lambert is known to have tried to win over Charlotte, the mother of his child, persuading her that he was not at fault. He has talked of selling their story to Hollywood. His approaches have been rather persistent, and Charlotte's lawyer has threatened to take out a harassment order against Lambert unless he ceases contact. For better or worse, he has also established a relationship with the son he never knew.

Lambert's professional life has taken a turn for the worse. Many of the invitations to make speeches appear to have dried up and Lambert has been obliged to leave an academic post as co-director of the European Muslim Research Centre at Exeter University. It was a major setback; he had been at the beginning of a decade-long programme of research. He retains his lecturing job at St Andrews where, embarrassingly, students staged a protest at one of his seminars, condemning his 'reprehensible' behaviour.

In one sense, Lambert always had the most to lose. He was a skilled manipulator, almost too accomplished for his own good. Having risen through the ranks of the SDS, he now knows he will be held to account for the misdemeanours of the spies who operated under his command. Lambert still socialises with these officers – his old team from back in the day. But even they must have detected a change in their old boss. He recently confided in friends that he planned to convert to Islam.

Lambert will need all of the spiritual guidance he can get in the days ahead. He knows he is the author of his own misfortune. His decision to pursue a new career as an academic, posing as a progressive liberal with a heart, meant that his downfall, when it came, was from an especially high pedestal.

Lambert knew the game was up in October 2011 – the day he was confronted by activists who turned up uninvited to one of his speeches in London. It was a humiliating start to his downfall. As activists handed out leaflets to the audience, entitled 'The Truth About Bob Lambert and his Special Branch Role', he left the stage and slipped out of a side entrance.

His heart must have sunk when he saw he was being pursued down the street by Helen Steel and Dave Morris, the tenacious London Greenpeace activists who took on McDonald's in the McLibel court case.

The ensuing chase was a curious event: Lambert at the front, scurrying along, pretending to ignore Steel and Morris and the camera they were pointing in his face. Saturday afternoon shoppers parted, as the former police spy and his activist friends made their way through the street.

'Come on, Bob. We would like to talk to you about your infiltration of London Greenpeace,' said Steel.

'All you have got to do is have a chat,' said Morris. 'What are you ashamed of?'

Lambert crossed the road and started running. Steel and Morris picked up their pace to stay in tow.

'Would you like to say sorry to any of the other women who had relationships with your undercover officers?' asked Steel. 'Are you proud of what you did?'

'It is all going to come out, yeah,' said Morris. 'All the infiltrators are being unmasked. Everyone knows that it's disgusting, yeah, using Stasi tactics against campaign groups.'

Lambert carried on walking.

'All you have to do is stop and say, "OK, it was wrong,"' Morris said.

'That it was abusive to people,' added Steel. 'It was damaging.'

It was clear that Lambert was not going to say a word. The procession continued along the street. He smiled, awkwardly.

'All you have got to do is stop and have a chat,' said Morris. 'You know us. We are good people. You knew us for five years.'

'You were quite happy to chat to us in the pub 15, 20 years ago,' said Steel.

Lambert stood by the road and hailed a taxi. Steel and Morris were still beside him, like apparitions from a previous life.

'So, nothing to say about abusing women campaigners?' said Steel.

'Will you apologise for the whole police operation against campaign groups?' said Morris.

The veteran spy said nothing. He entered the taxi and slammed the door. He would have heard the final shouts from those familiar faces, the people he had called his friends all those years before.

'Shame on you!' they shouted. 'Shame on you!'

AUTHORS' NOTE AND ACKNOWLEDGEMENTS

For two years we have delved into a particularly secretive part of the secret state. It is not possible, for obvious reasons, to acknowledge in public the many people who went out of their way to enable this story to be told. They know who they are. There were some, however, who did not help at all. Mark Kennedy did not co-operate with this book. On the occasions he or his family are quoted, the remarks are taken from published interviews with the *Mail on Sunday*, *Guardian*, BBC and *Rolling Stone*. The Metropolitan Police officially refused to co-operate and answered virtually none of our questions. We asked for an interview with a senior officer who could give the official view of these undercover operations, or assistance 'on background', which is almost always provided for projects on this scale. The force refused, saying undercover policing 'is by definition a covert activity and it is imperative that we safeguard our working practices and certain aspects of our decision making, to protect the men and women who undertake this dangerous work.'

In the face of official obstruction, we relied on the courage of confidential sources. A number of 'insiders', past and present, have helped us, but we owe particular thanks to Pete Black. This book could never have been written without his bravery. Pete has not received any payment for this book. At his request, a portion of the royalties is being donated to a local branch of the mental health charity, Mind. We thank Tony Thompson for introducing us to Pete, who was at the time known as Officer A.

A number of people spoke on the condition of anonymity, either to protect their privacy or because they feared retribution from police. As a rule, all references to people by first names only (e.g. 'Megan') are pseudonyms. We are grateful to the many other activists who agreed to break with tradition to be named on the record.

Our book was made possible by senior executives at the *Guardian* who allowed us the time and freedom to investigate these stories and then turn them into a book. Particular thanks to Alan Rusbridger, Ian Katz, Dan Roberts, Dan Sabbagh, Jan Thompson, Sara Montgomery and Katie Roden. We would like to thank our main researcher, Sorcha Pollack, and three reporters who helped along the way: Rowenna Davis, who worked briefly at the *Guardian*, and Meirion Jones and Richard Watson, from BBC *Newsnight*. Thanks also to our friends at ITN Productions.

We're grateful to three solicitors who represent the targets of the undercover operations – Mike Schwarz, Jules Carey and Harriet Wistrich – and two media lawyers who facilitated publication, Sean McTernan and Gill Phillips. We are also indebted to the careful skill of Lindsay Davies, who edited the manuscript, and Tom Lewis, whose advice early on helped shape it.

We have in places been greatly helped by journalists and researchers who have gone before us. In chapter two, we quoted from Peter Taylor's BBC 2002 series on MI5 and the Special Branch, and his accompanying *Guardian* article of October 23 2002, which disclosed the existence of the Special Demonstration Squad. We also drew from a BBC *Newsnight* programme on May 28 2008 on the policing of the 1968 anti-Vietnam war protests. Solomon Hughes passed on documents he had uncovered in the National Archives in Kew, London, about those protests. We also quoted from a BBC Radio Four *File on Four* programme broadcast on October 2 2012 and, in chapter five, drew on two books: *McLibel – Burger Culture on Trial* by John Vidal (Macmillan, 1997) and *Secret Manoeuvres in the Dark – Corporate and Police Spying on Activists* by Eveline Lubbers (Pluto Press, 2012).

Authors regularly acknowledge the tolerance of their partners while they disappear for some time. We are no different. Rob would like to thank his wife Caroline for her forbearance and support. She may have got bored of him talking about undercover police, but she did not show it. Paul would like to thank Kay for encouraging him to pursue his obsessions. She was unwaveringly supportive, right from when the story first broke.

Finally, like all journalism, this book is merely a first draft of the history. We recognise we have only scratched the surface. If you can help us improve the record, then we would urge you to get in touch via Rob.Evans@guardian.co.uk or Paul.Lewis@guardian.co.uk. We hope this book will be an incentive, in particular, to the South African resident, the Scottish hotelier, the pensioner in Lincolnshire and the second spy who learned the consequences of fathering a child undercover.

Paul Lewis and Rob Evans, May 2013

INDEX